*Dedicated to Joe Colquhoun.
Of all the great artists I've worked with,
he was the greatest.*

Pat Mills

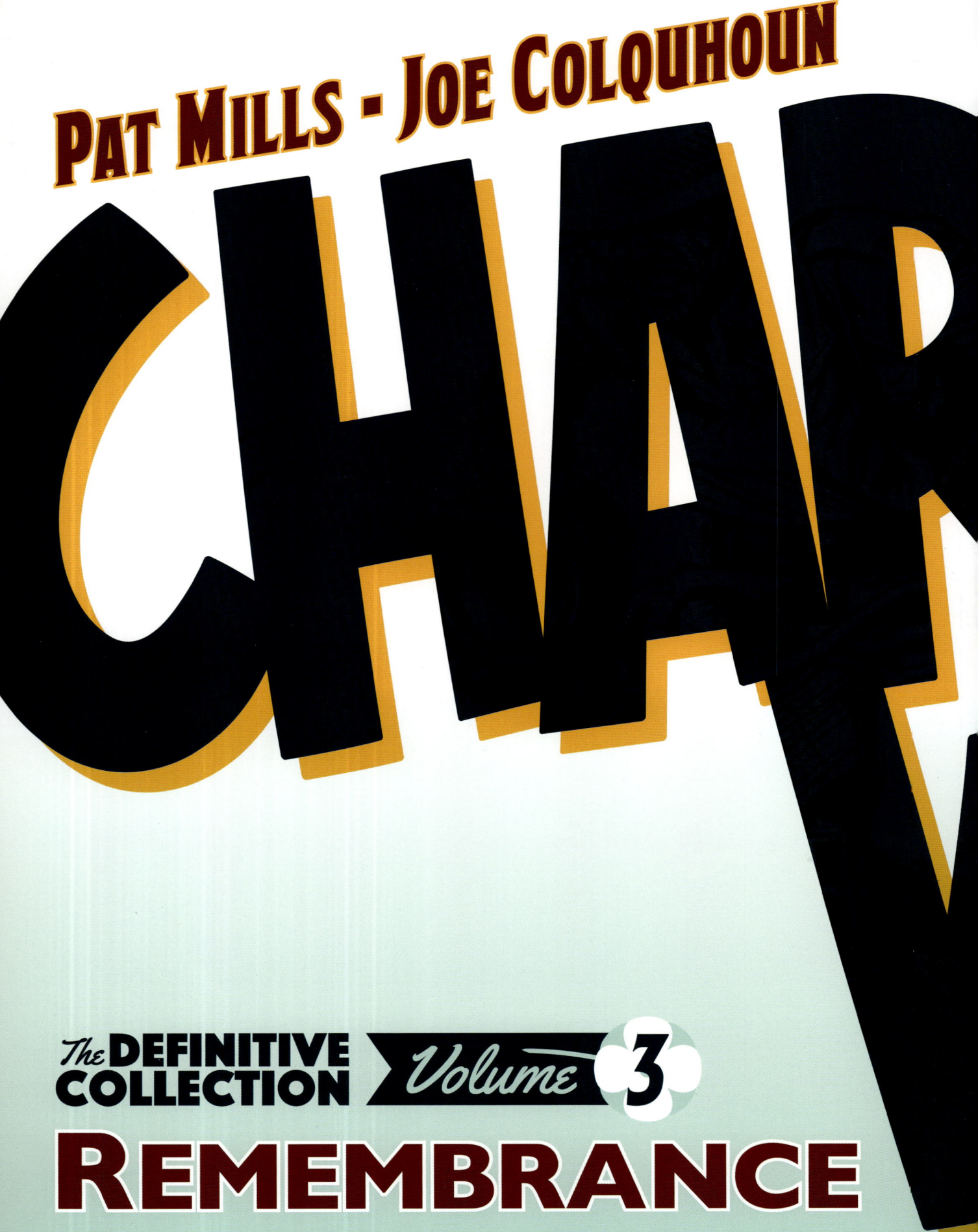

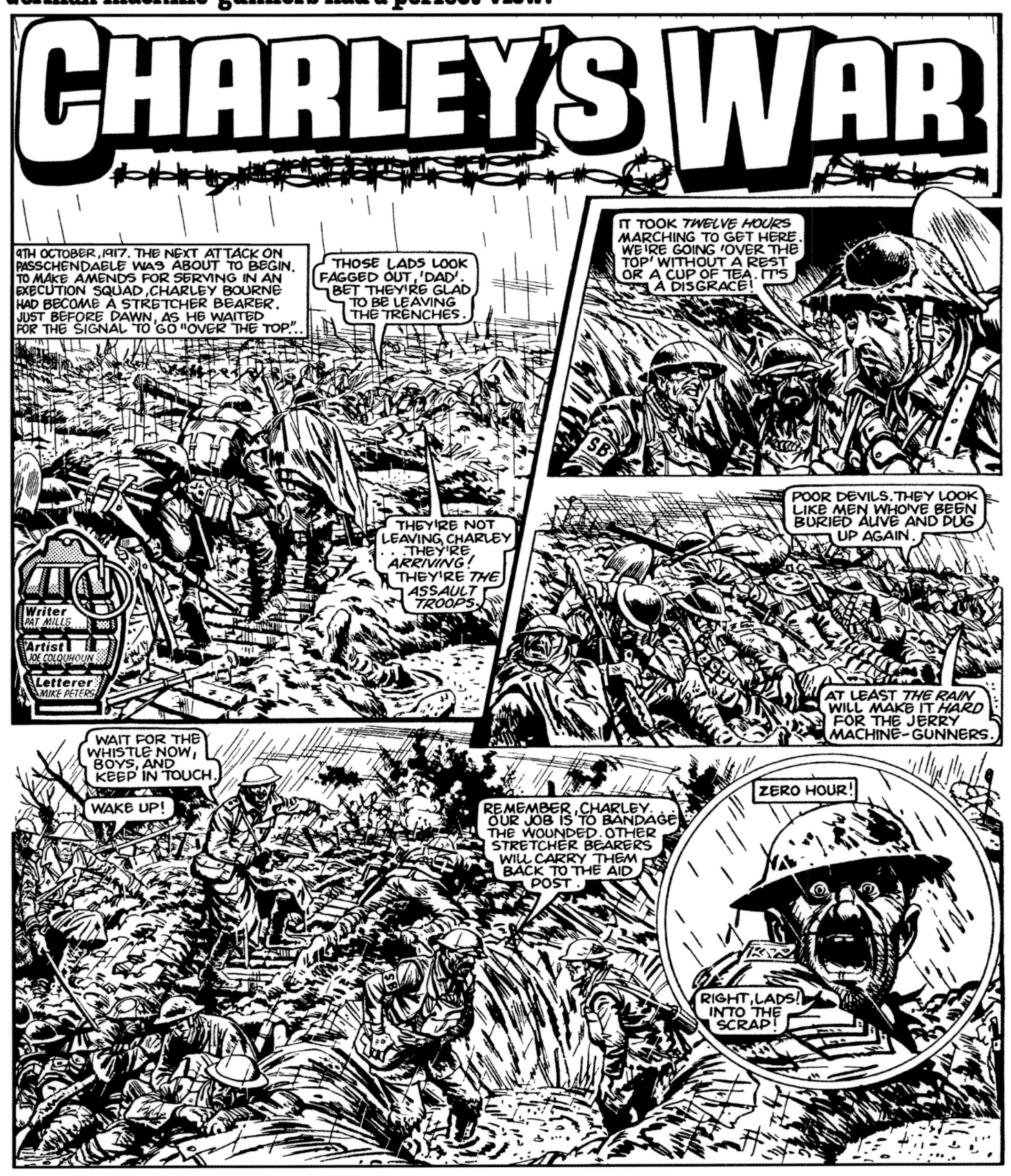

"PROMISE ME YOU'LL HAVE A GREAT TIME!" "ALL RIGHT, CHUM."	"HE'S GONE... I'LL HAND HIS MONEY IN LATER. PROBABLY GOT SOME NEXT-OF-KIN WHO COULD USE IT."
SUDDENLY... "FIRE SHELLS!" "FRITZ HAS SPOTTED US!"	"SMITHY!"

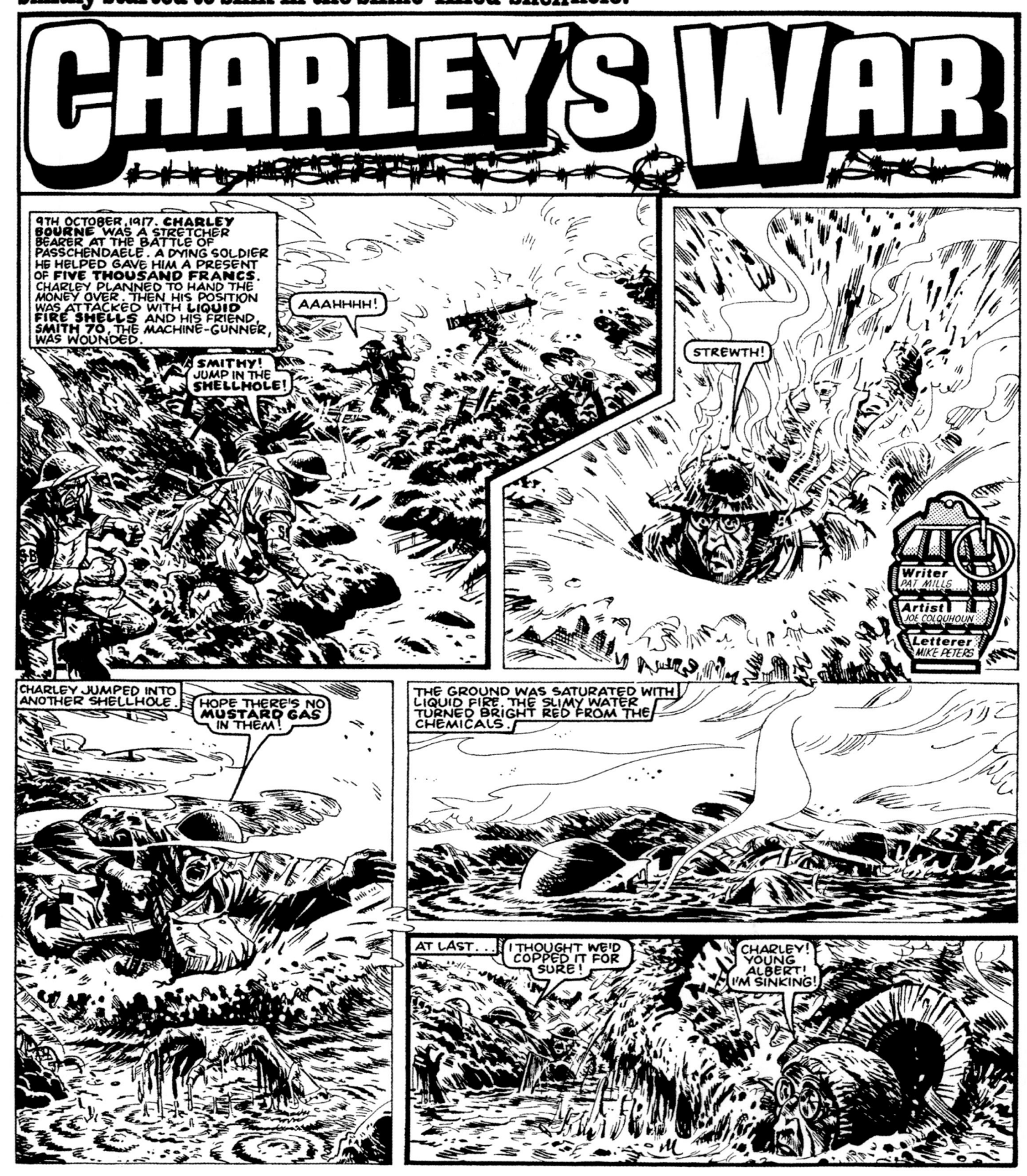

"Serves him right if his own gas chokes him!"

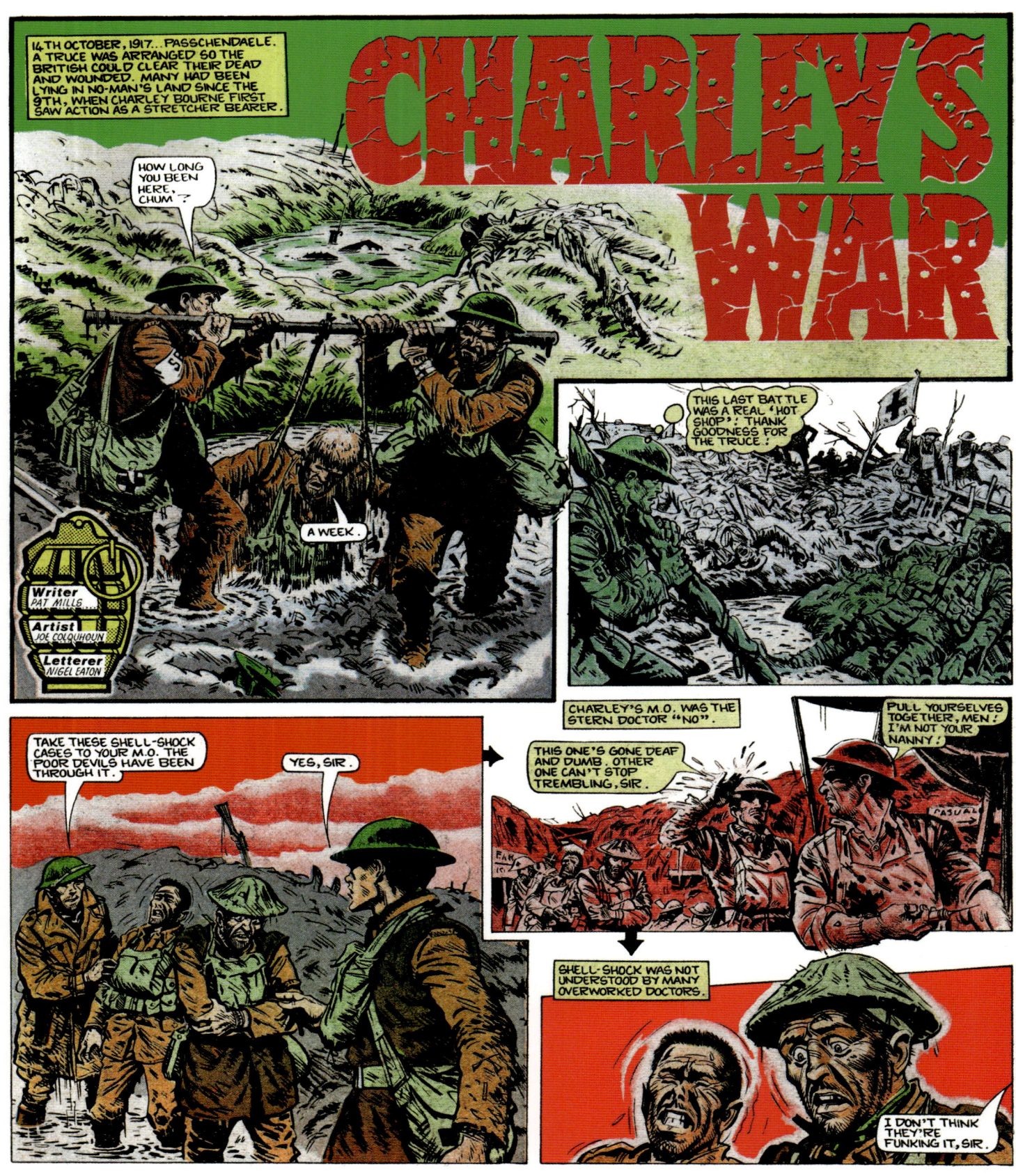

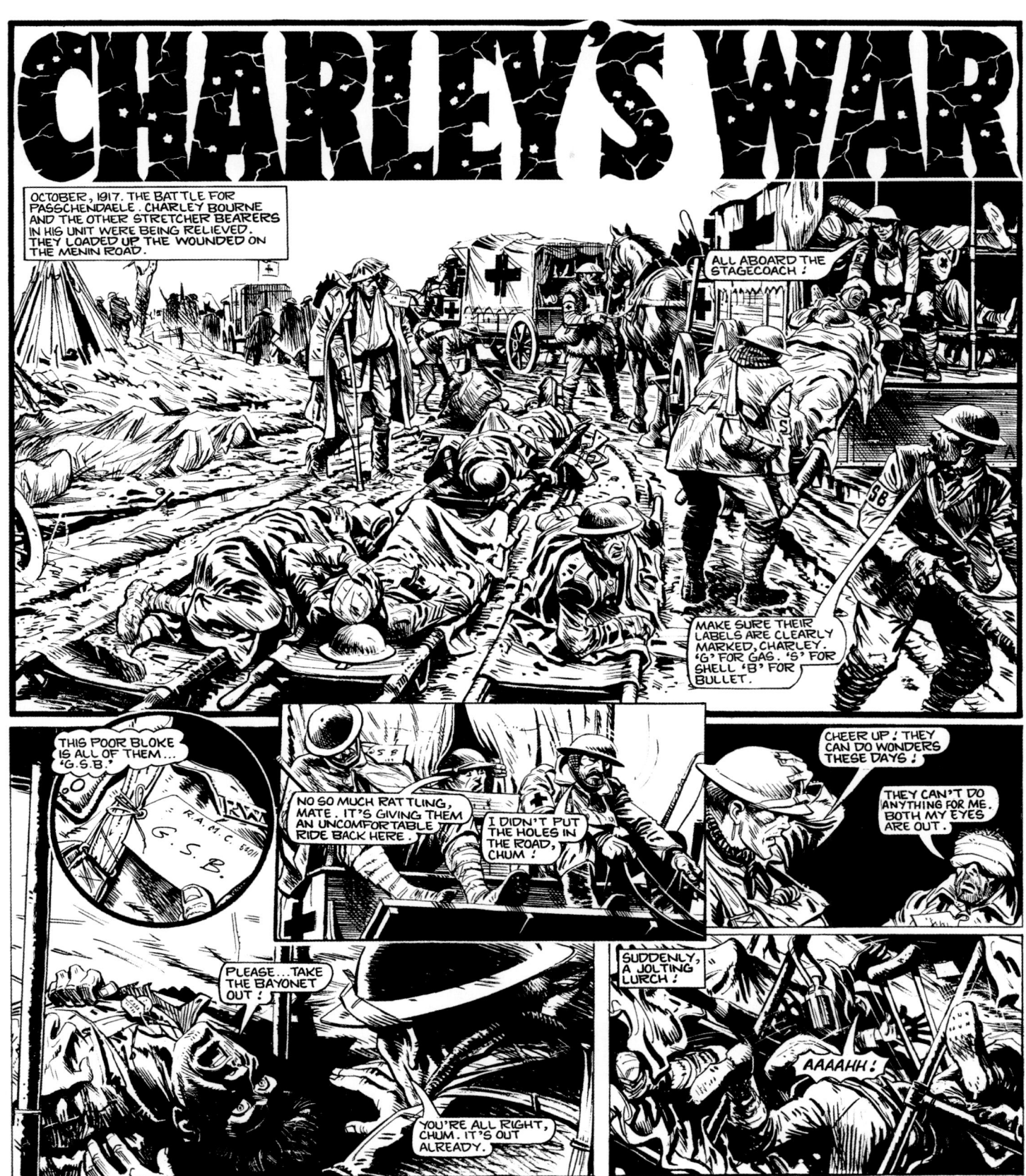

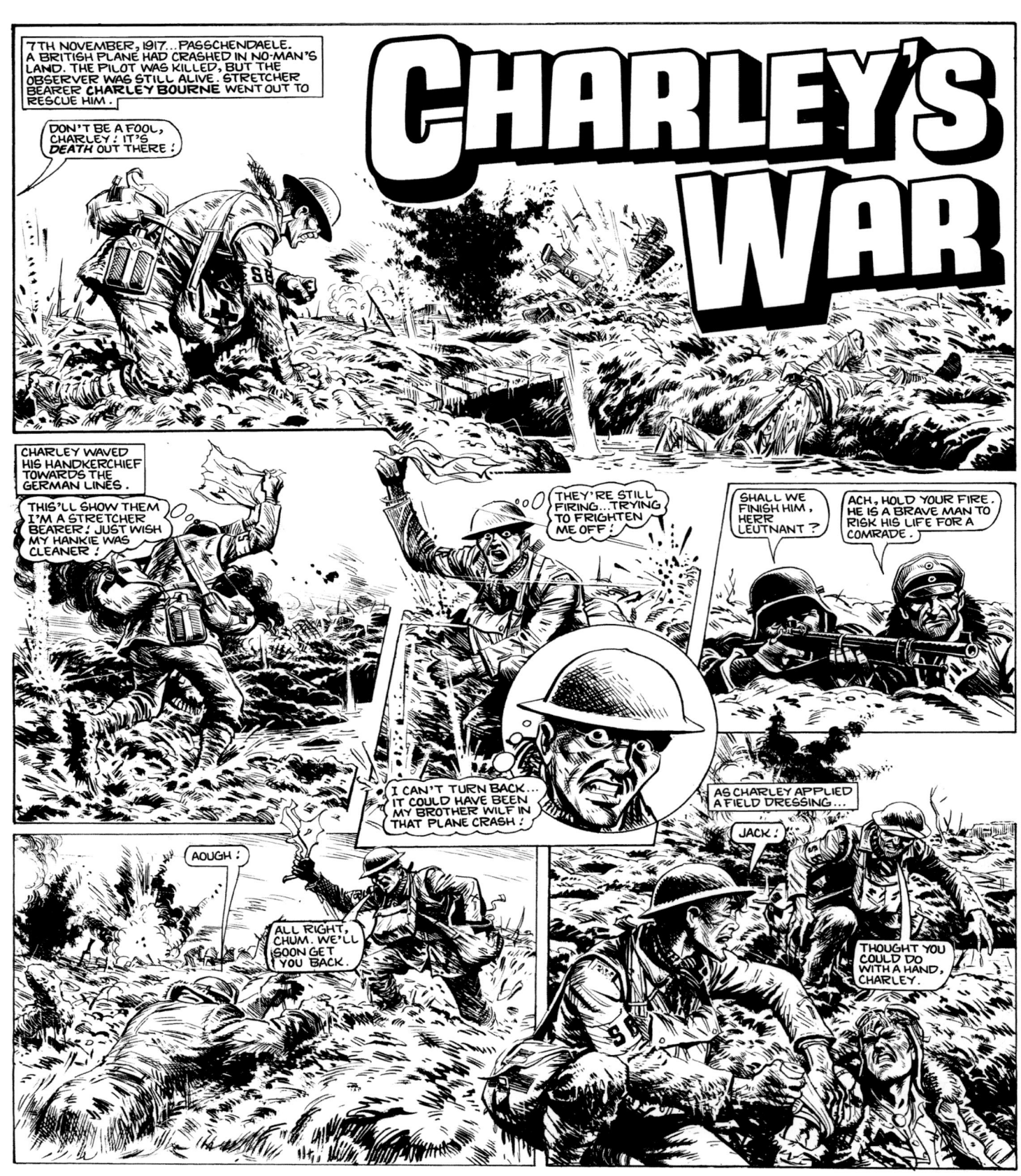

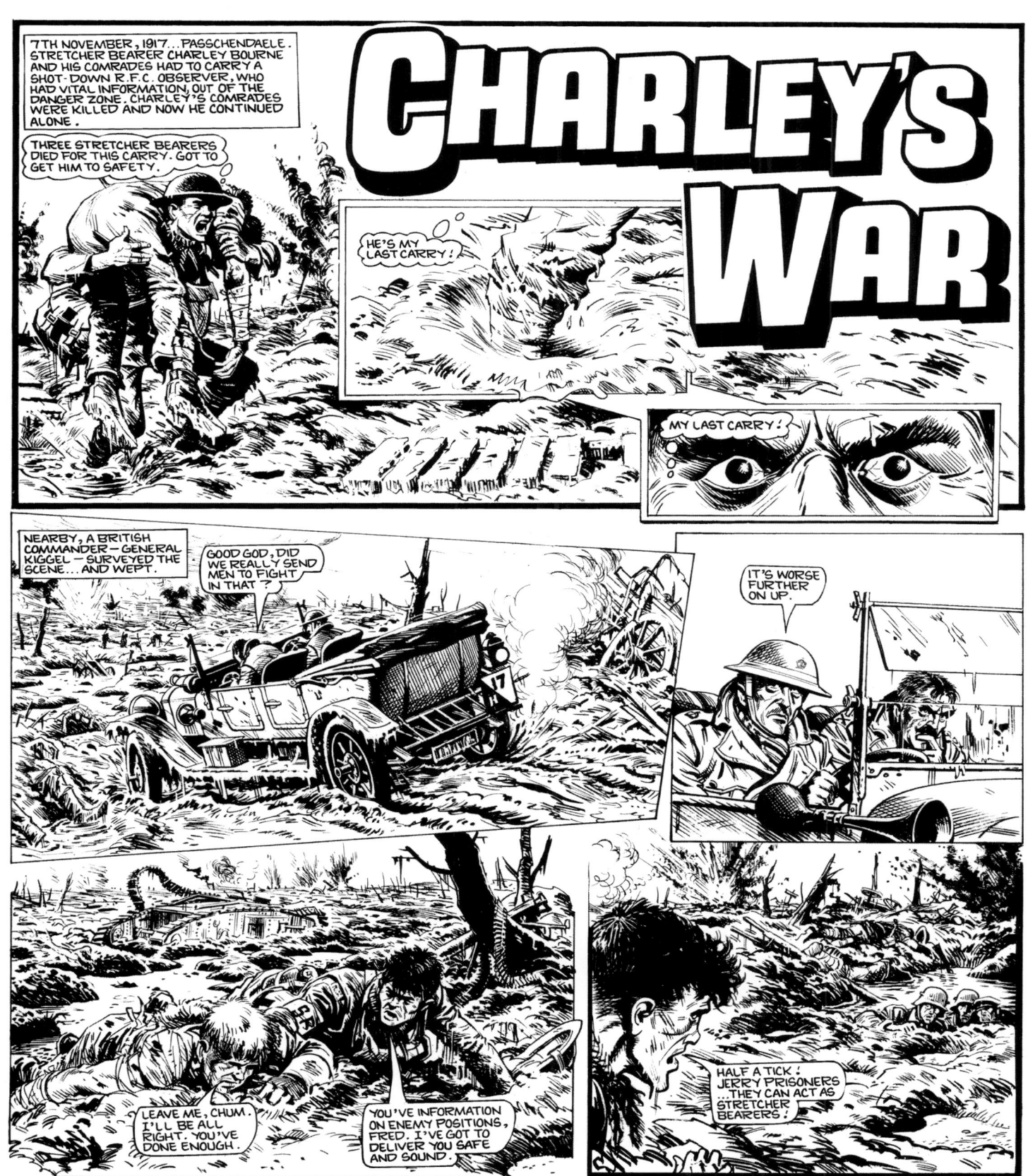

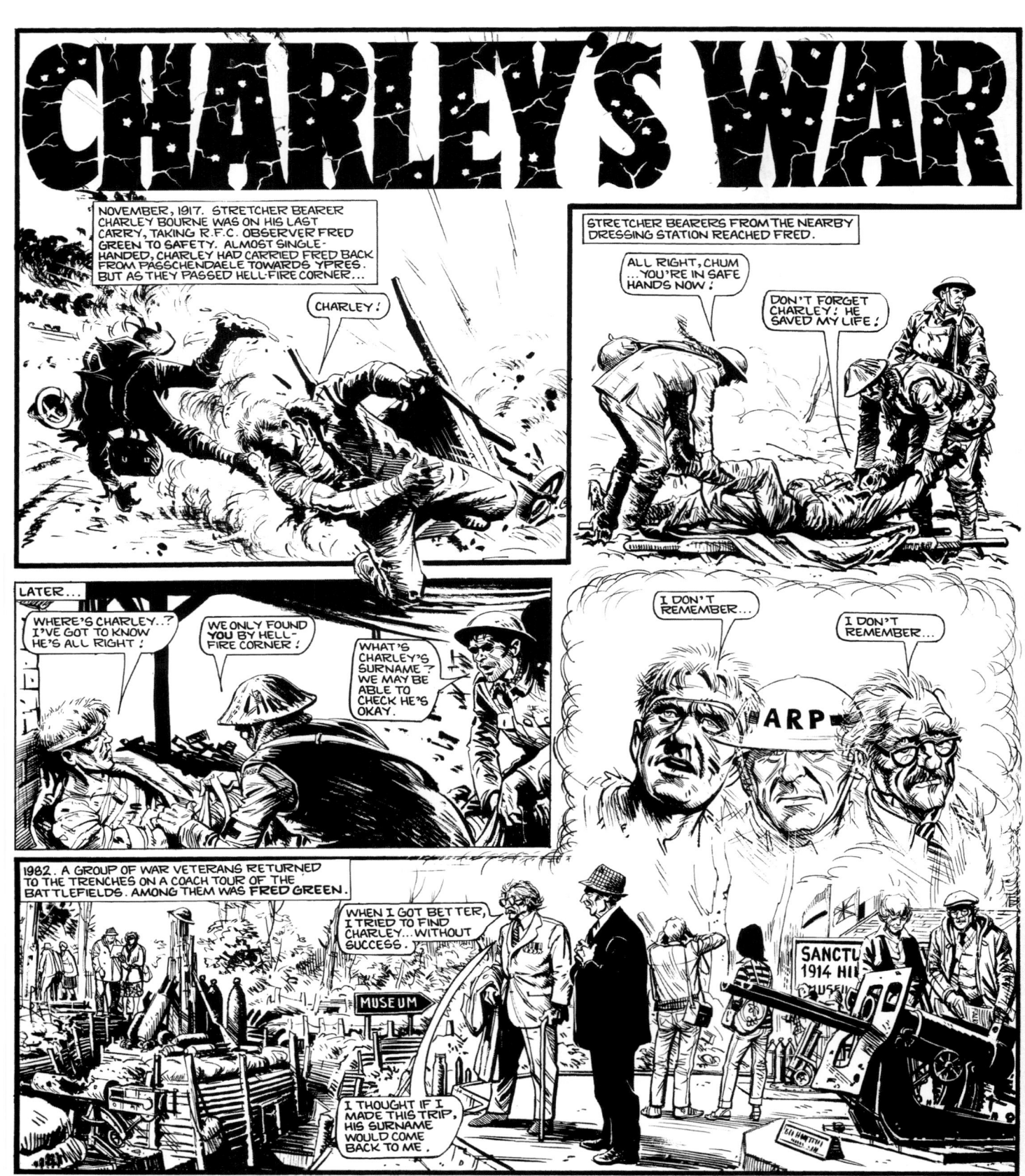

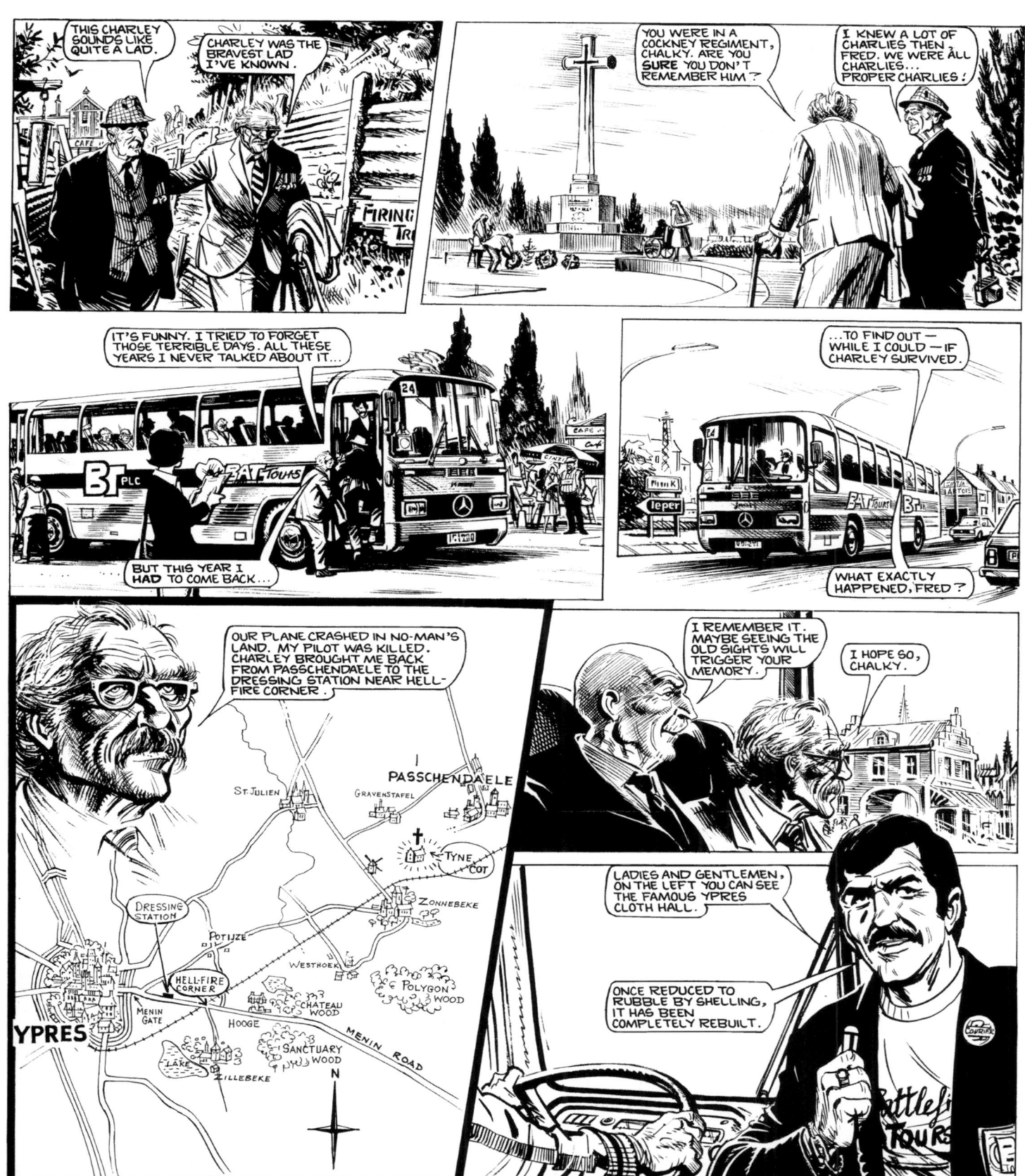

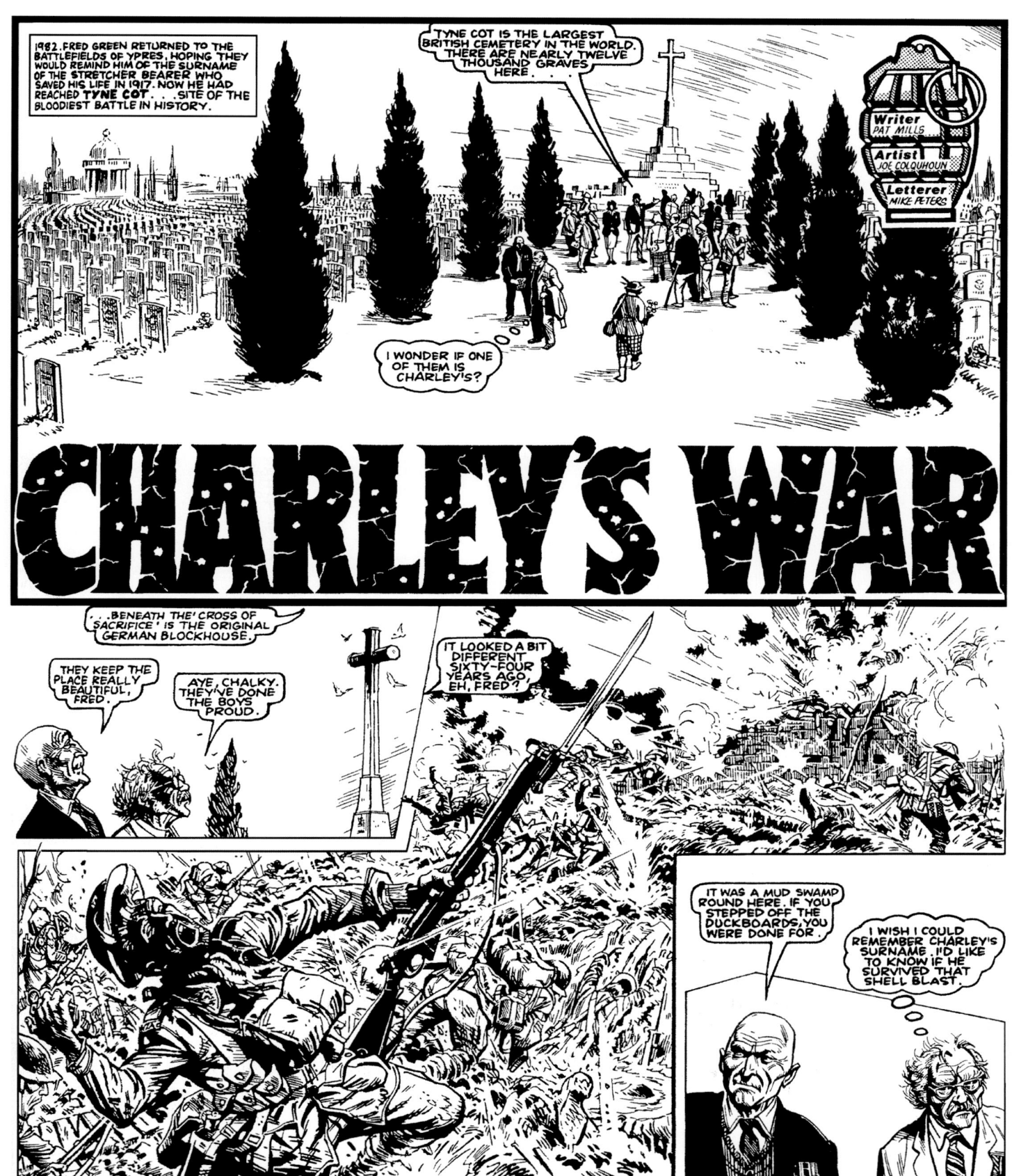

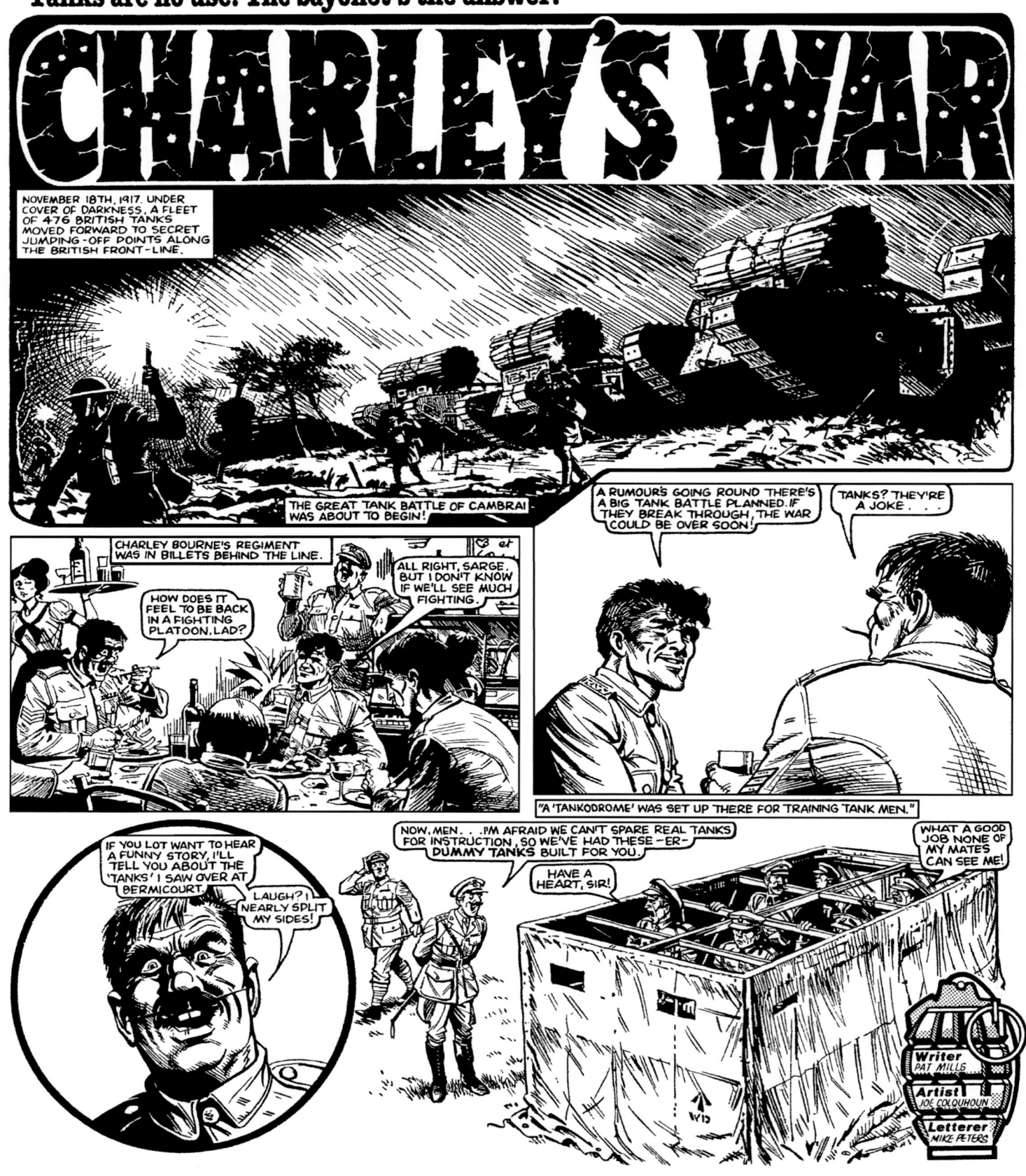

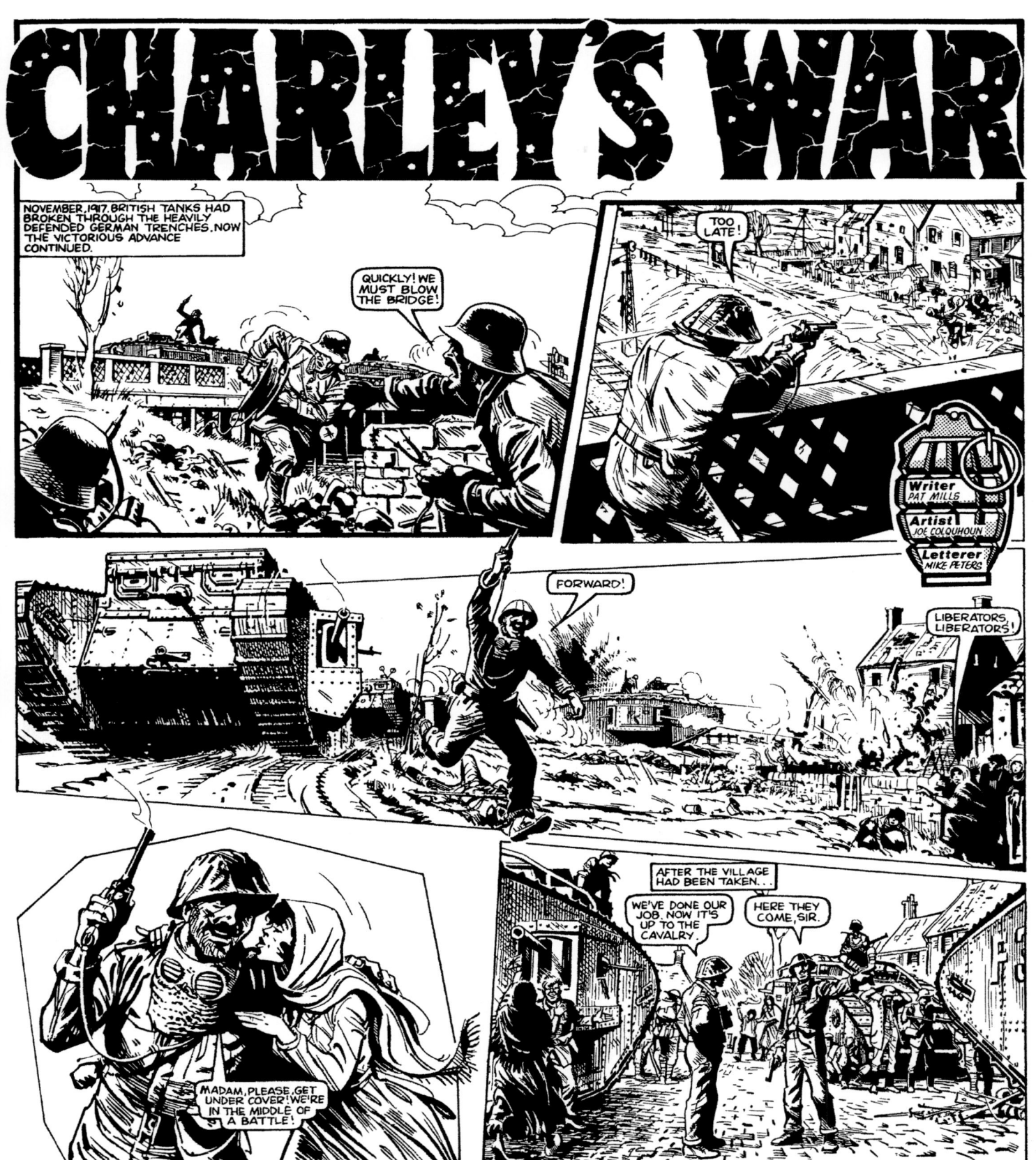

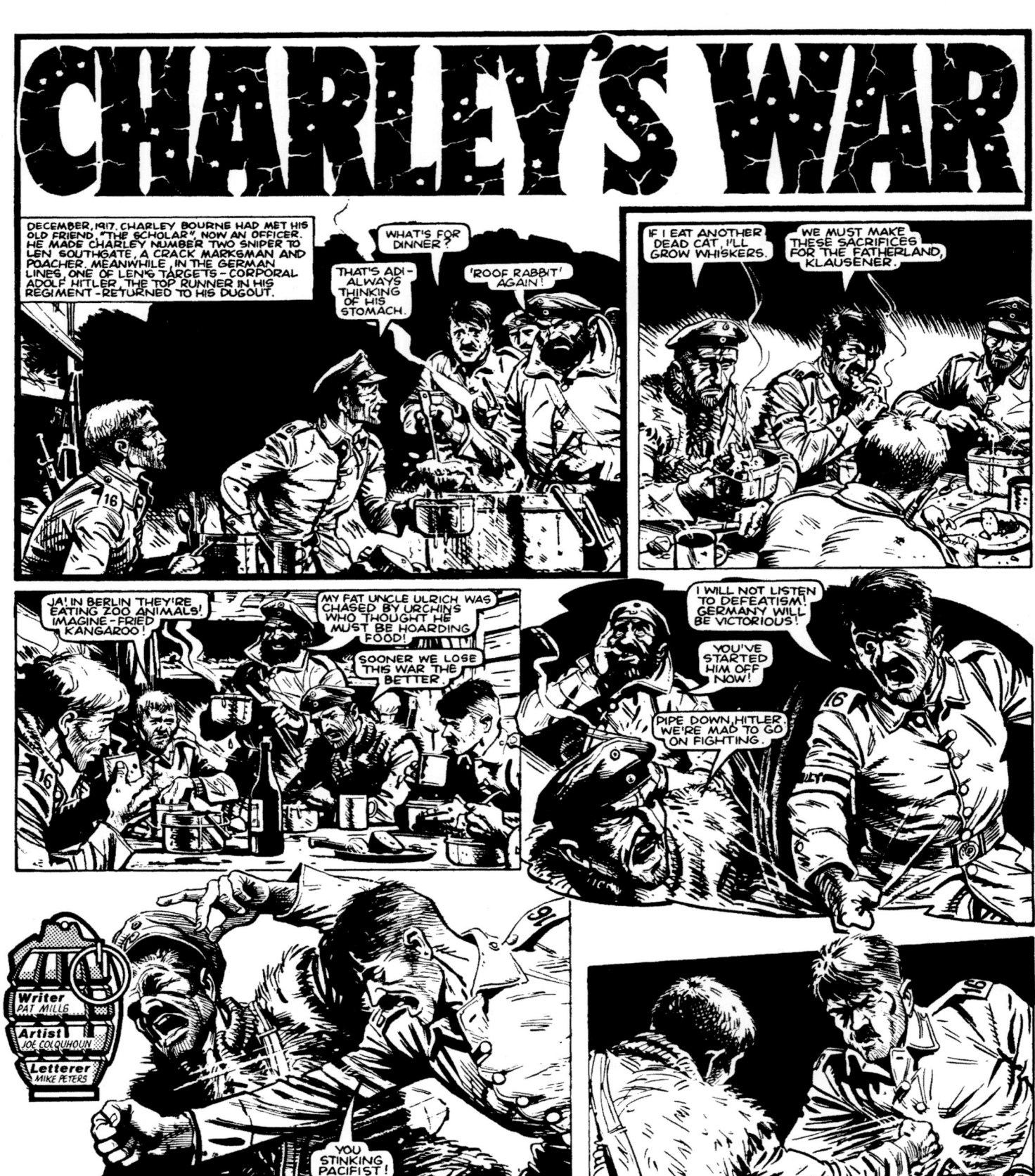

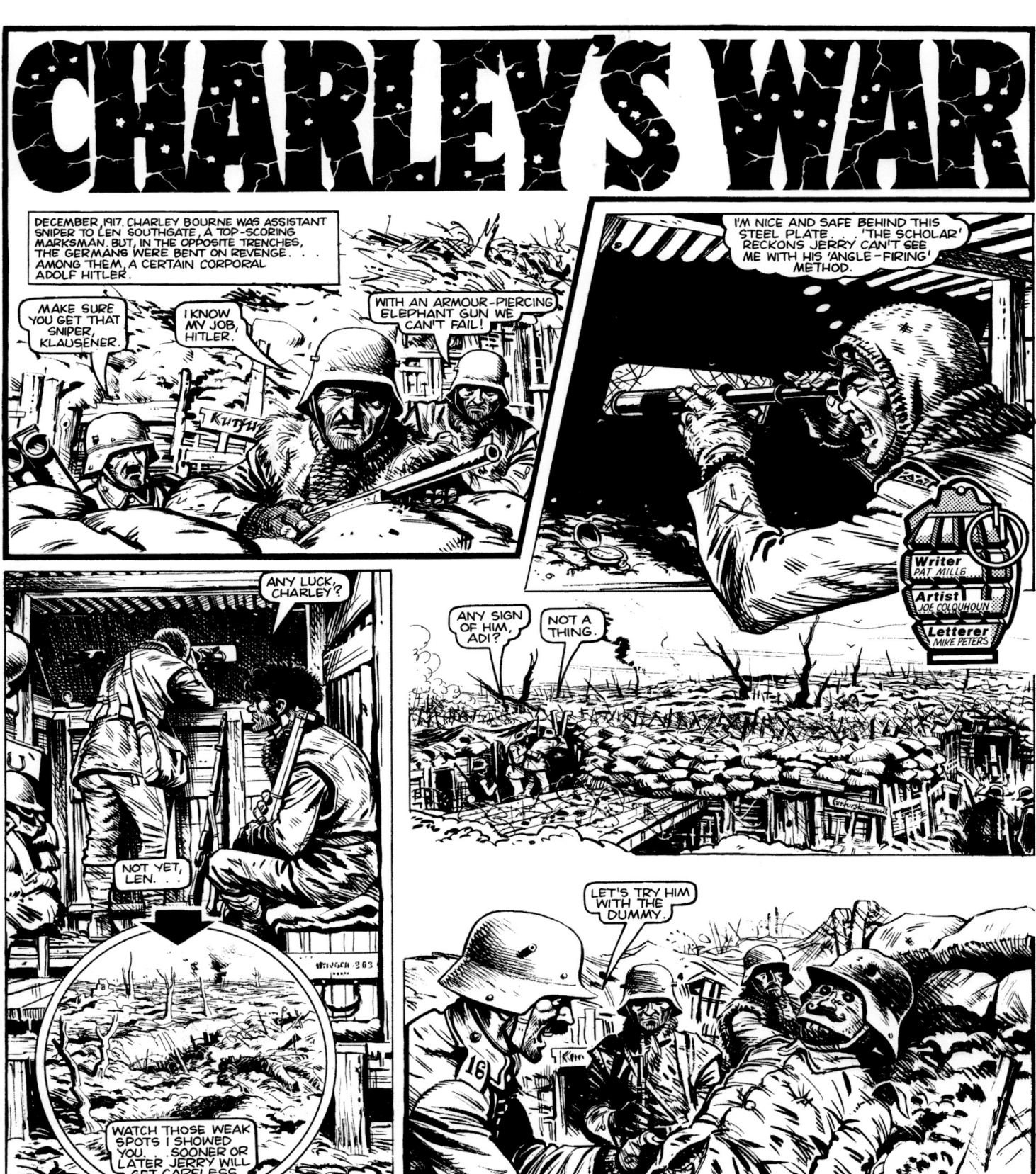

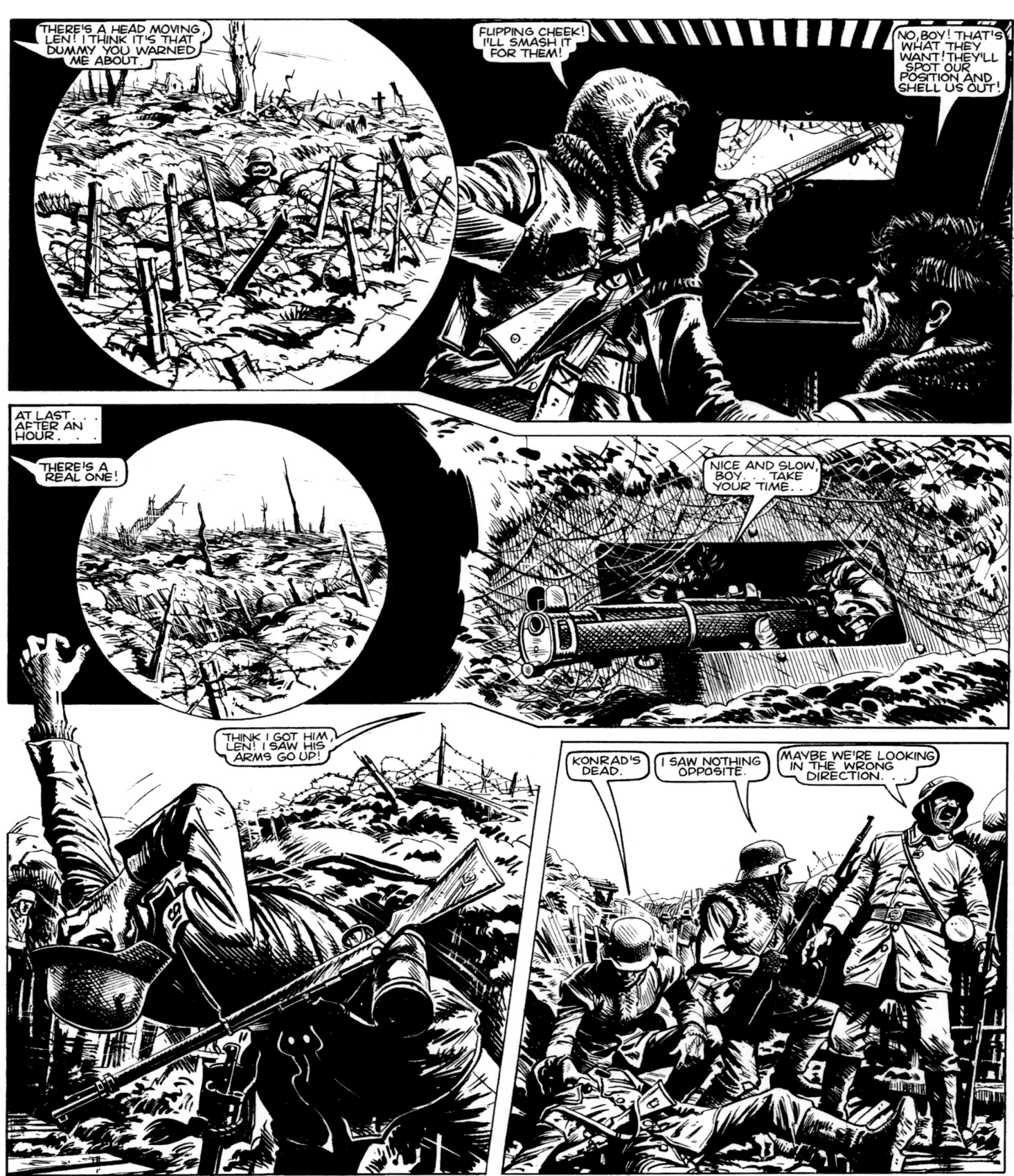

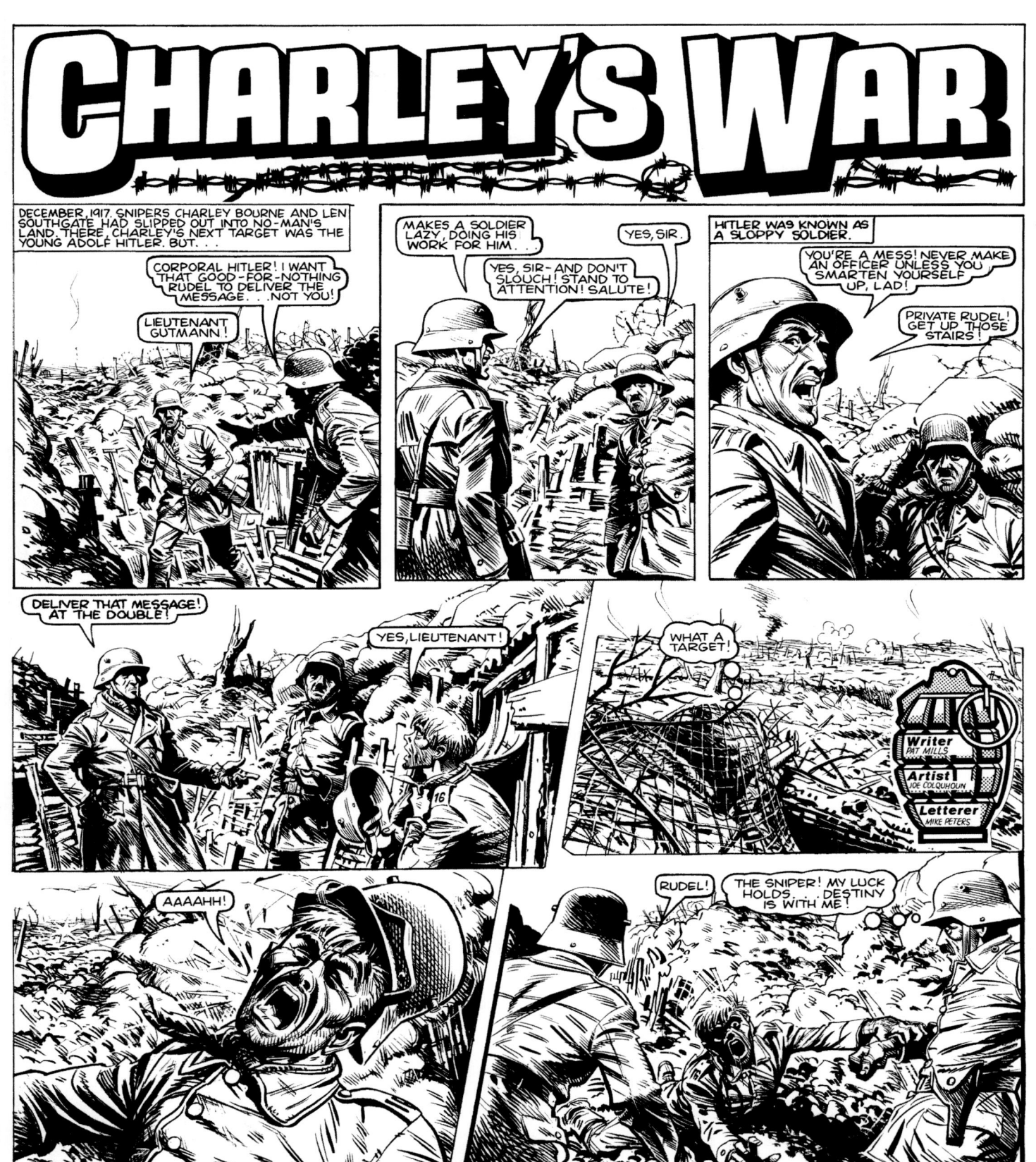

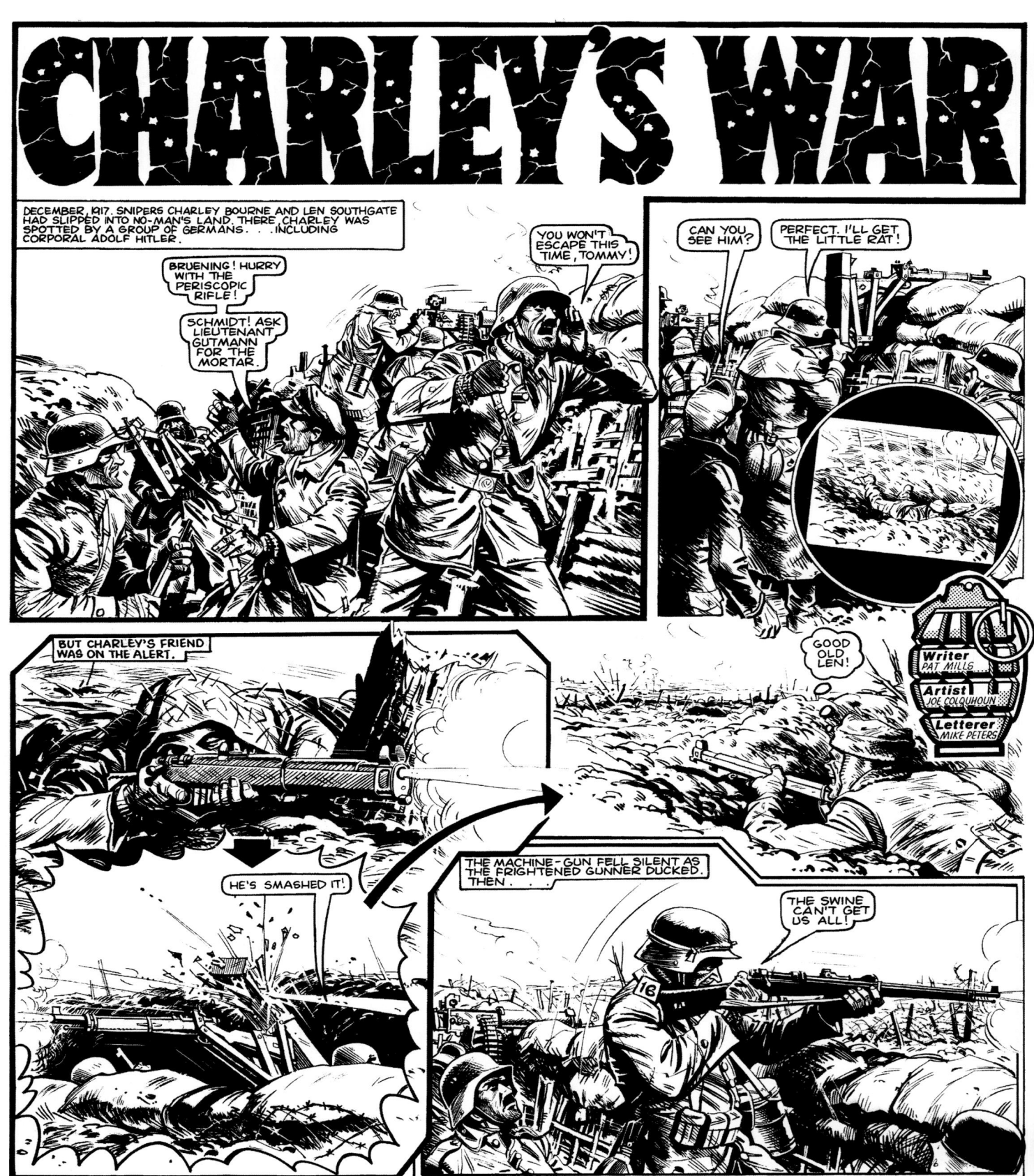

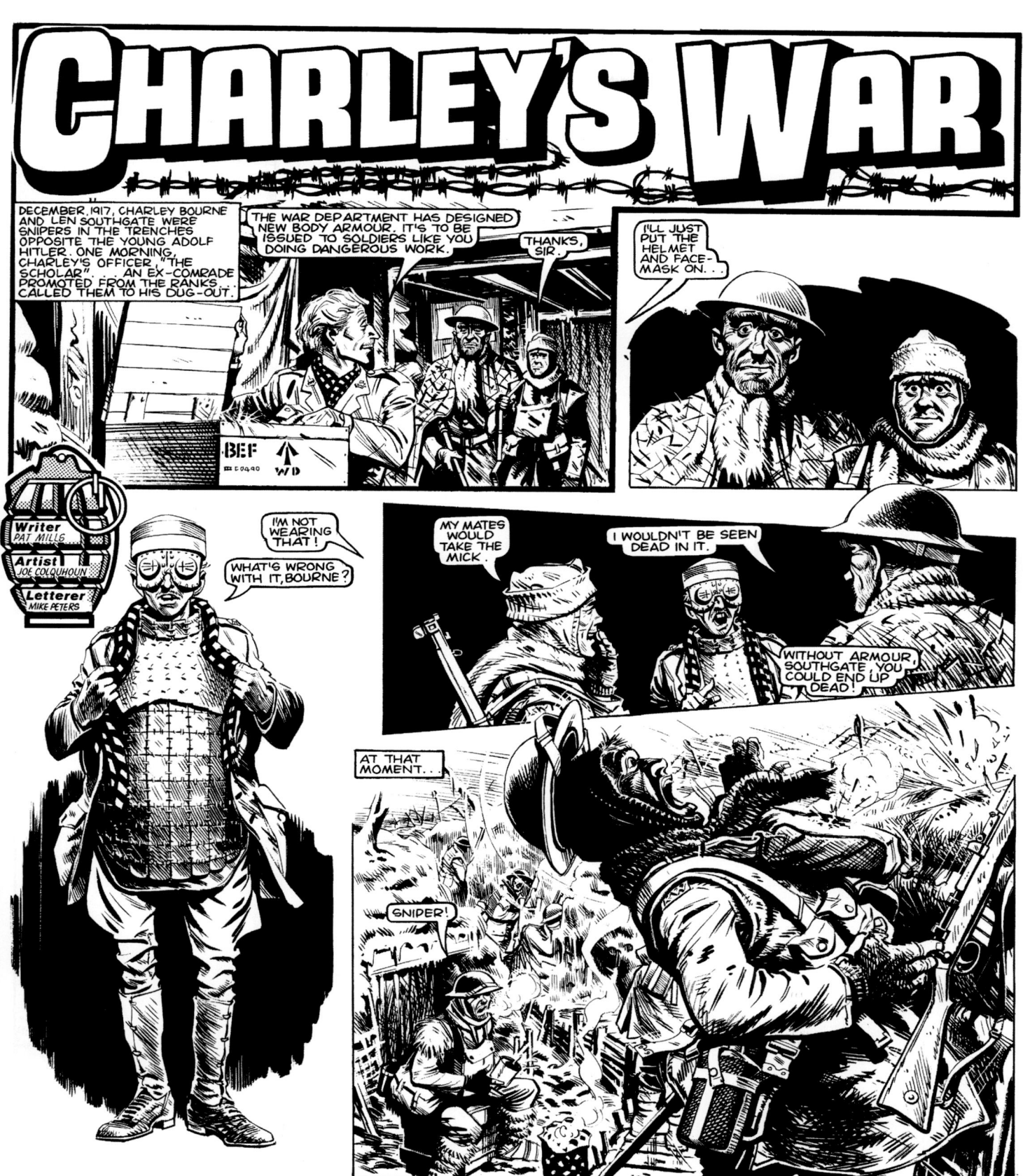

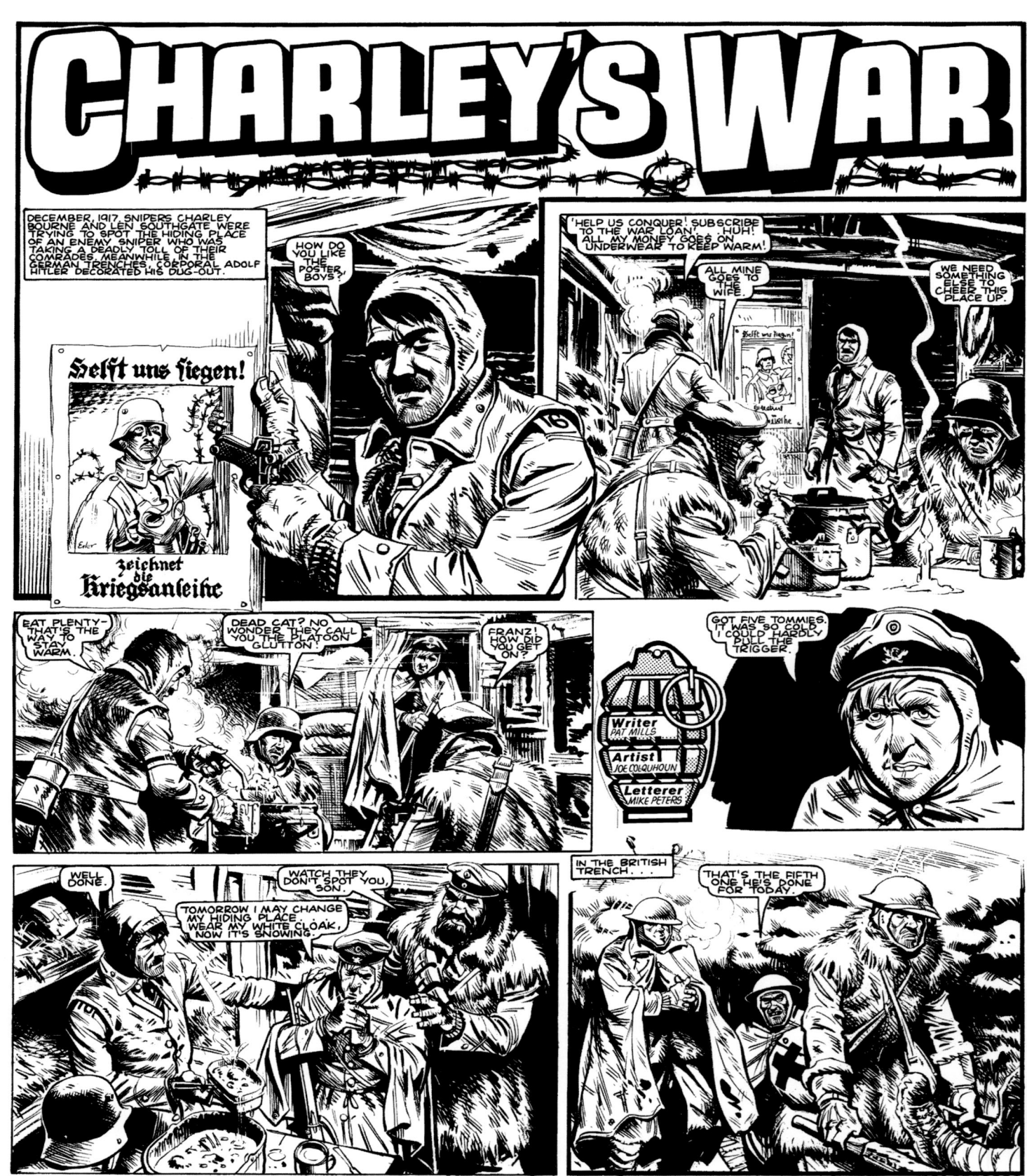

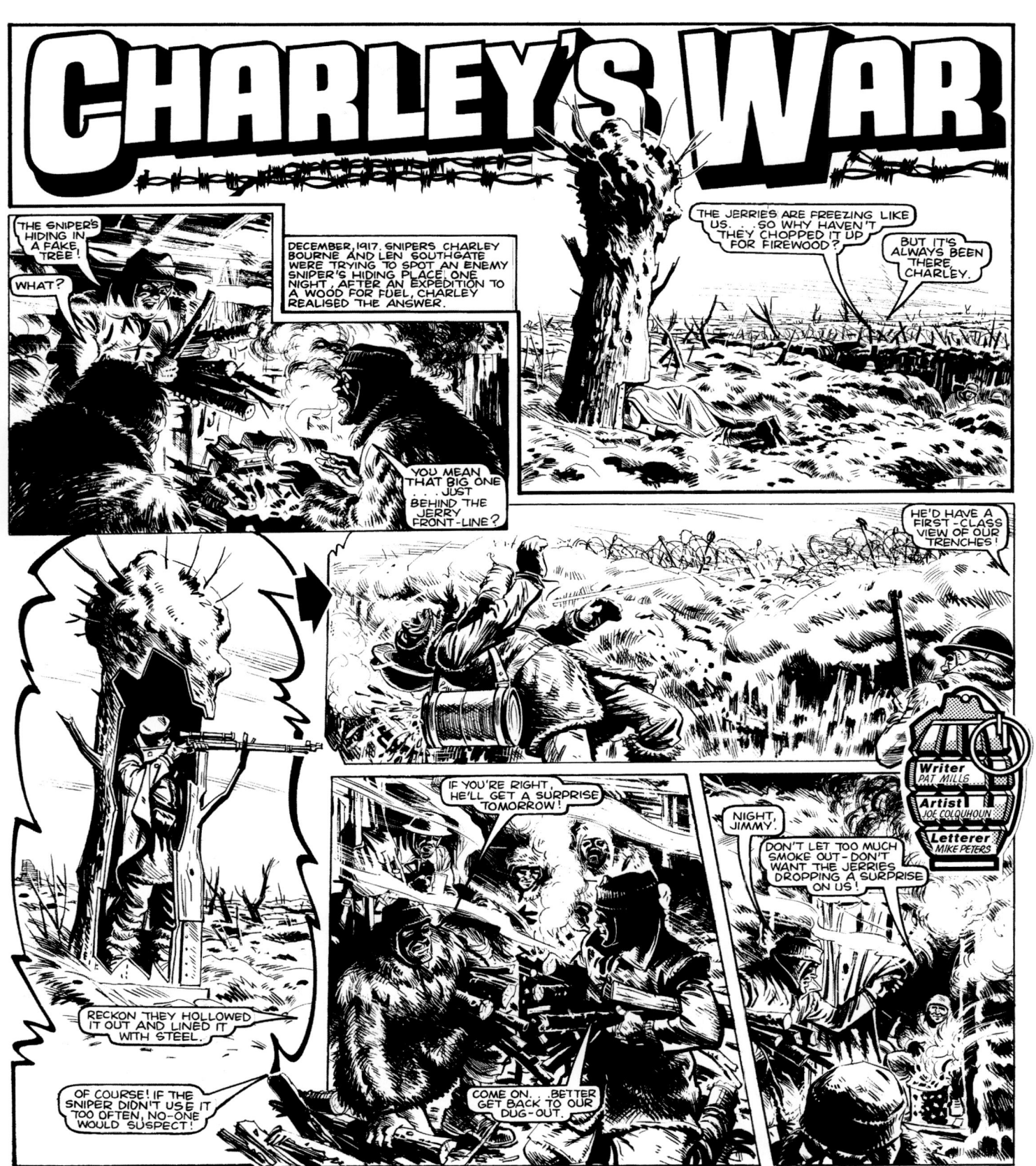

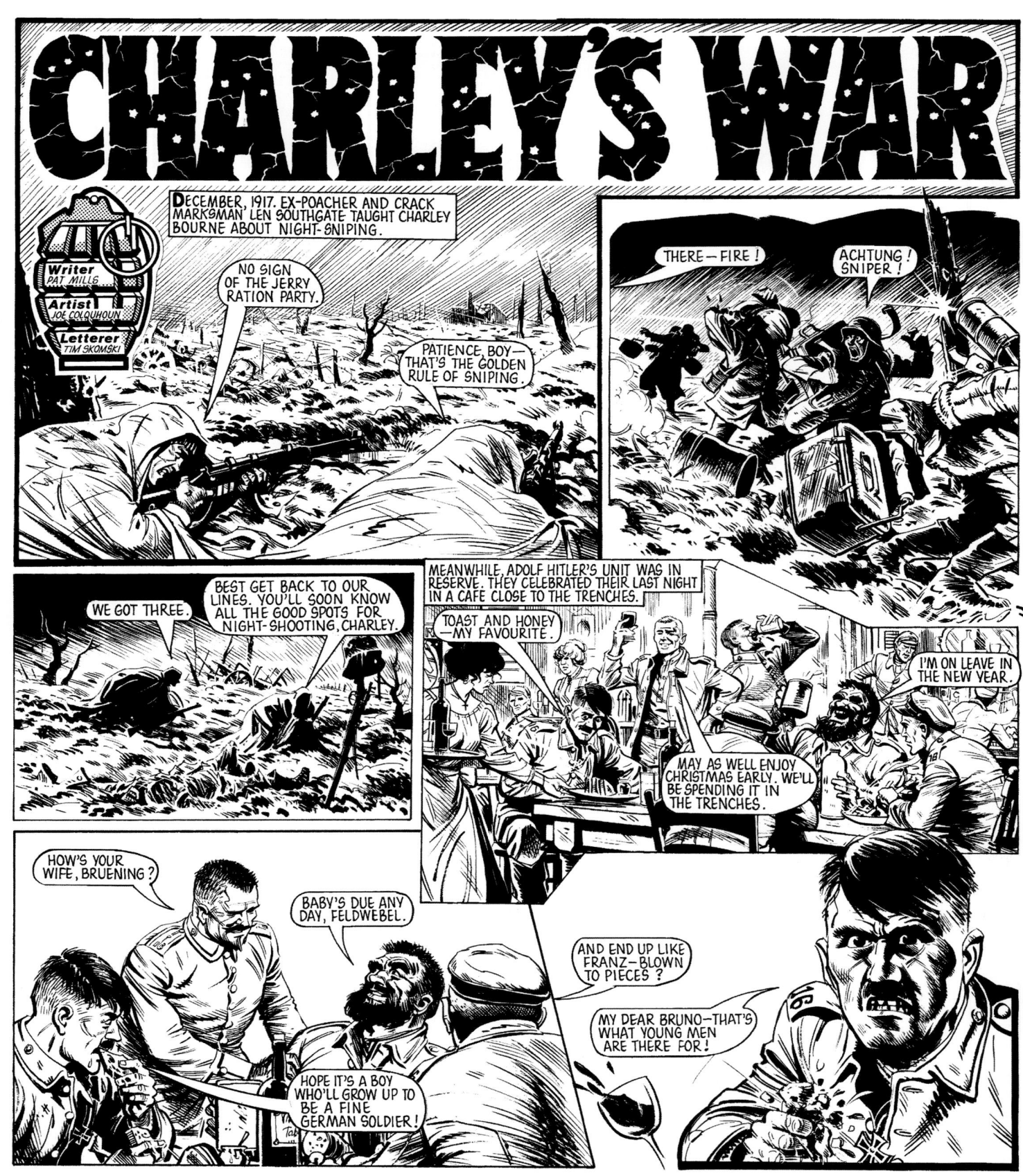

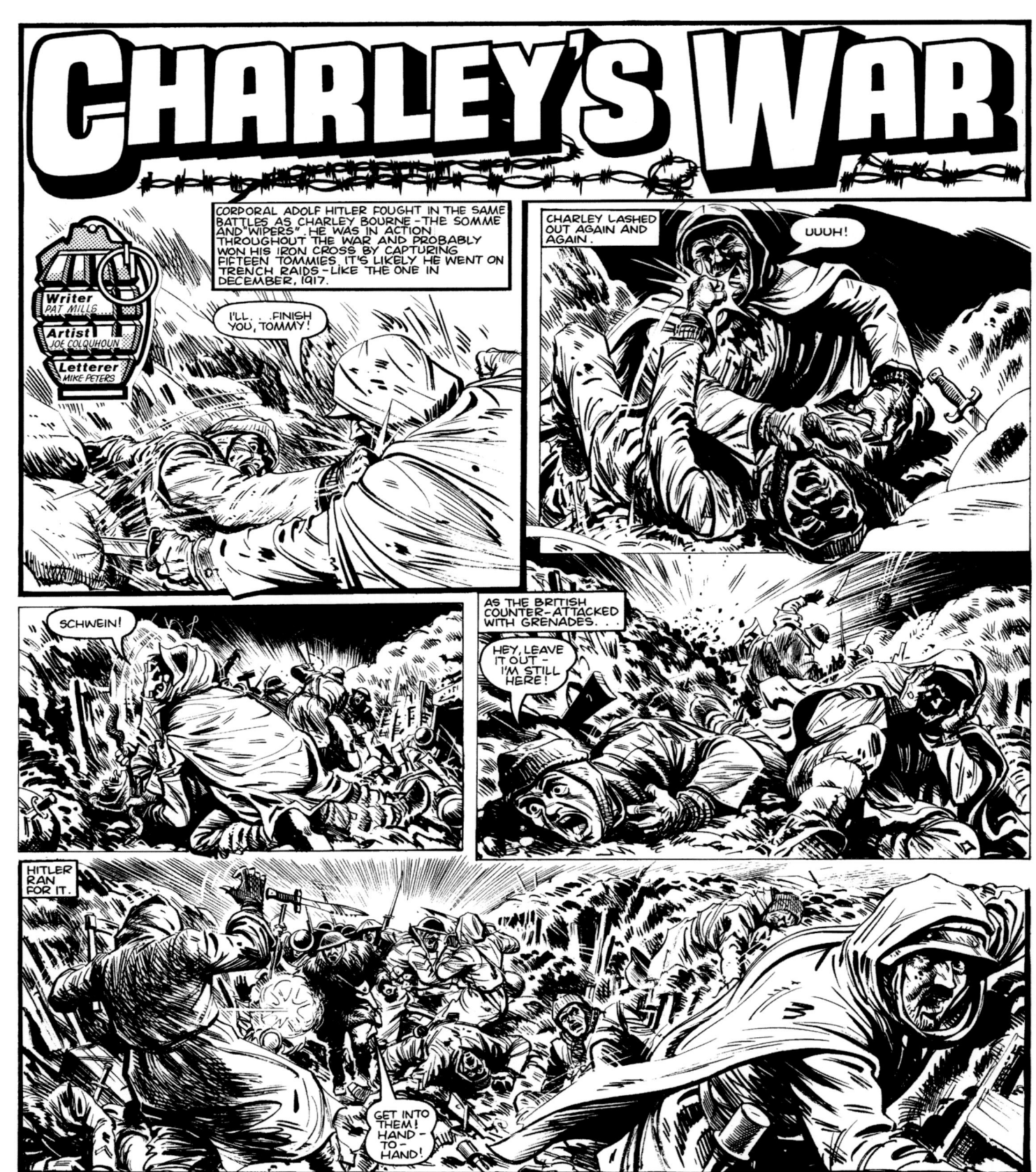

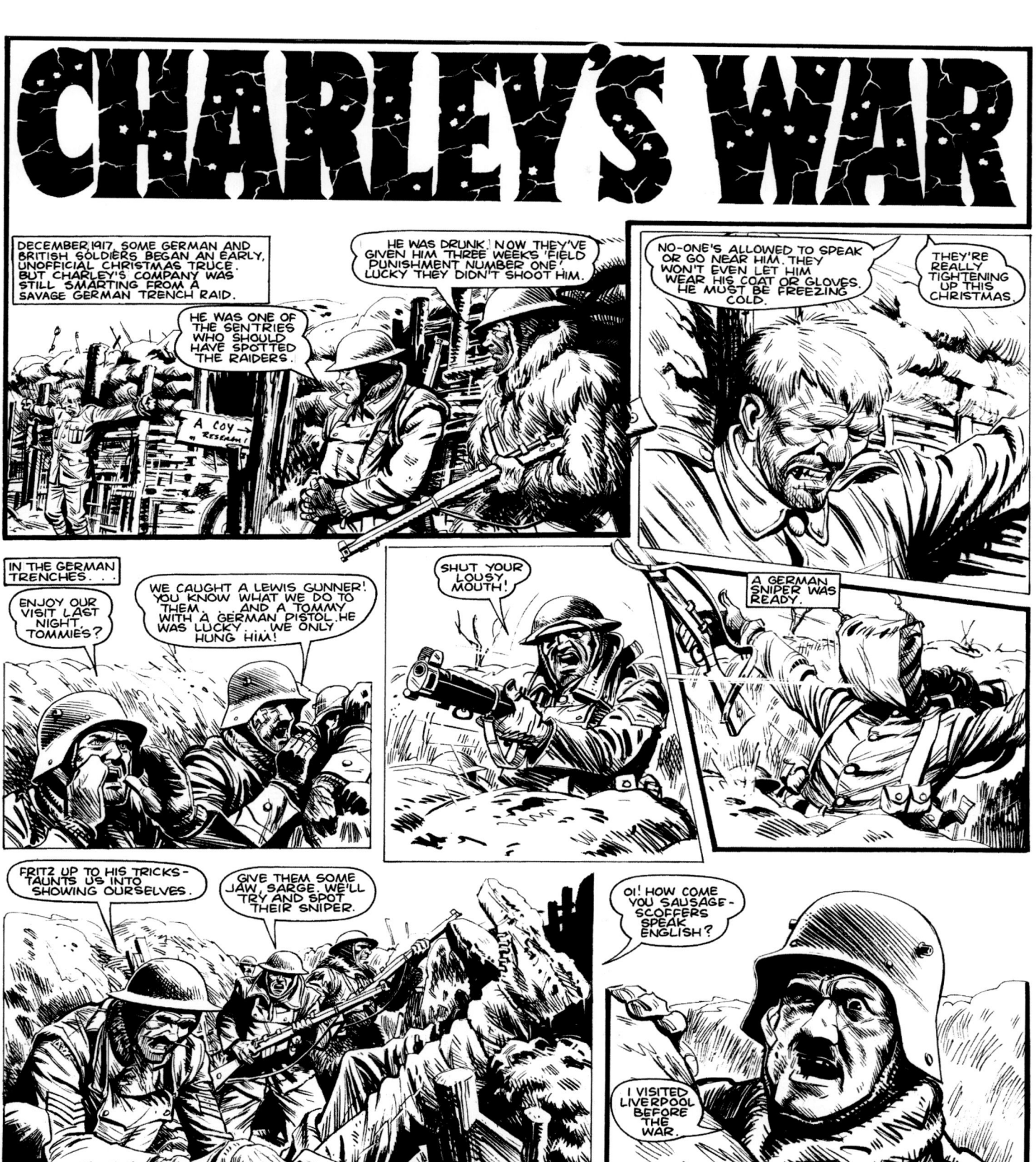

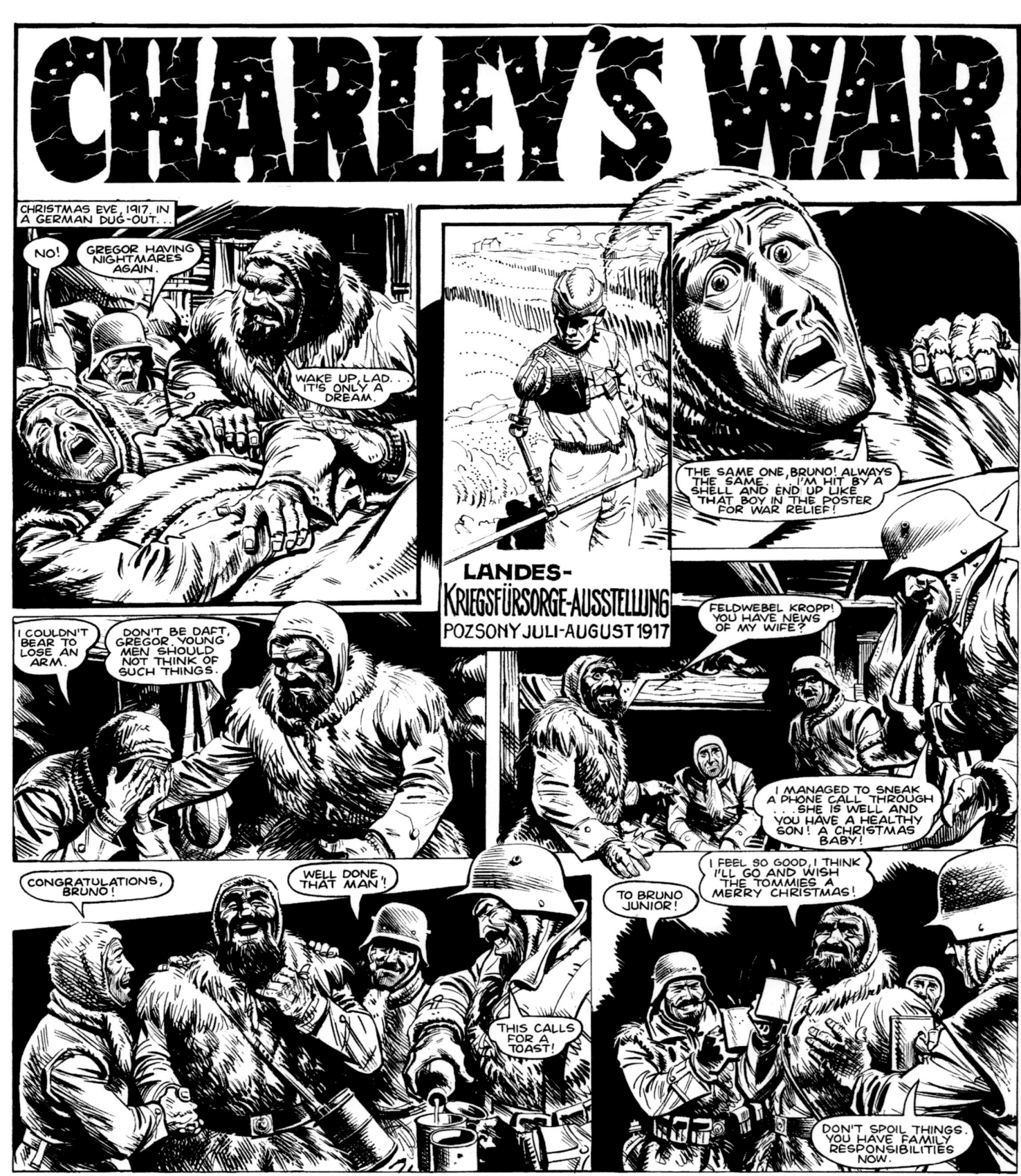

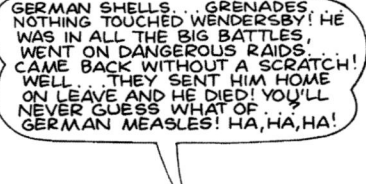

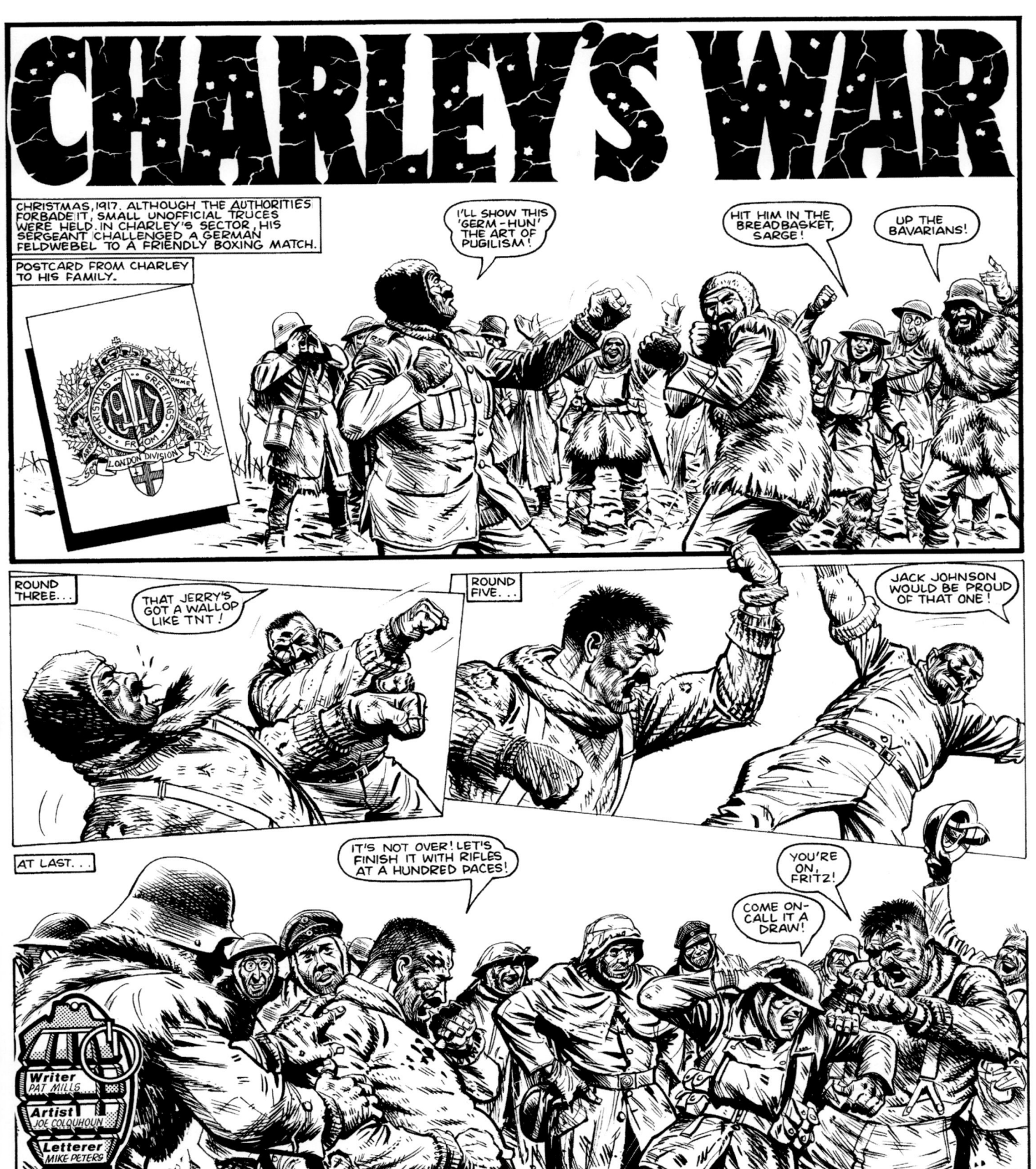

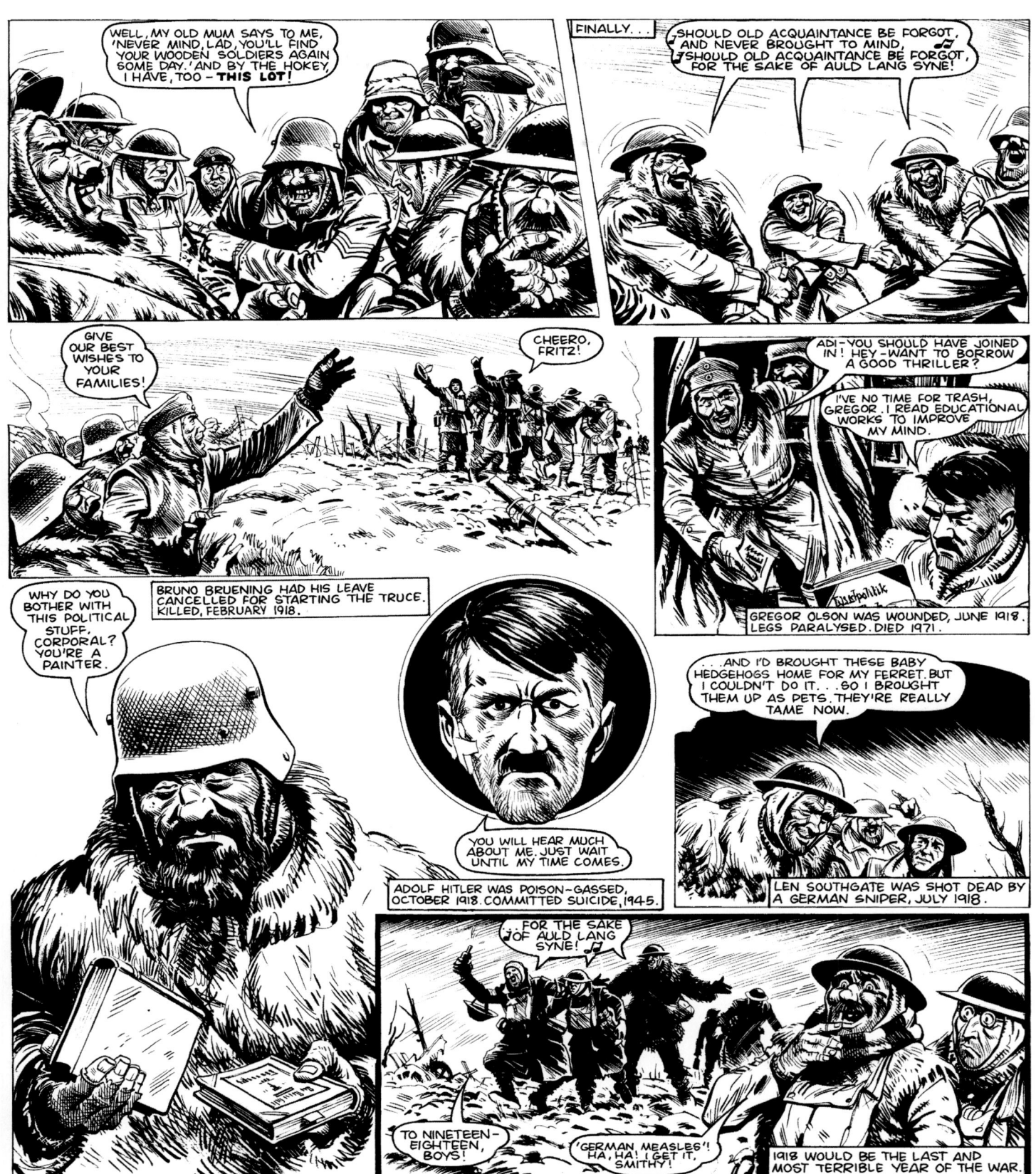

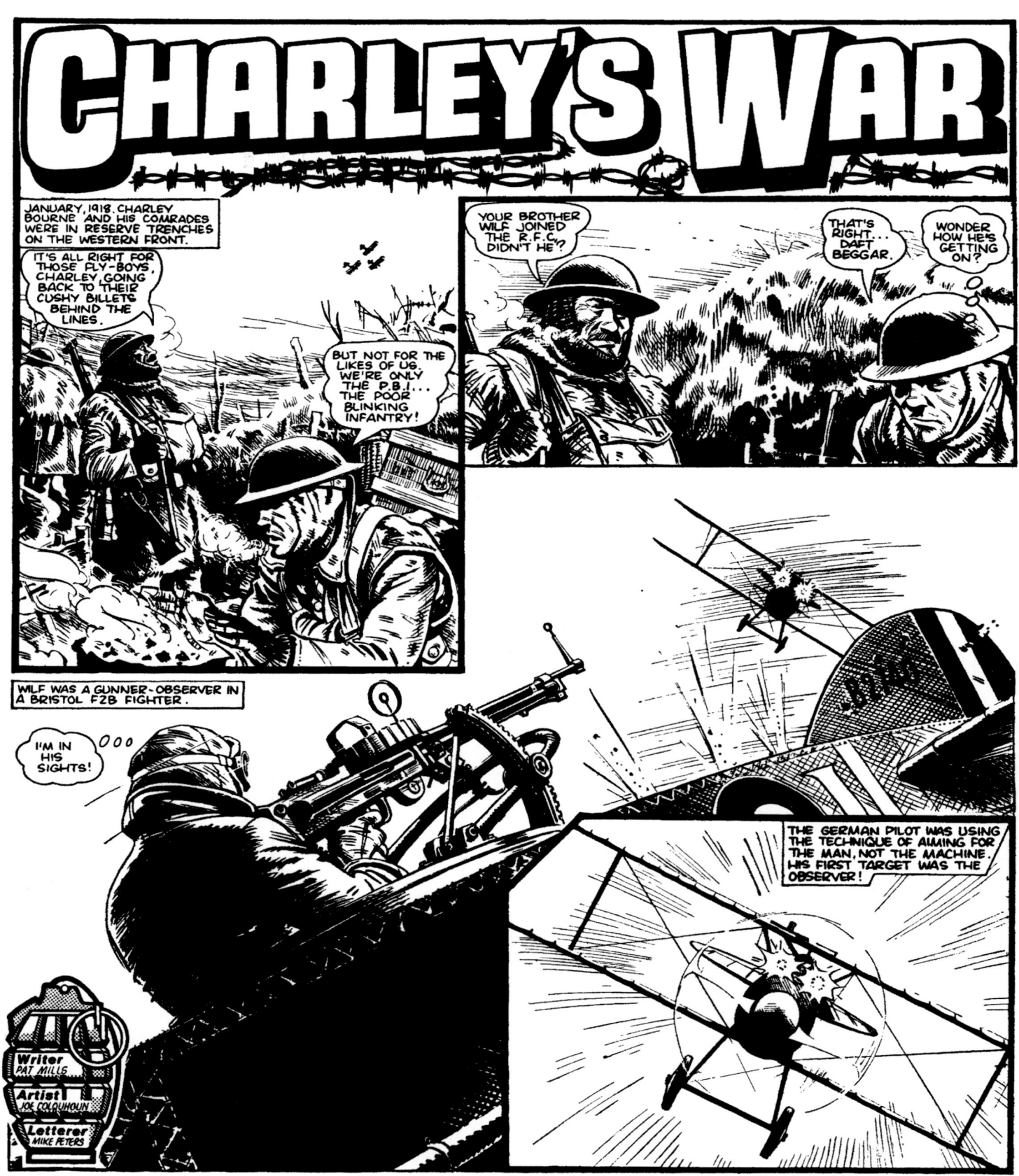

CHARLEY'S WAR

JANUARY, 1918. WILF — CHARLEY BOURNE'S YOUNGER BROTHER — WAS P.B.O. (POOR BLINKING OBSERVER) TO CAPTAIN MORGAN. IN A DOGFIGHT WITH RICHTOFEN'S "TRIPES", WILF'S LEWIS GUN JAMMED.

CARTRIDGE IS STUCK IN THE BREECH! NEVER GET IT FREE IN TIME!

HELP CAME FROM "JANKER" REED.

THAT WAS CLOSE!

MORGAN'S PLANE PULLED OUT OF THE FIGHT.

FIX IT! HURRY!

HANDS NUMB WITH COLD, WILF STRIPPED THE GUN DOWN.

THAT'S DONE IT. HELLO! WE'VE GOT COMPANY!

MORGEY'S GOING TO RAM HIM!

Writer PAT MILLS
Artist JOE COLQUHOUN
Letterer MIKE PETERS

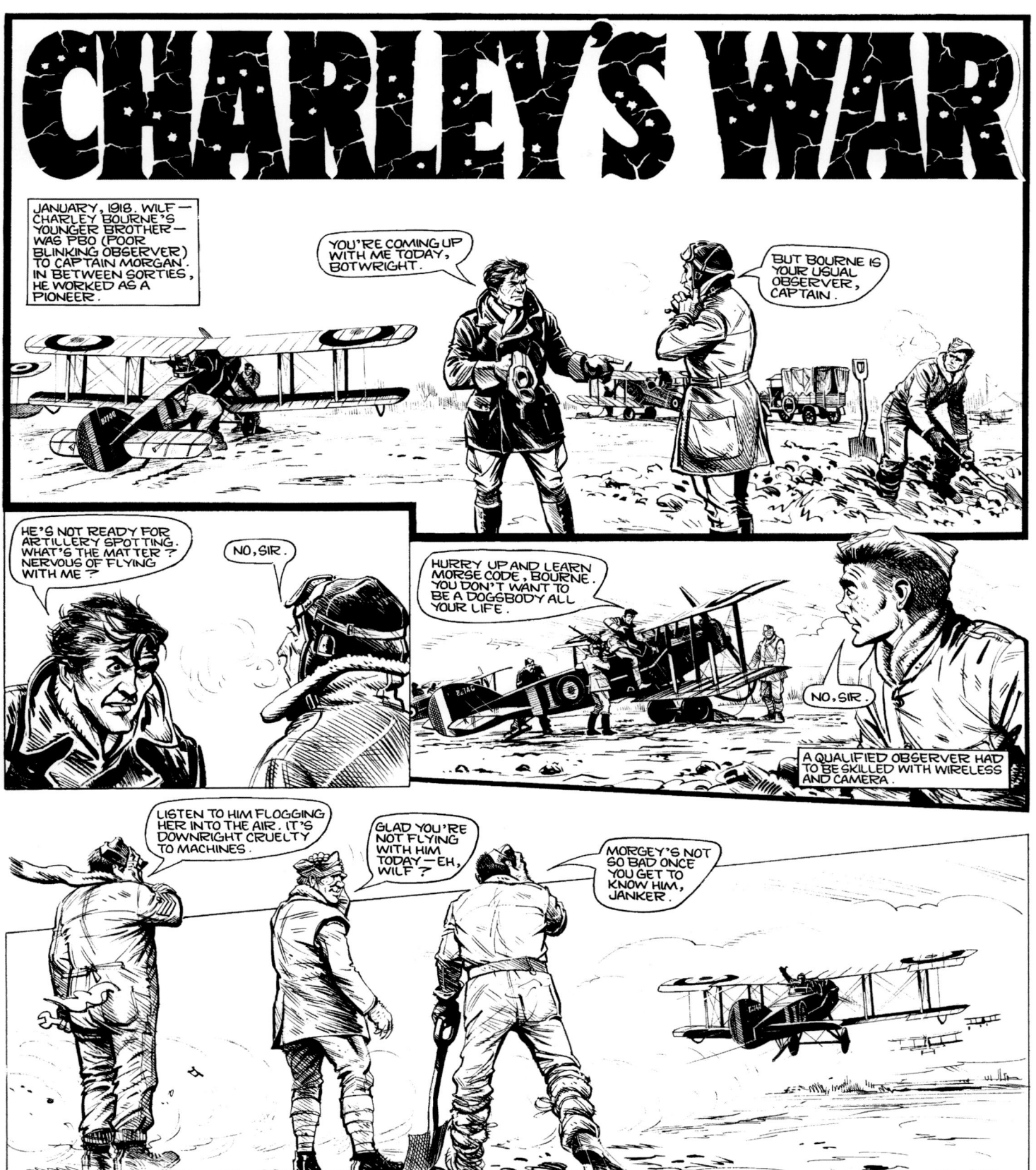

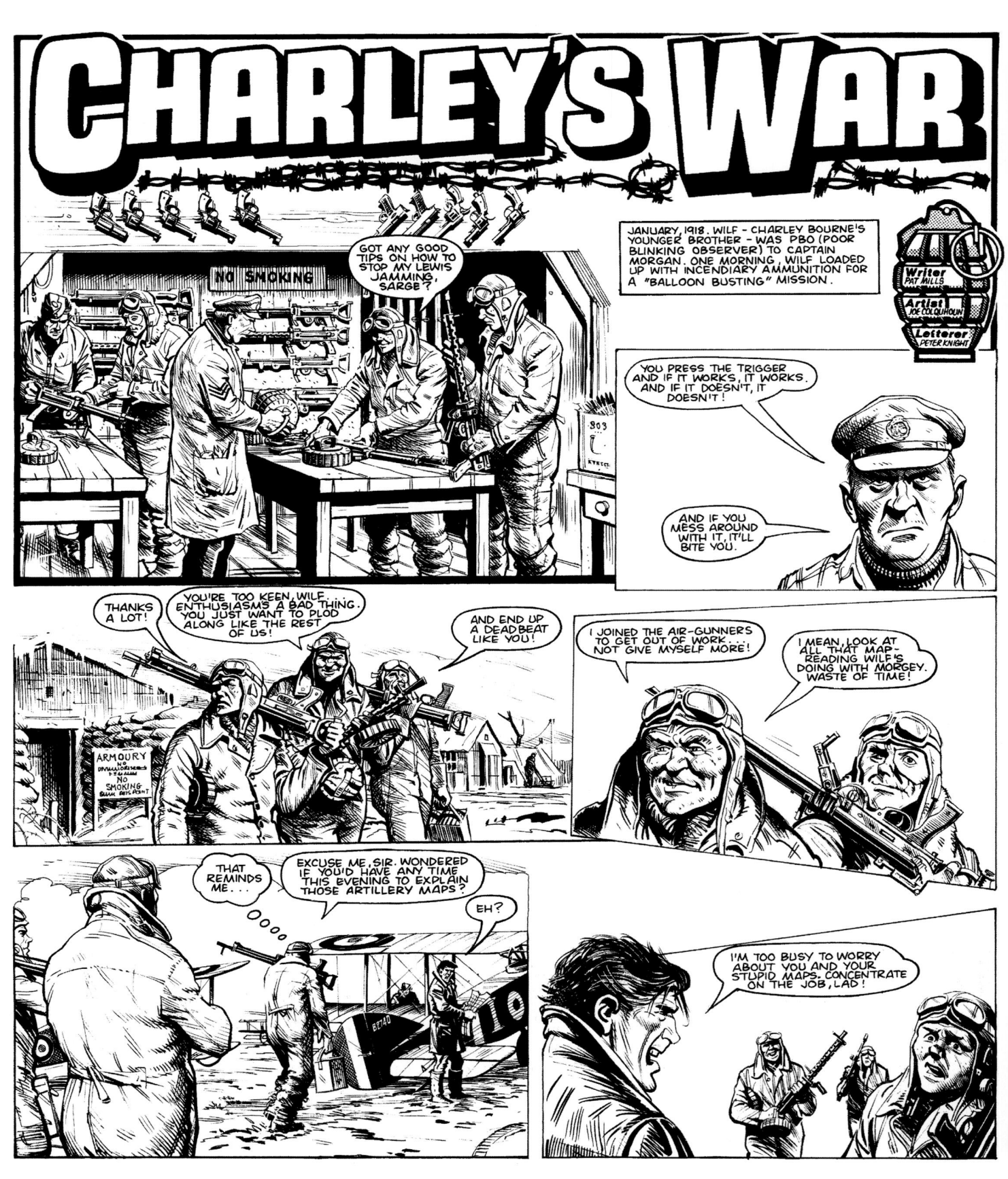

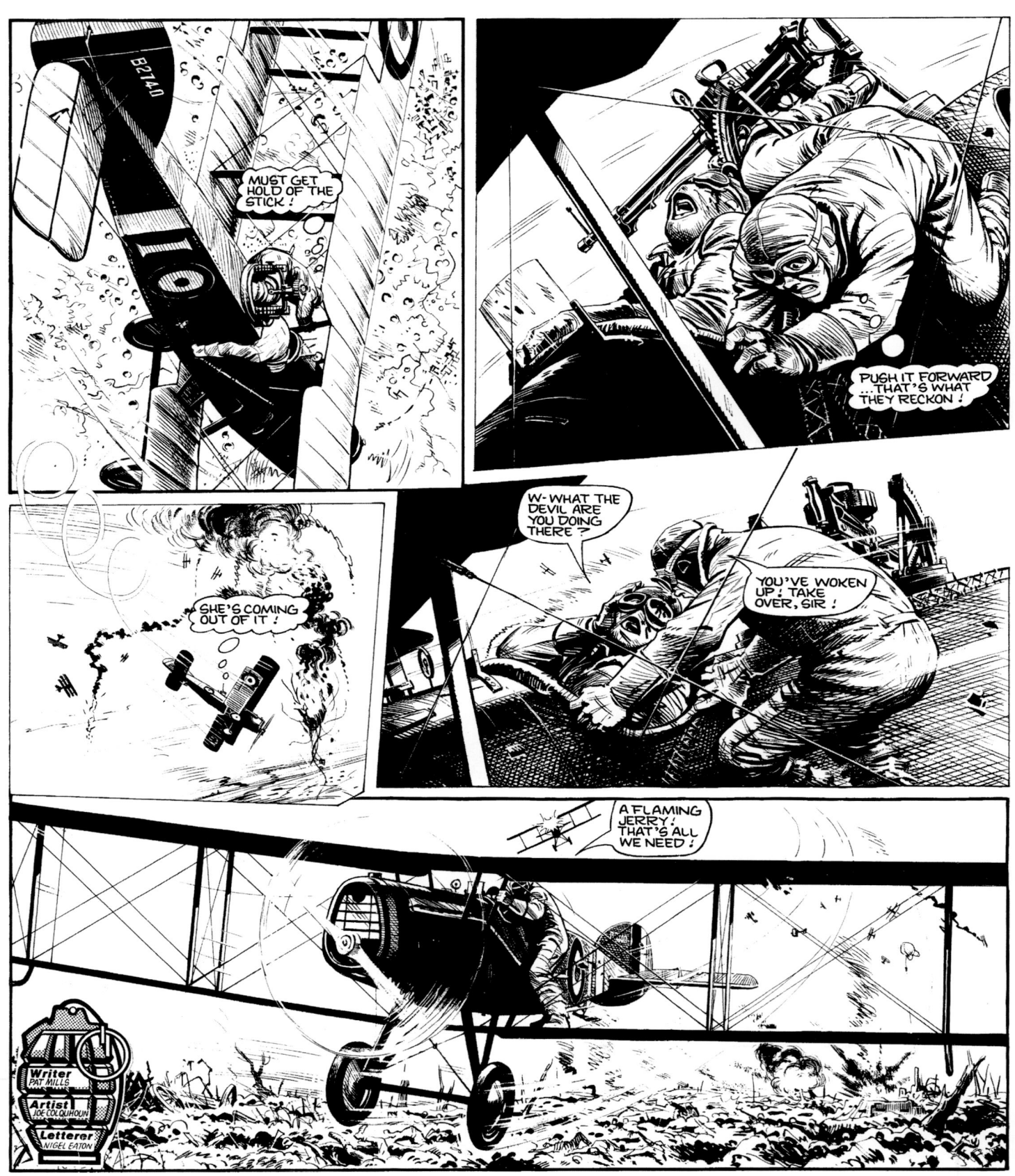

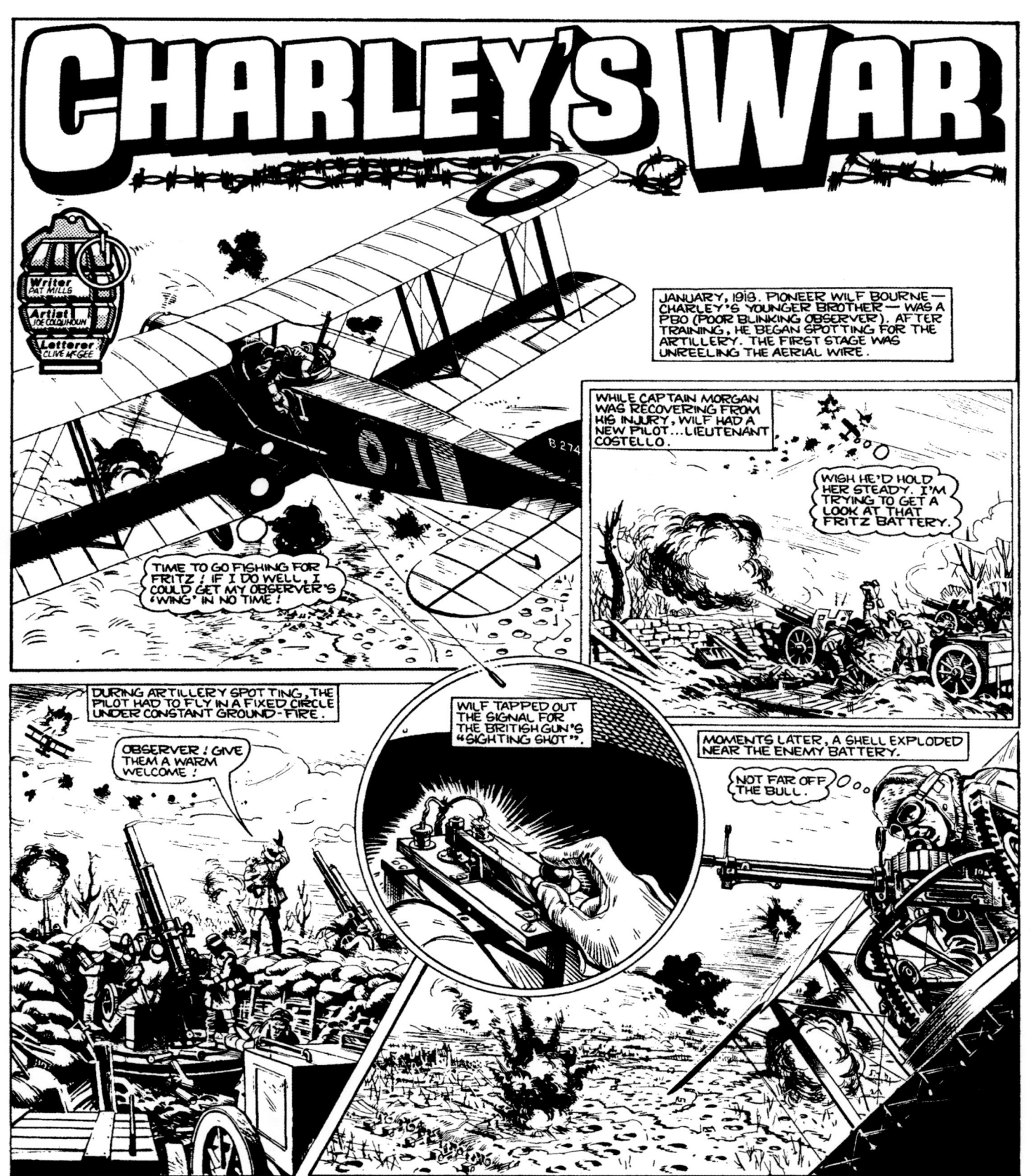

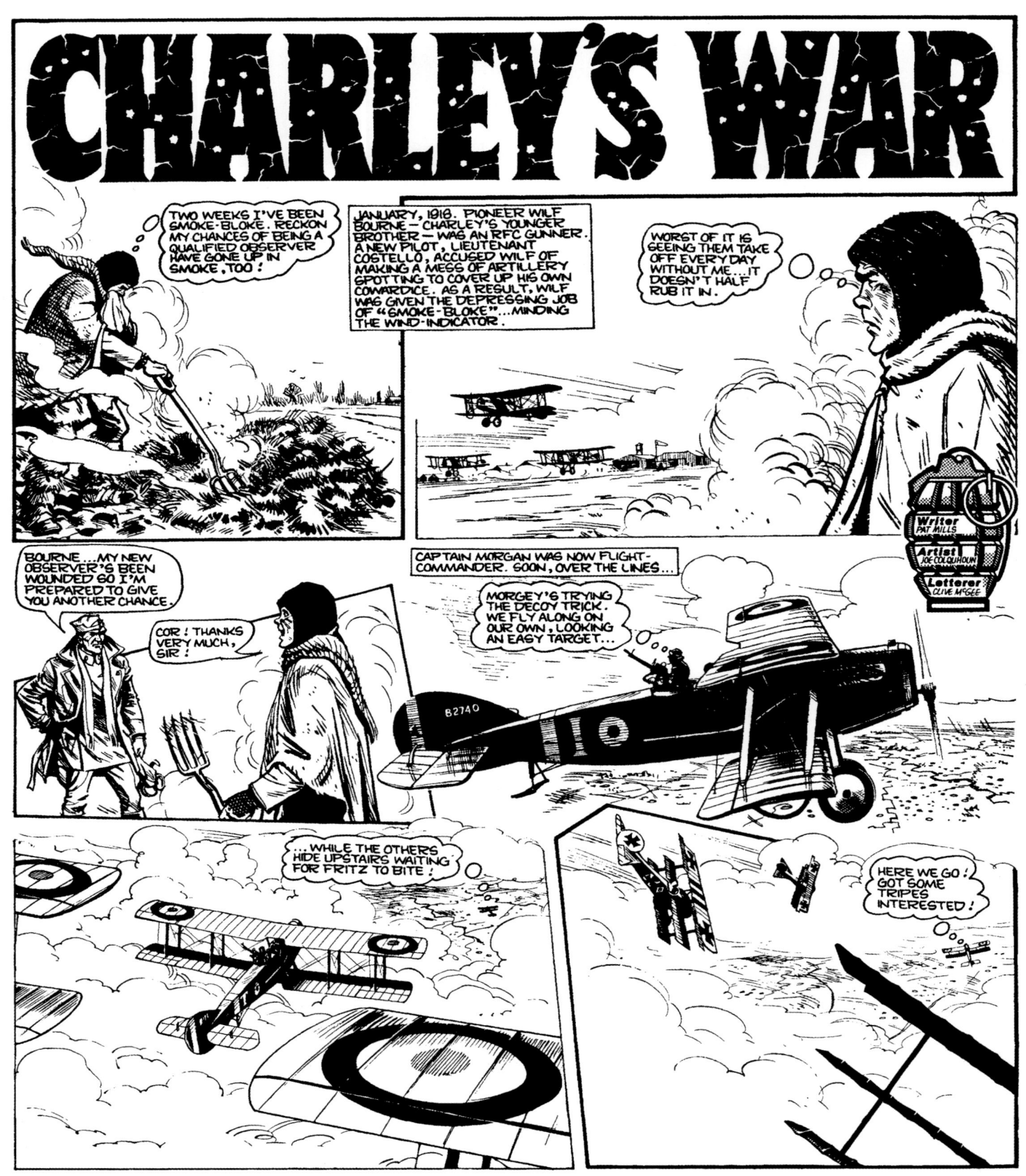

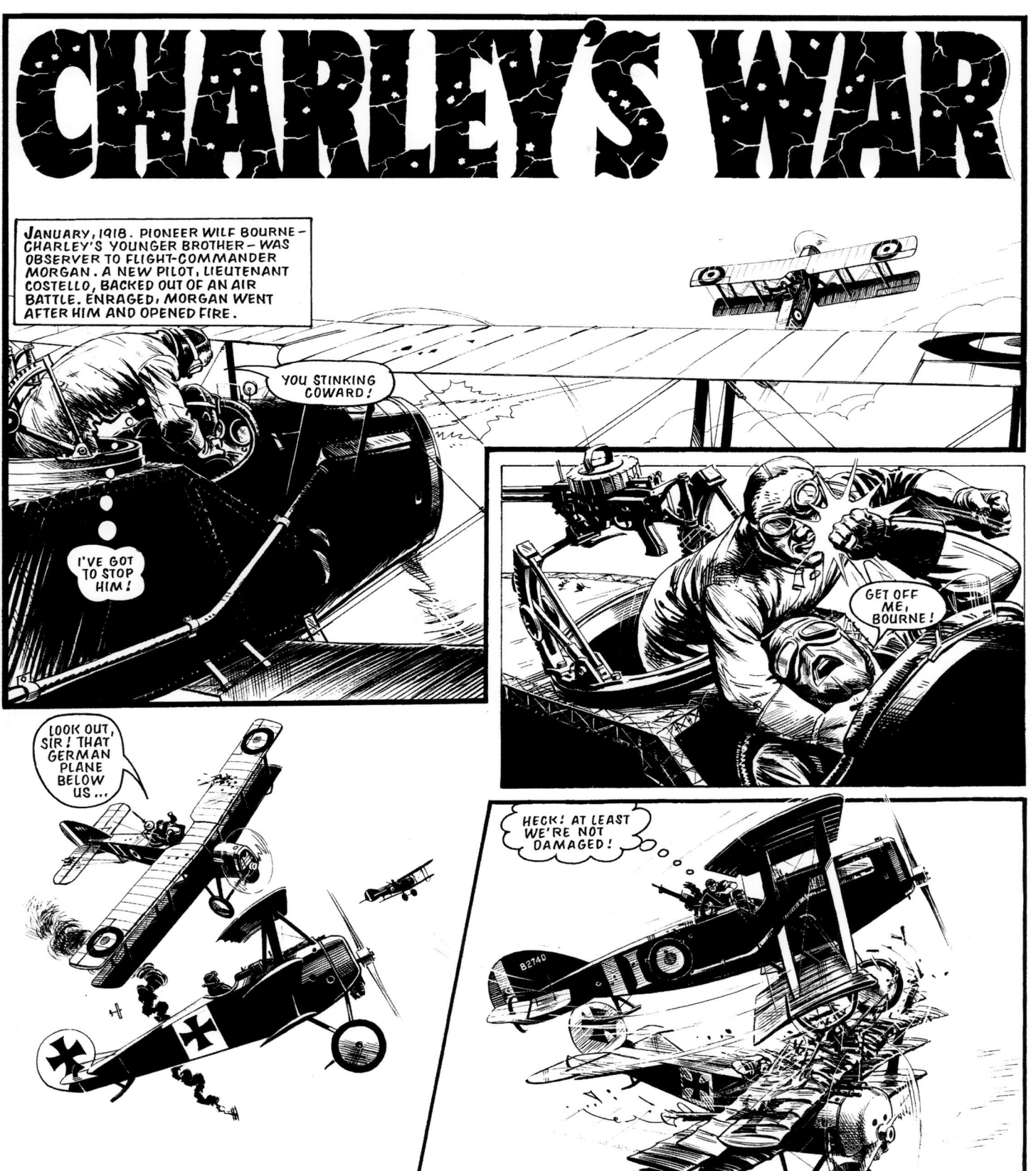

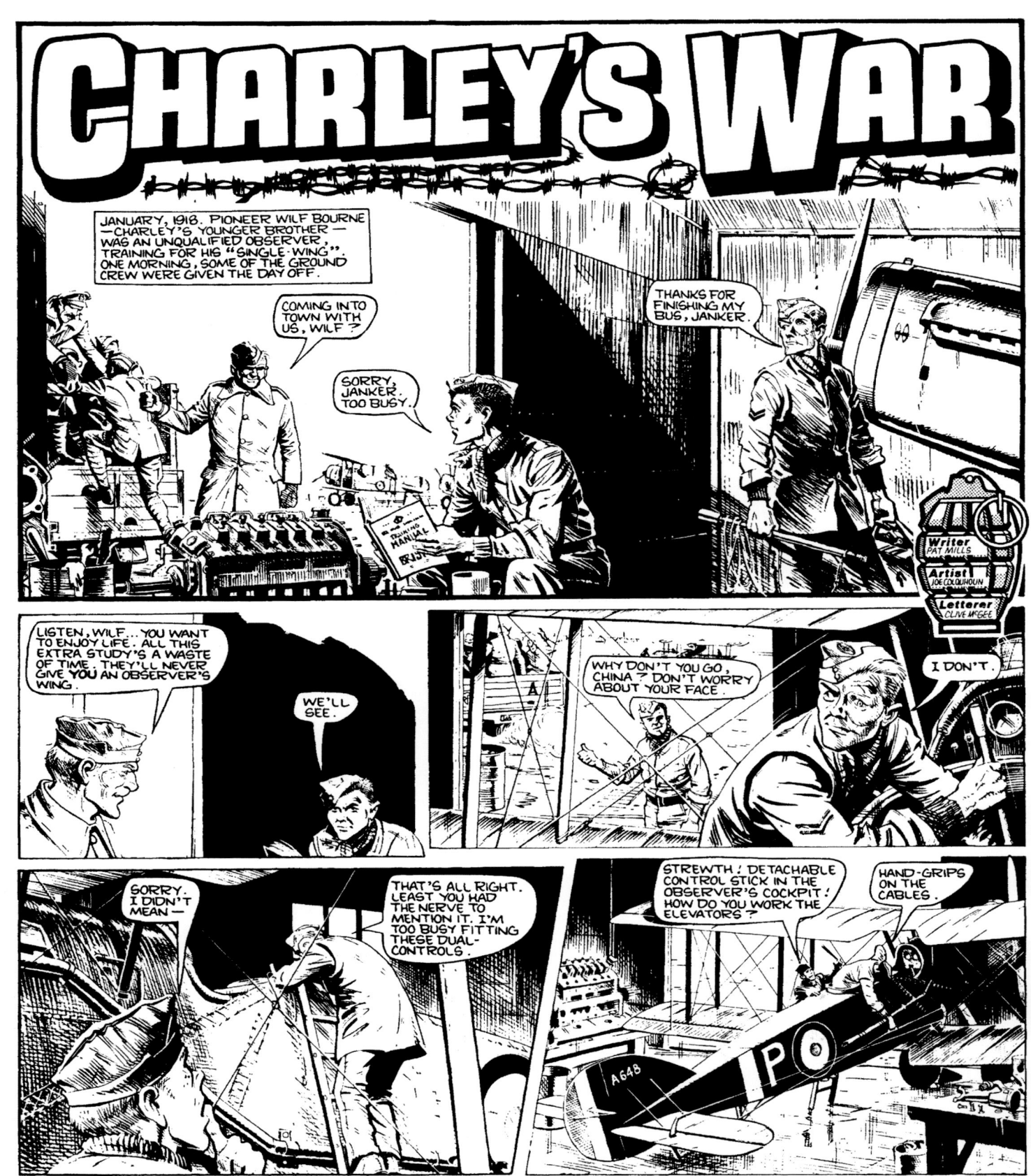

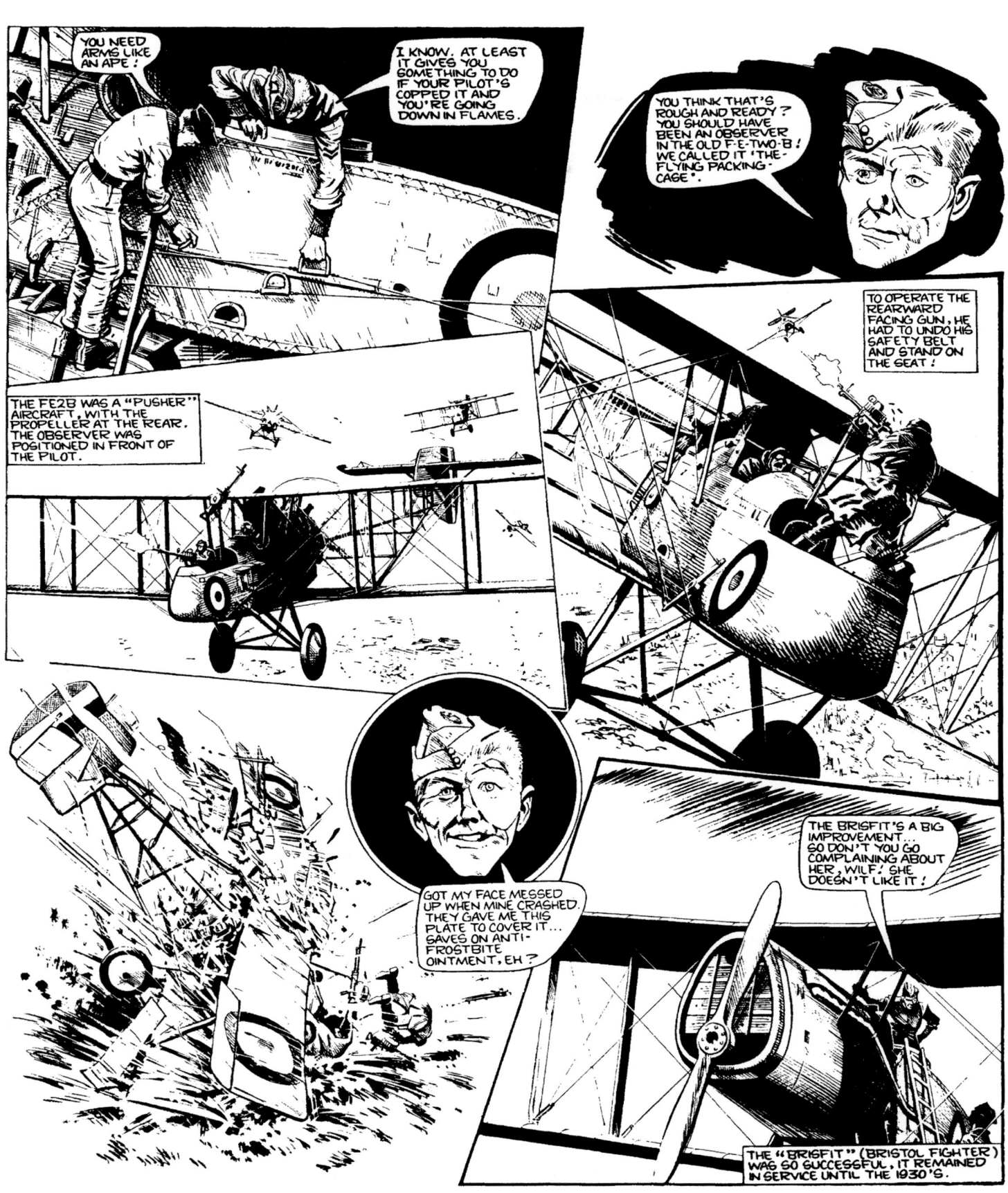

Panel 1	Panel 2
"BIT DIFFICULT TO CONCENTRATE!"	"TAKE HER ROUND ONCE MORE, CAPTAIN MORGAN! I'VE SPOTTED SOMETHING!" "HURRY UP!"

"RIGHT! LAST PHOTO!"

NEXT DAY, CAPTAIN MORGAN HAD GOOD NEWS FOR WILF.
"PHOTOGRAPHIC OFFICER'S DELIGHTED WITH YOUR PICTURES! HE'S LOCATED THE BATTERY ON THEM! WELL DONE, LAD!"
"THANK YOU, SIR."

"SHOULD GET YOUR SINGLE-WING NOW. WHAT'S WRONG..? I THOUGHT YOU'D BE PLEASED."
"I AM, SIR!"
"ONLY I DON'T DESERVE IT!"

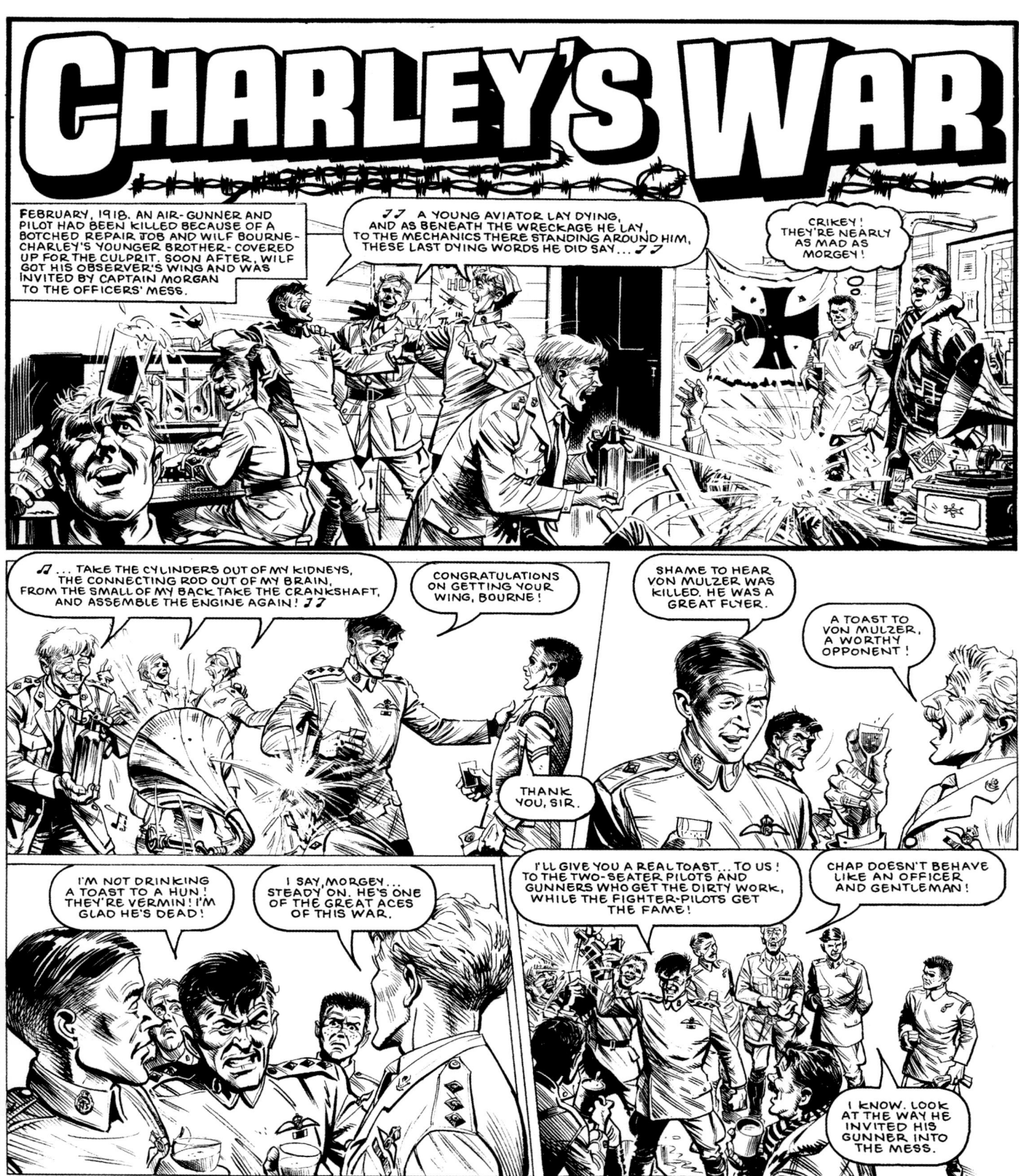

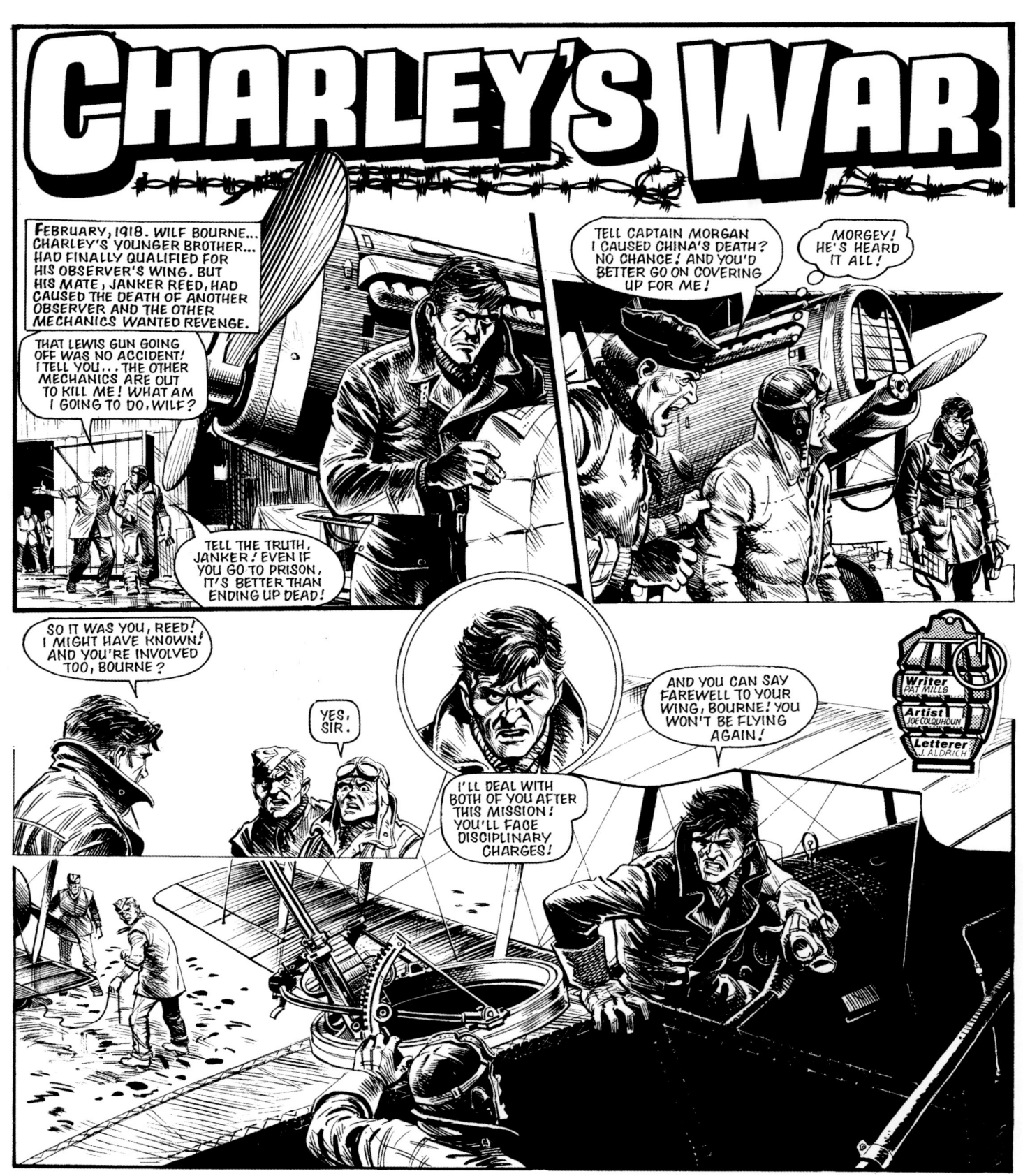

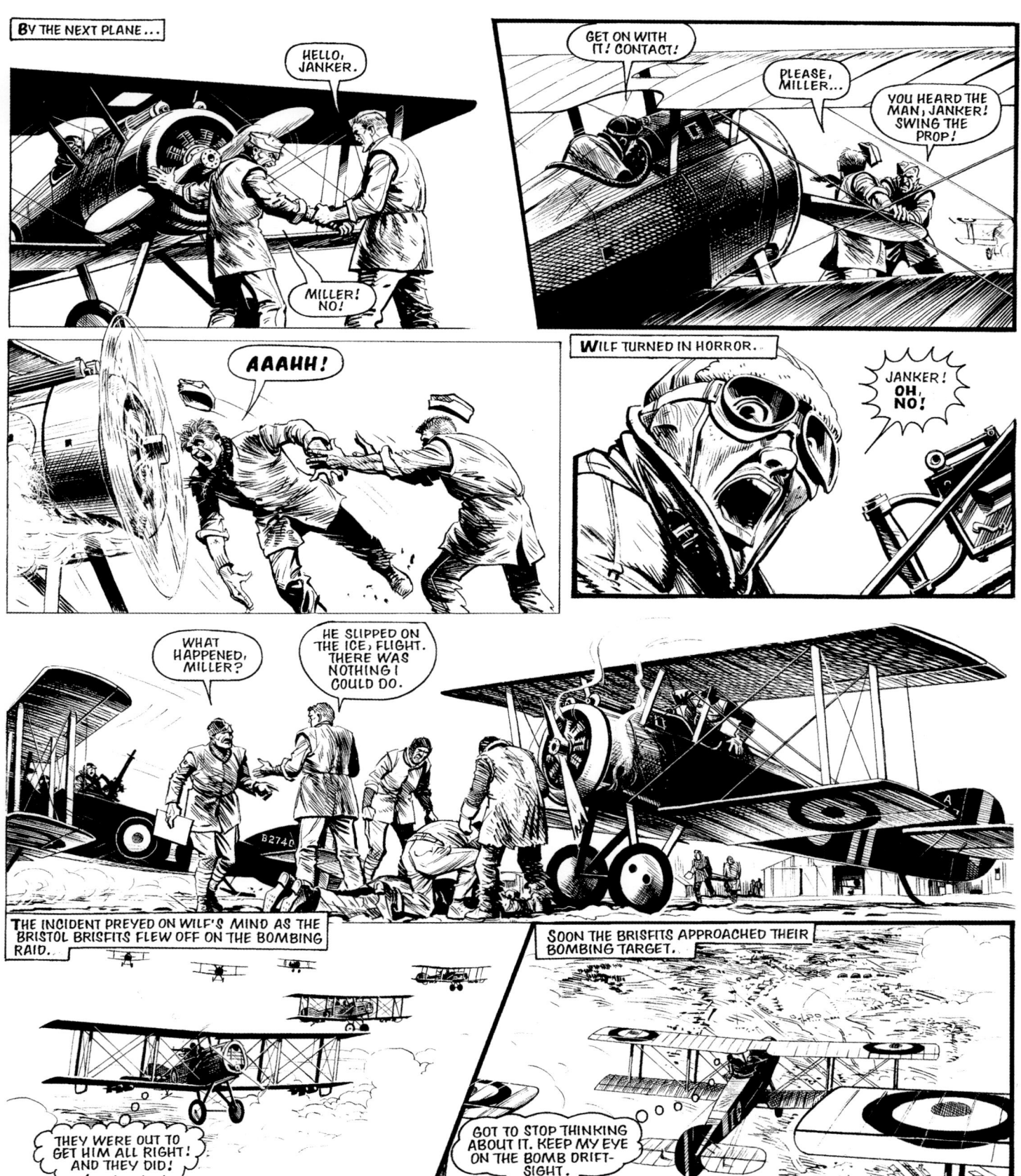

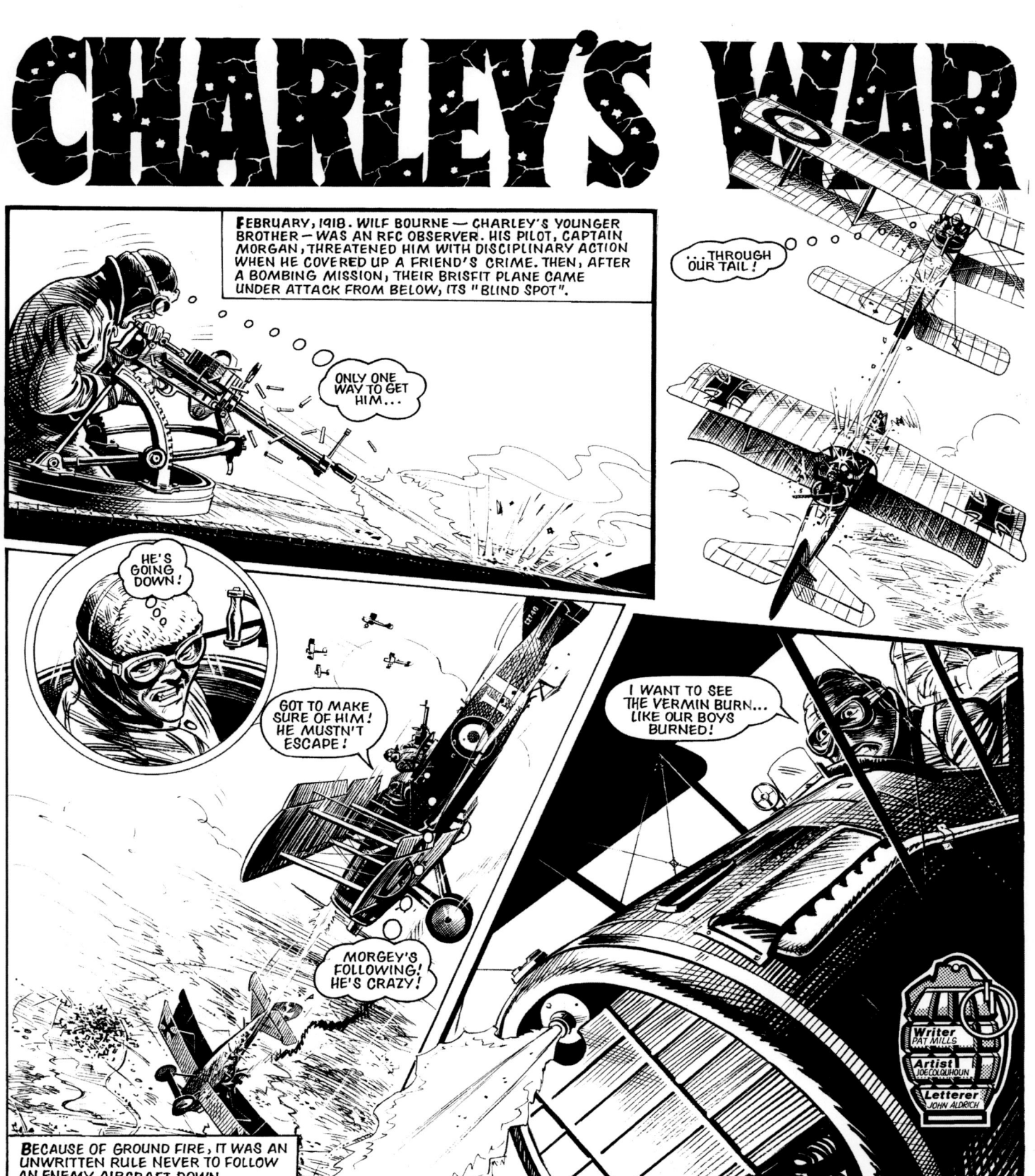

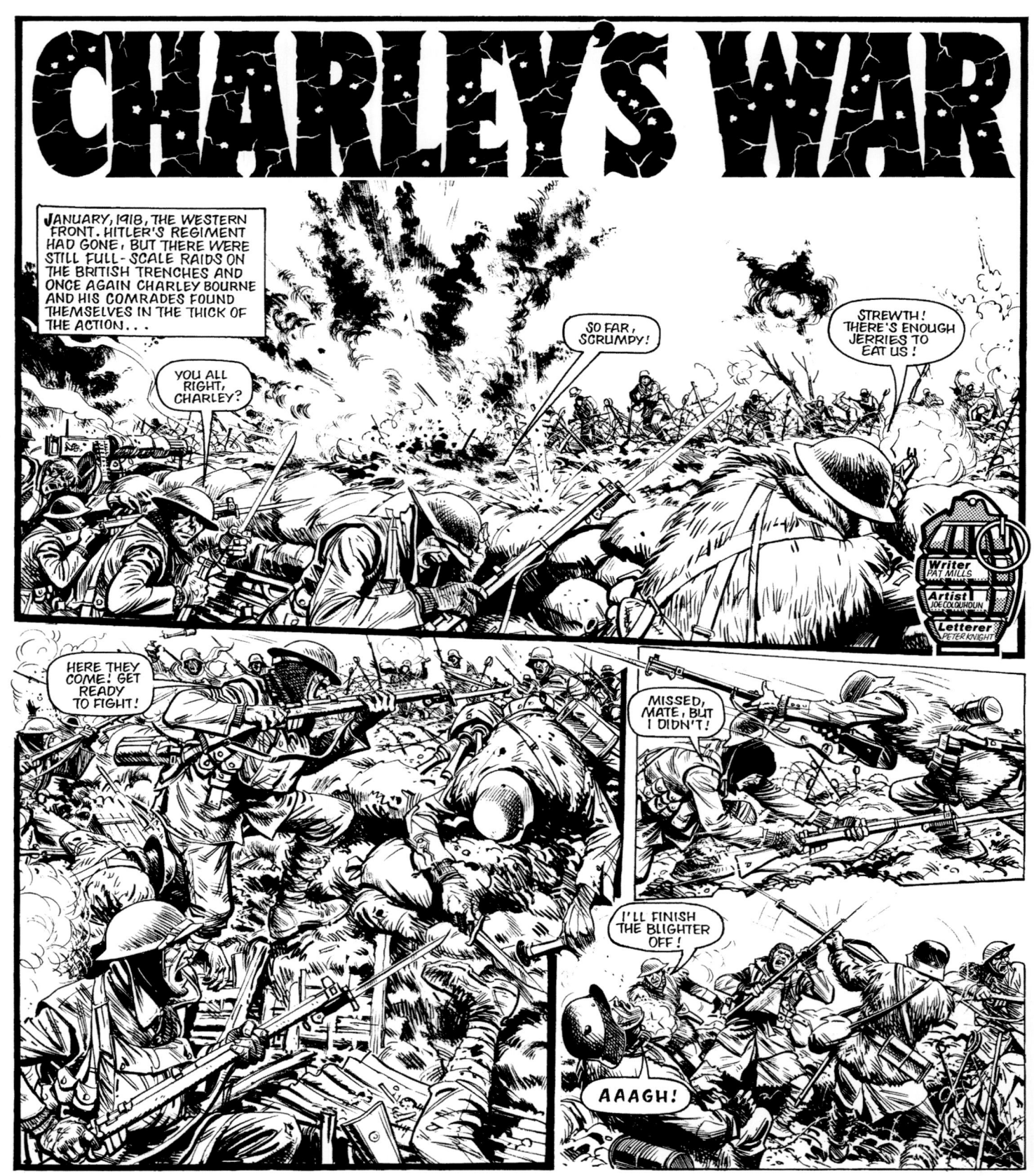

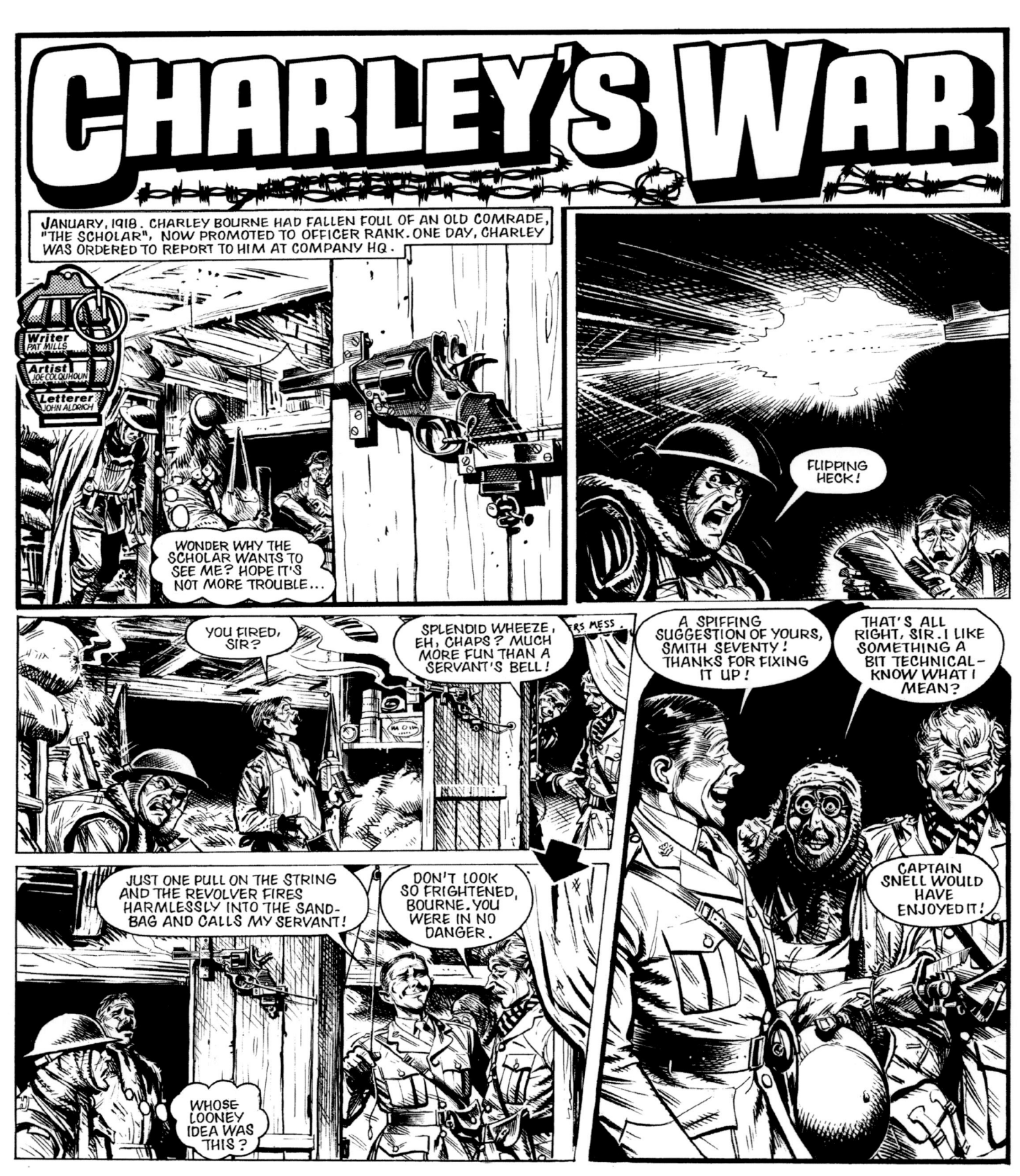

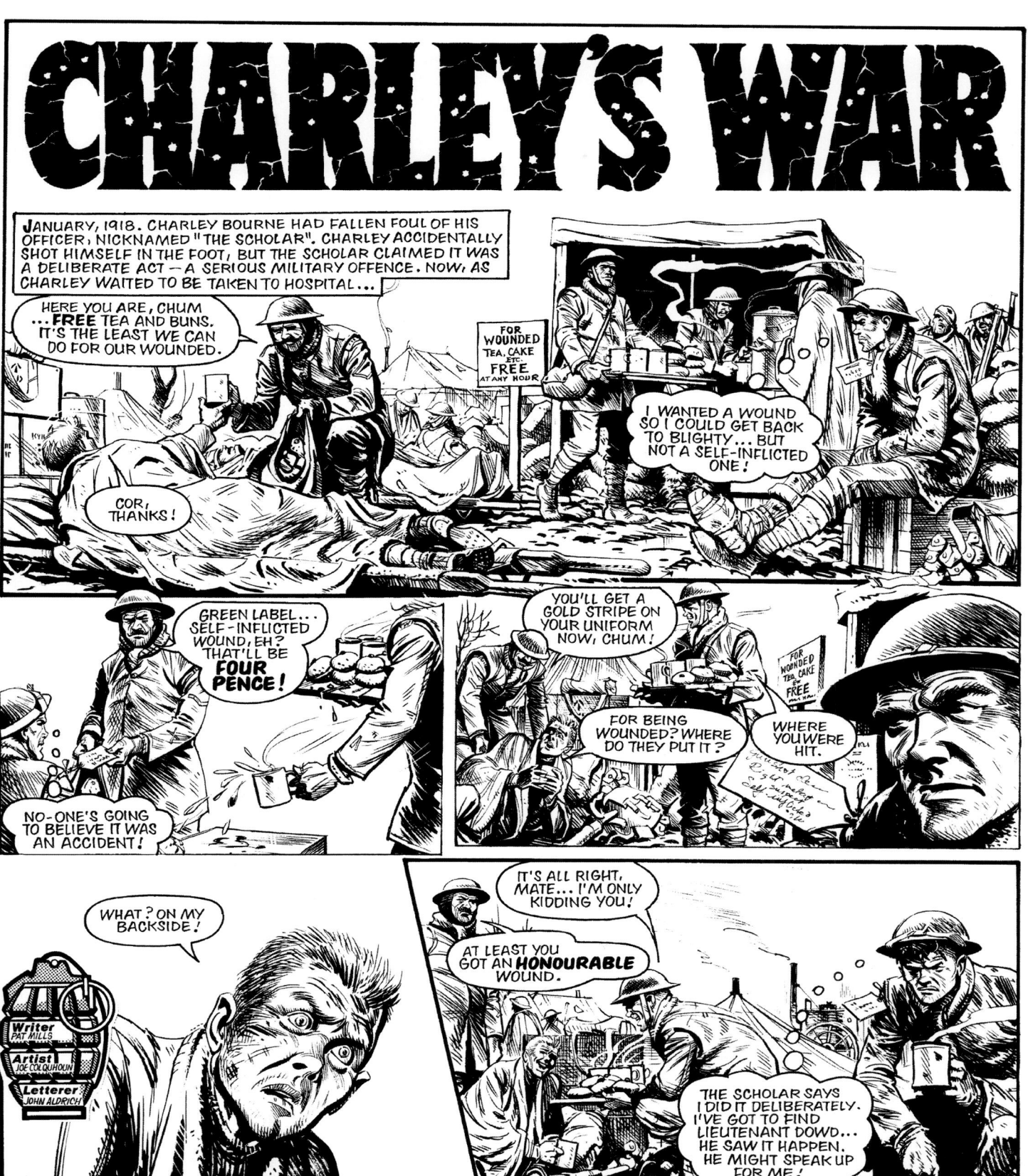

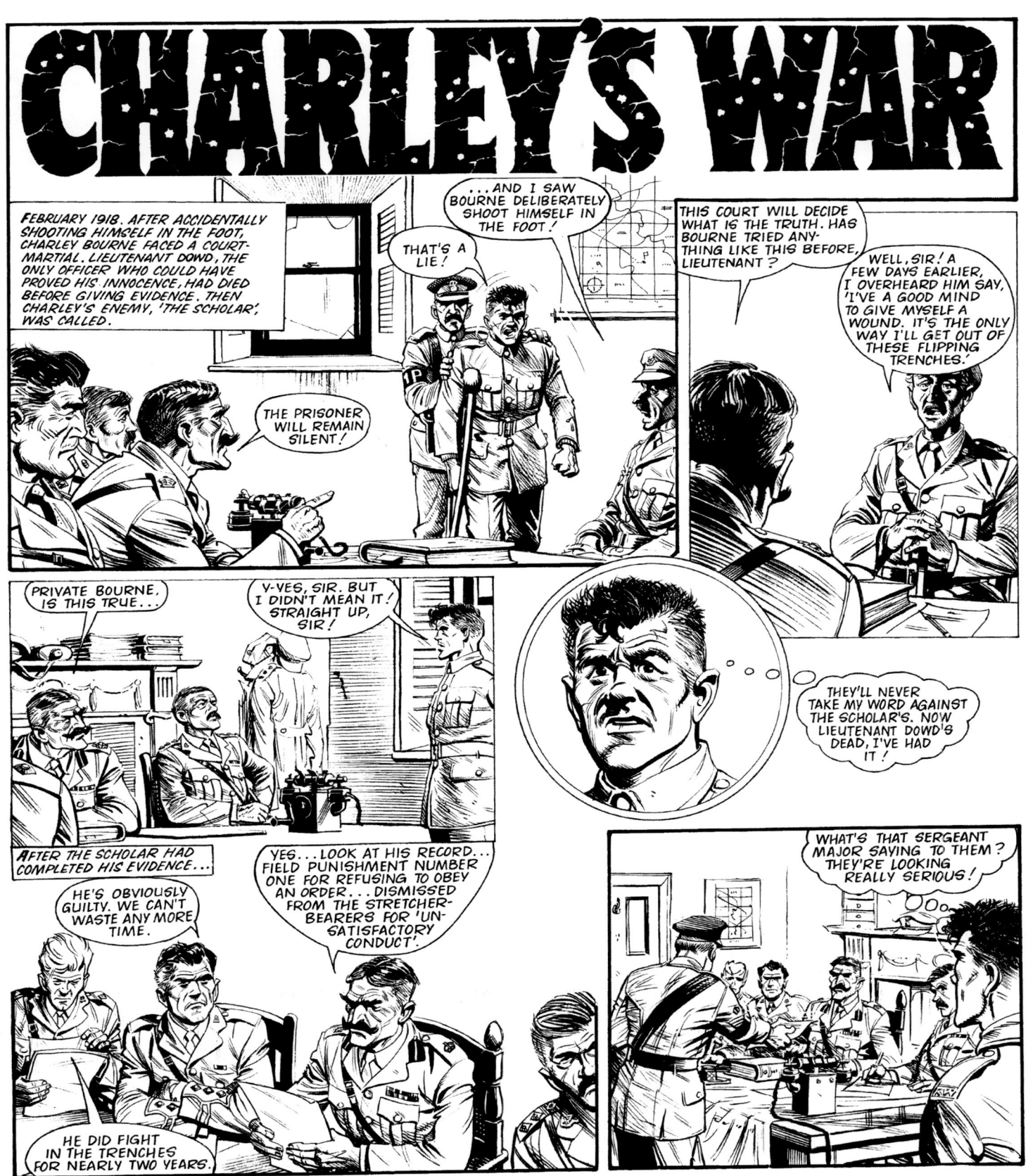

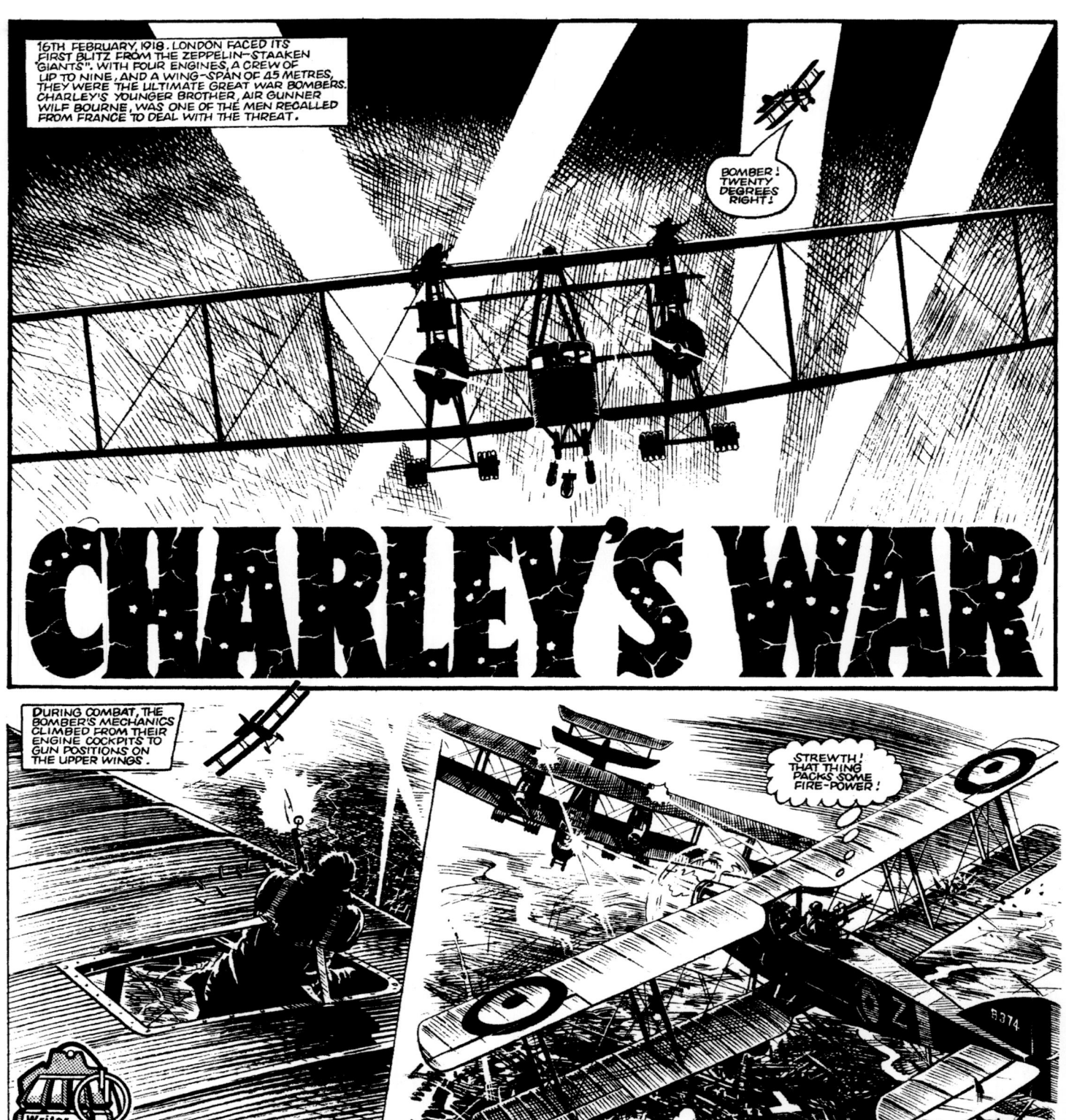

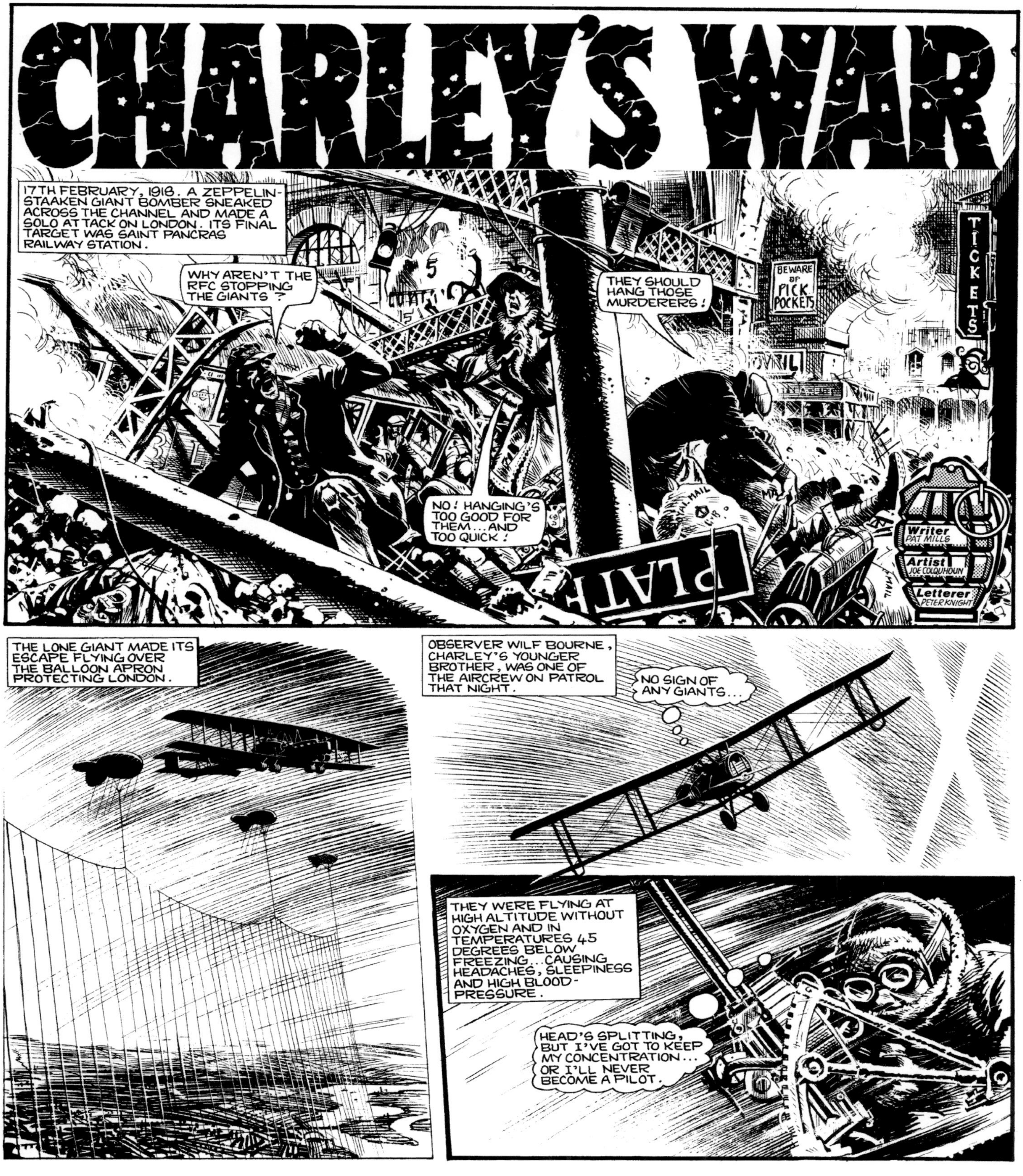

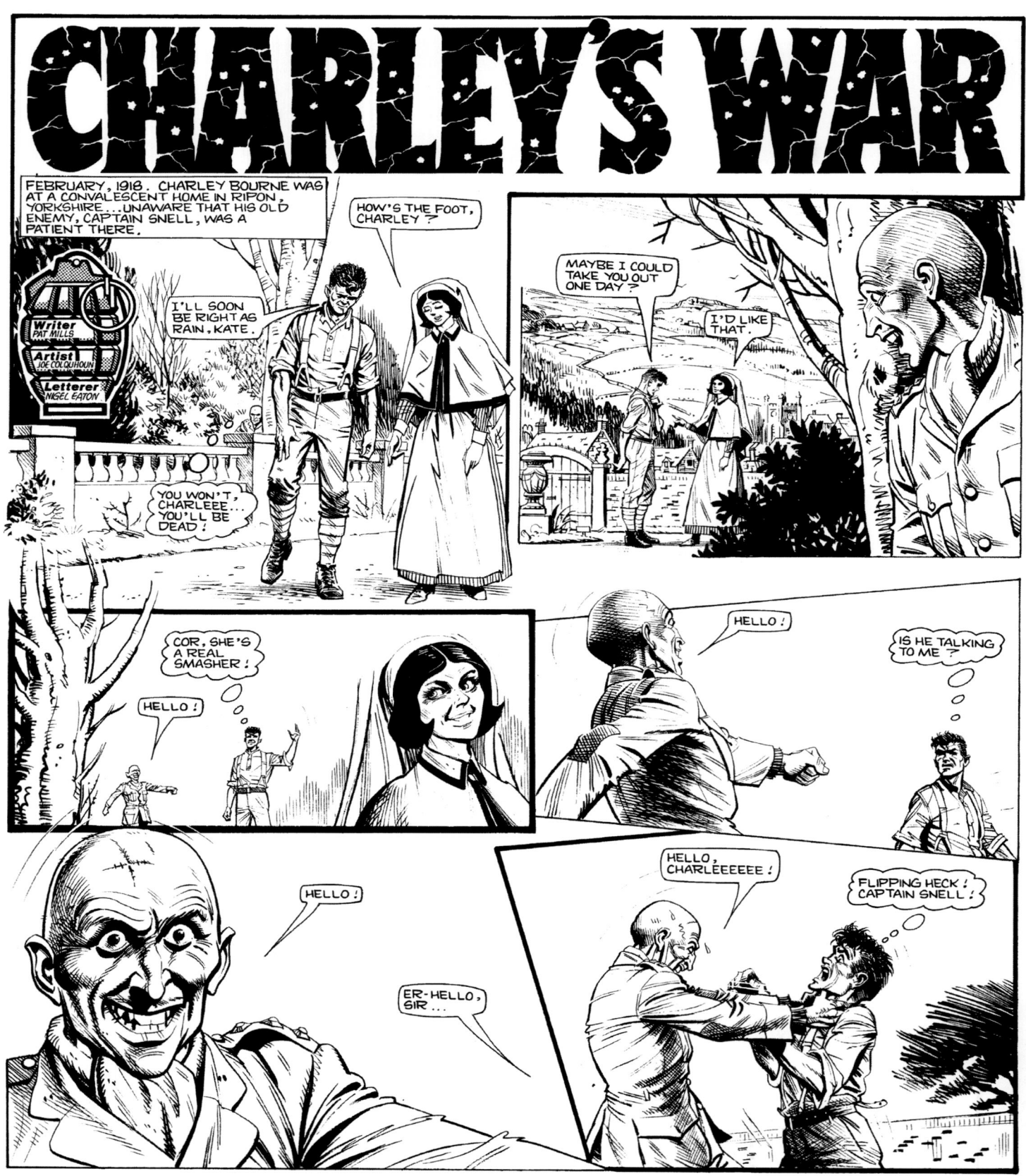

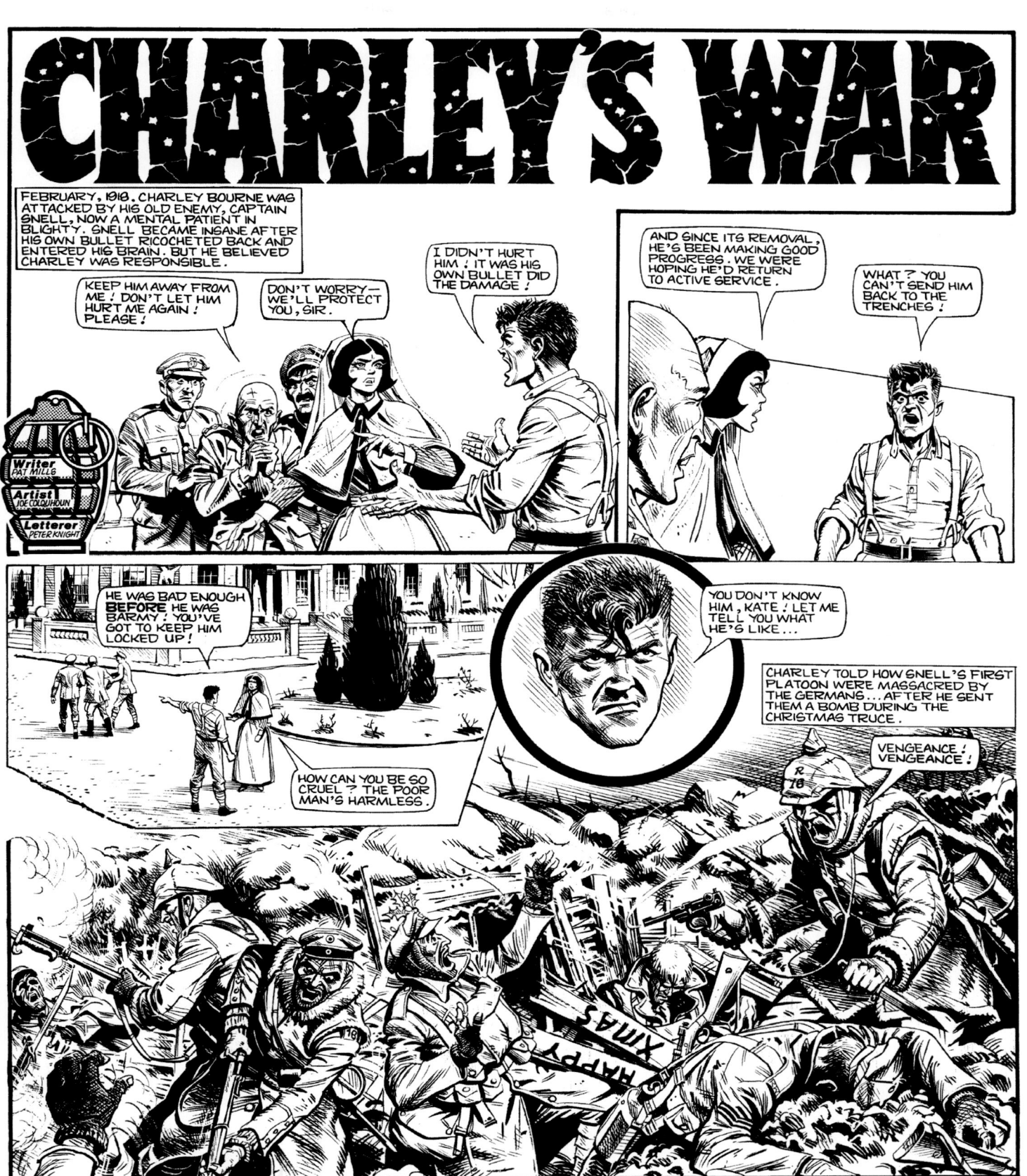

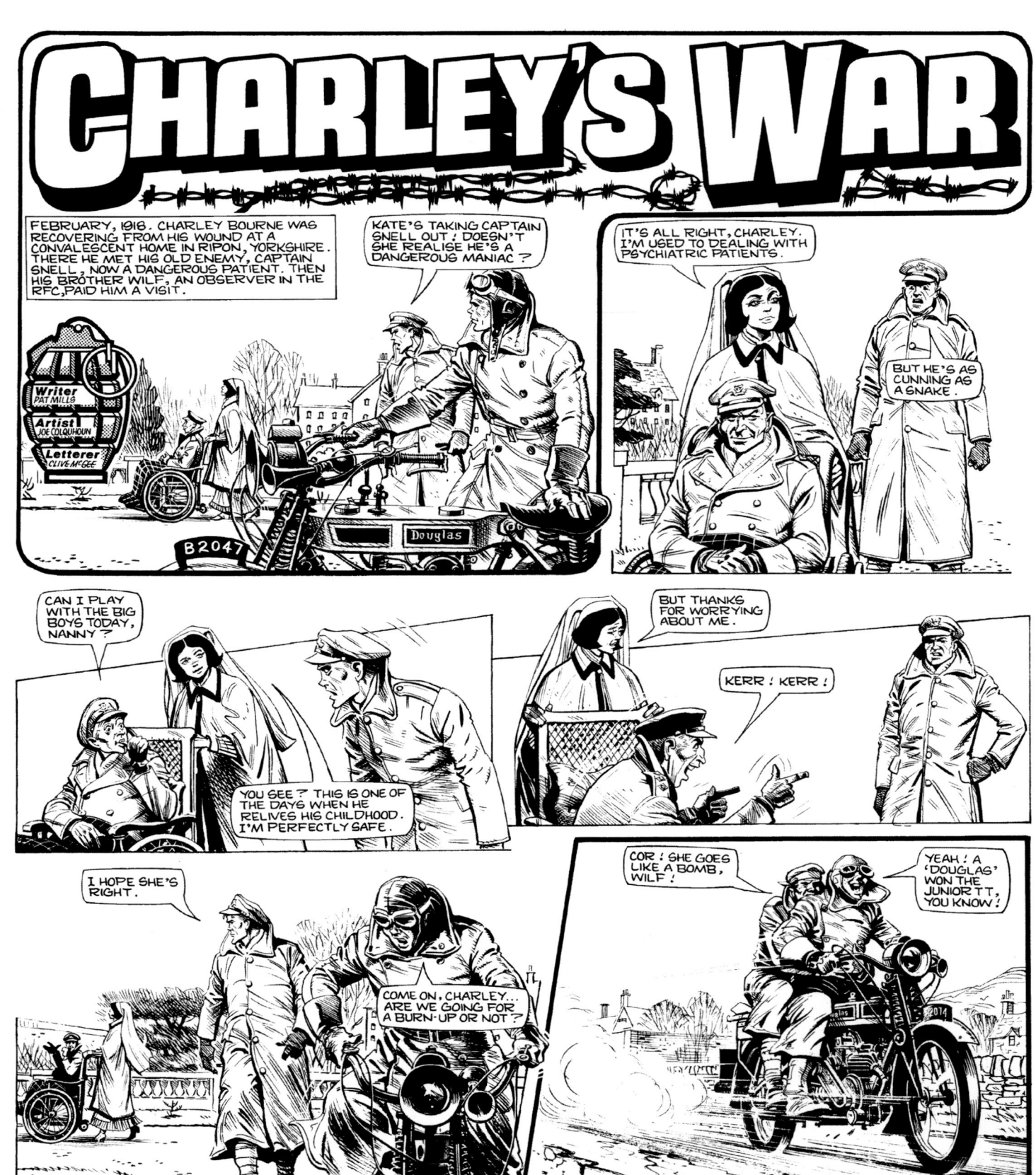

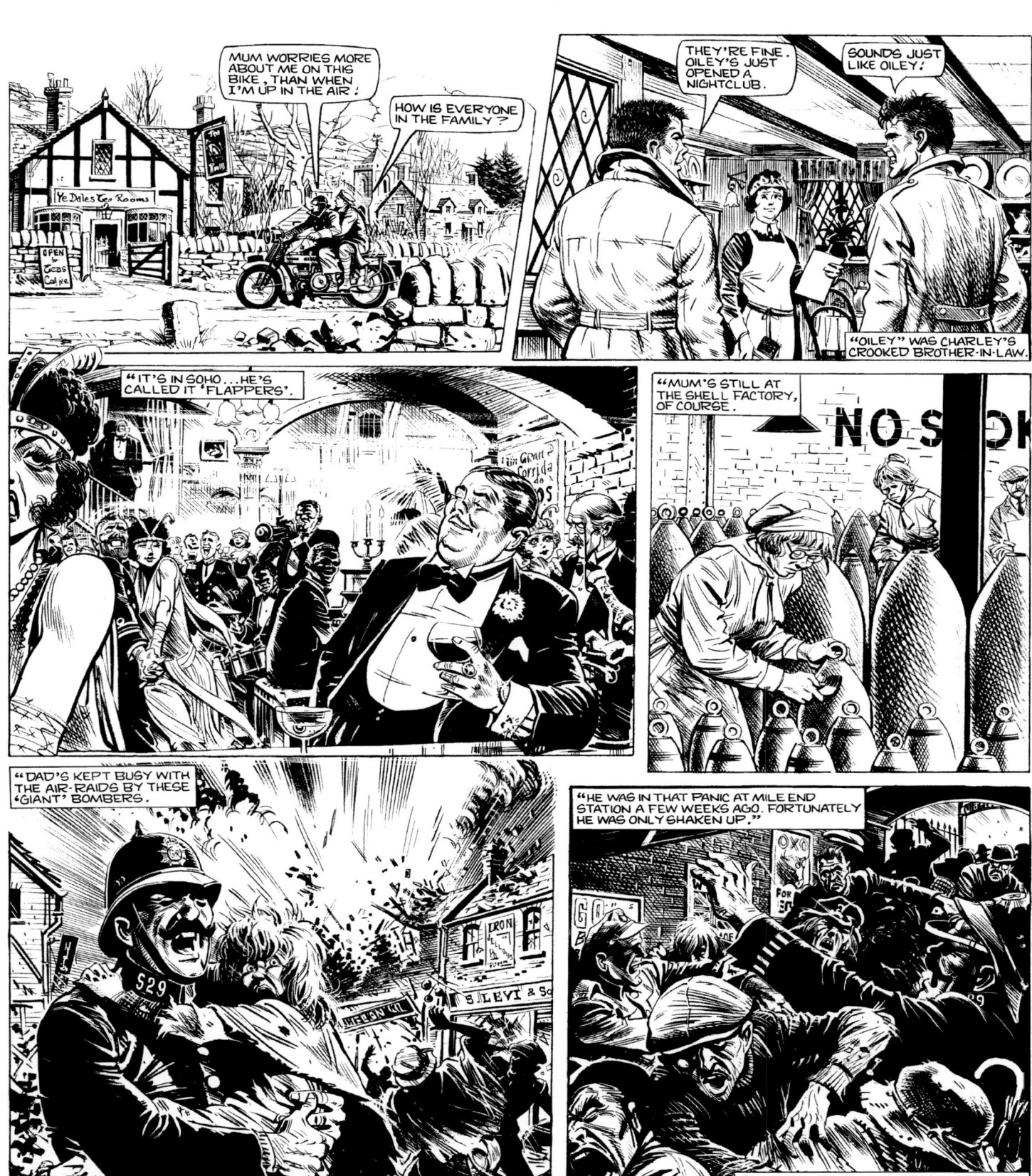

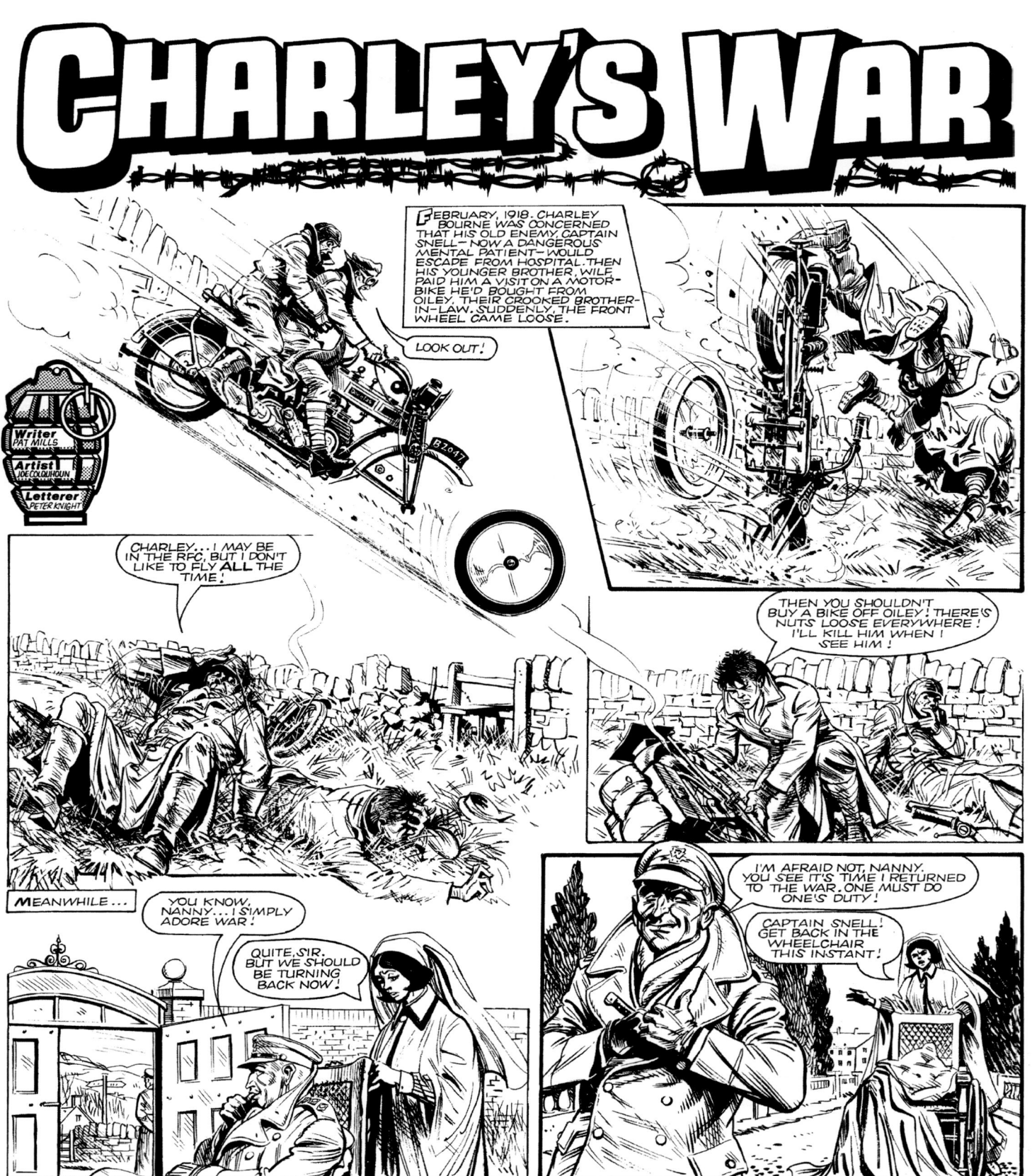

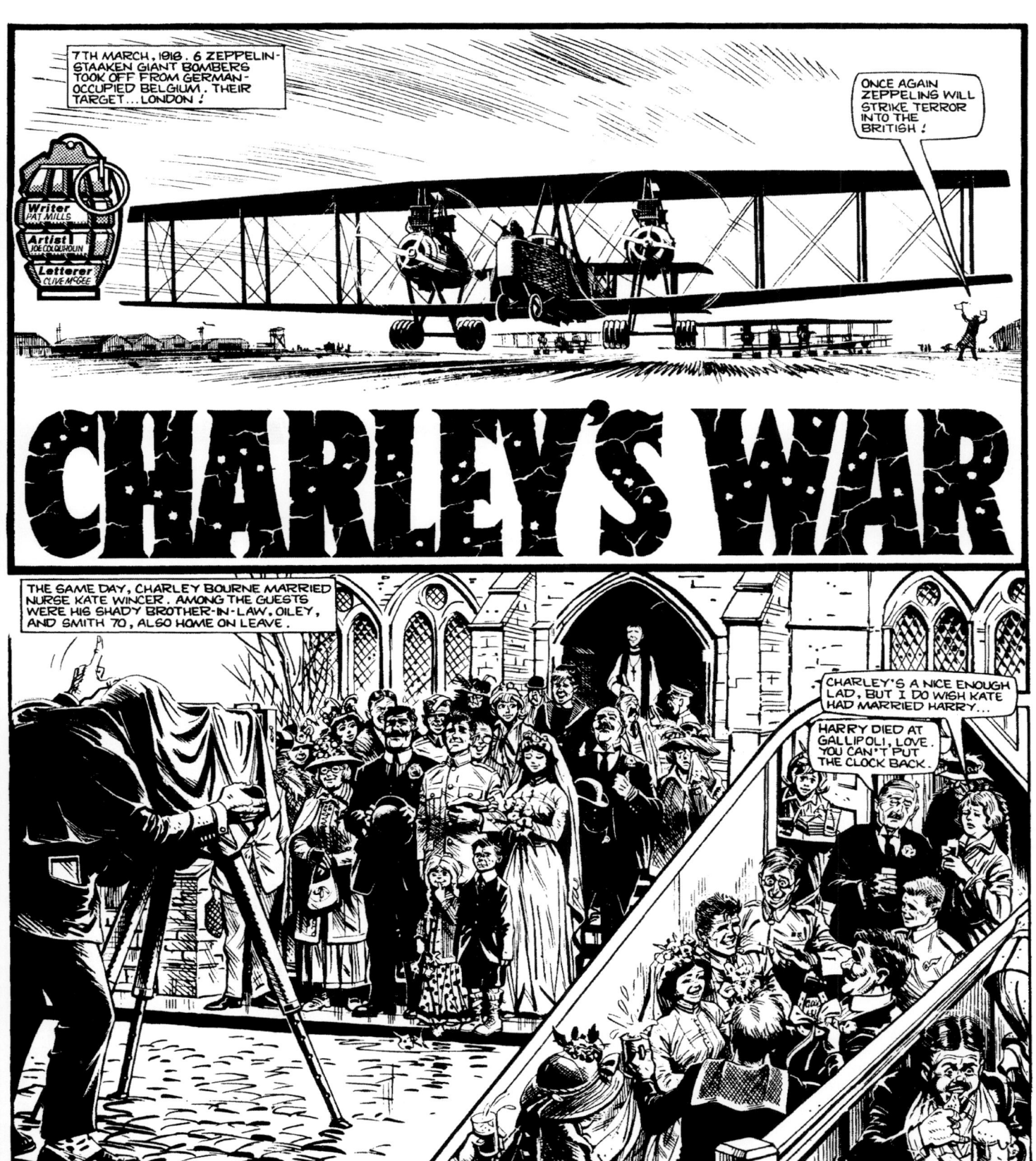

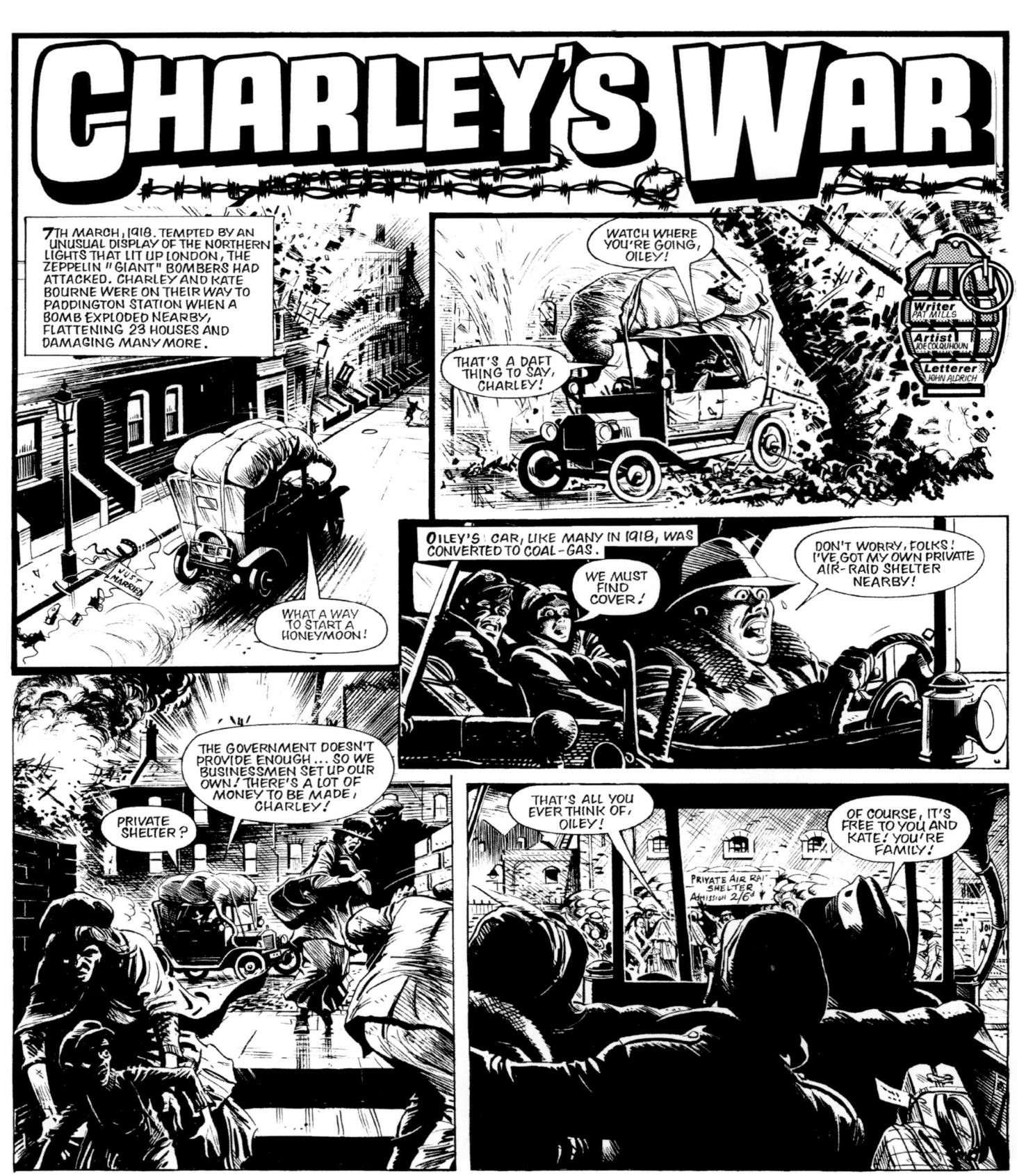

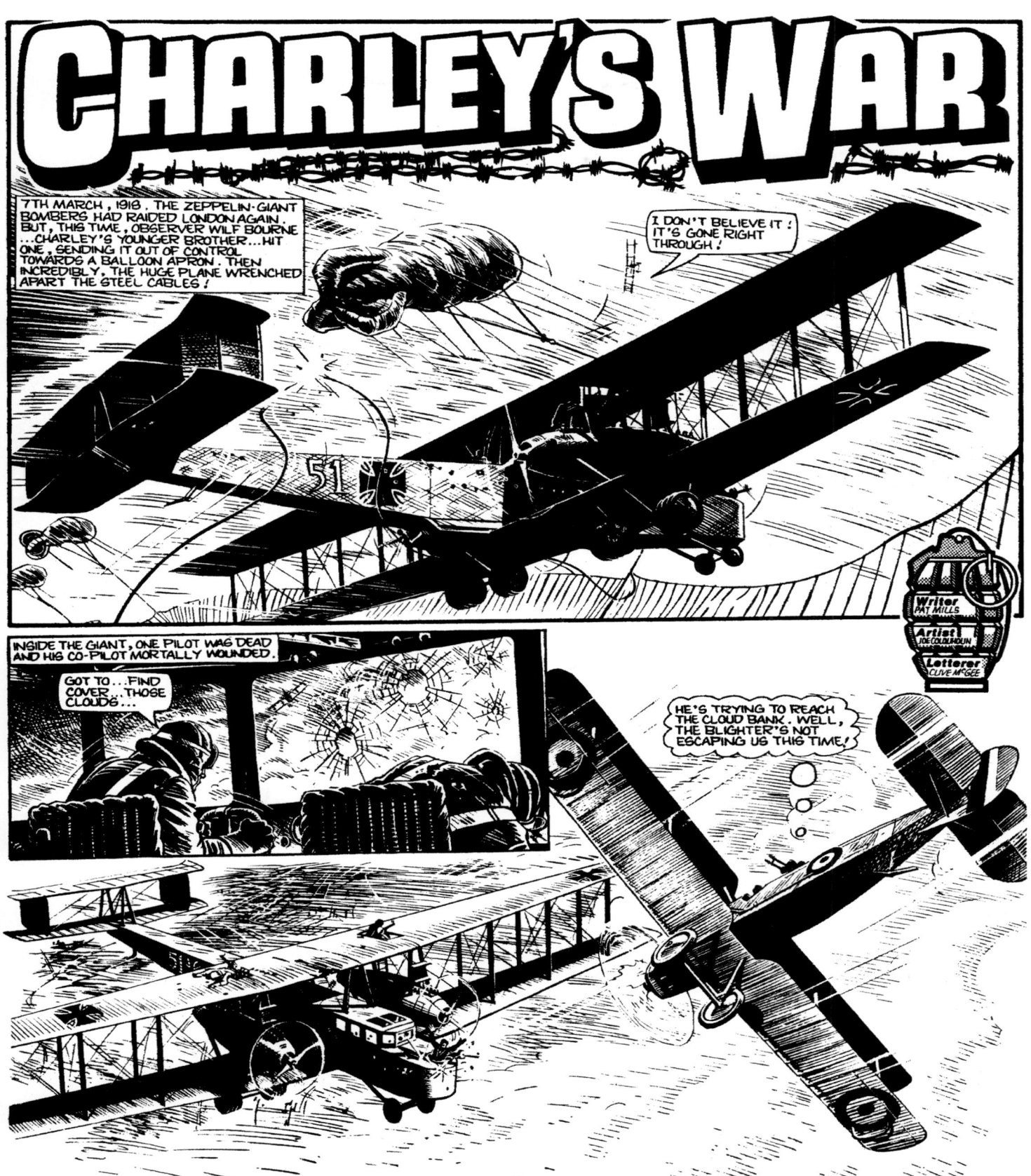

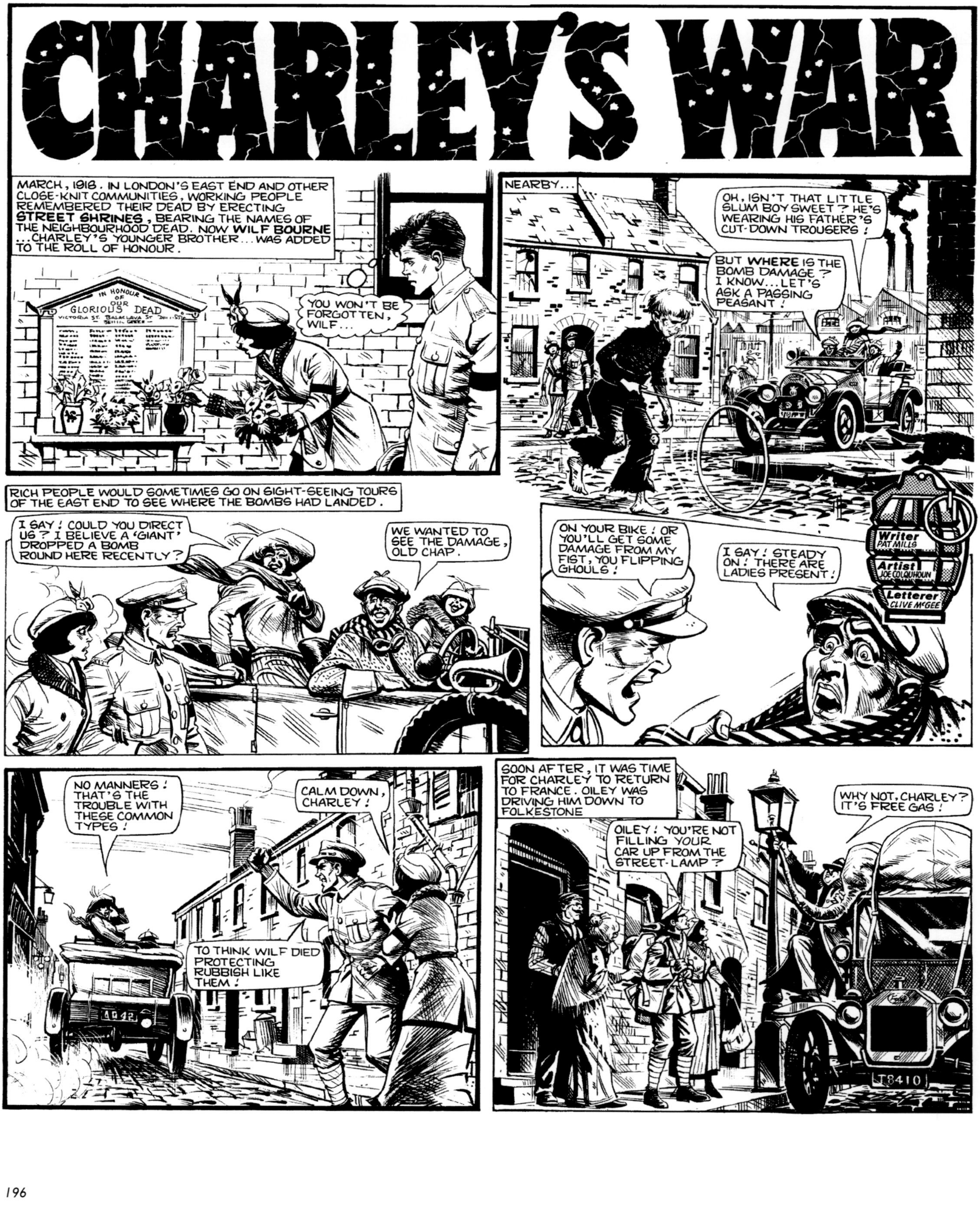

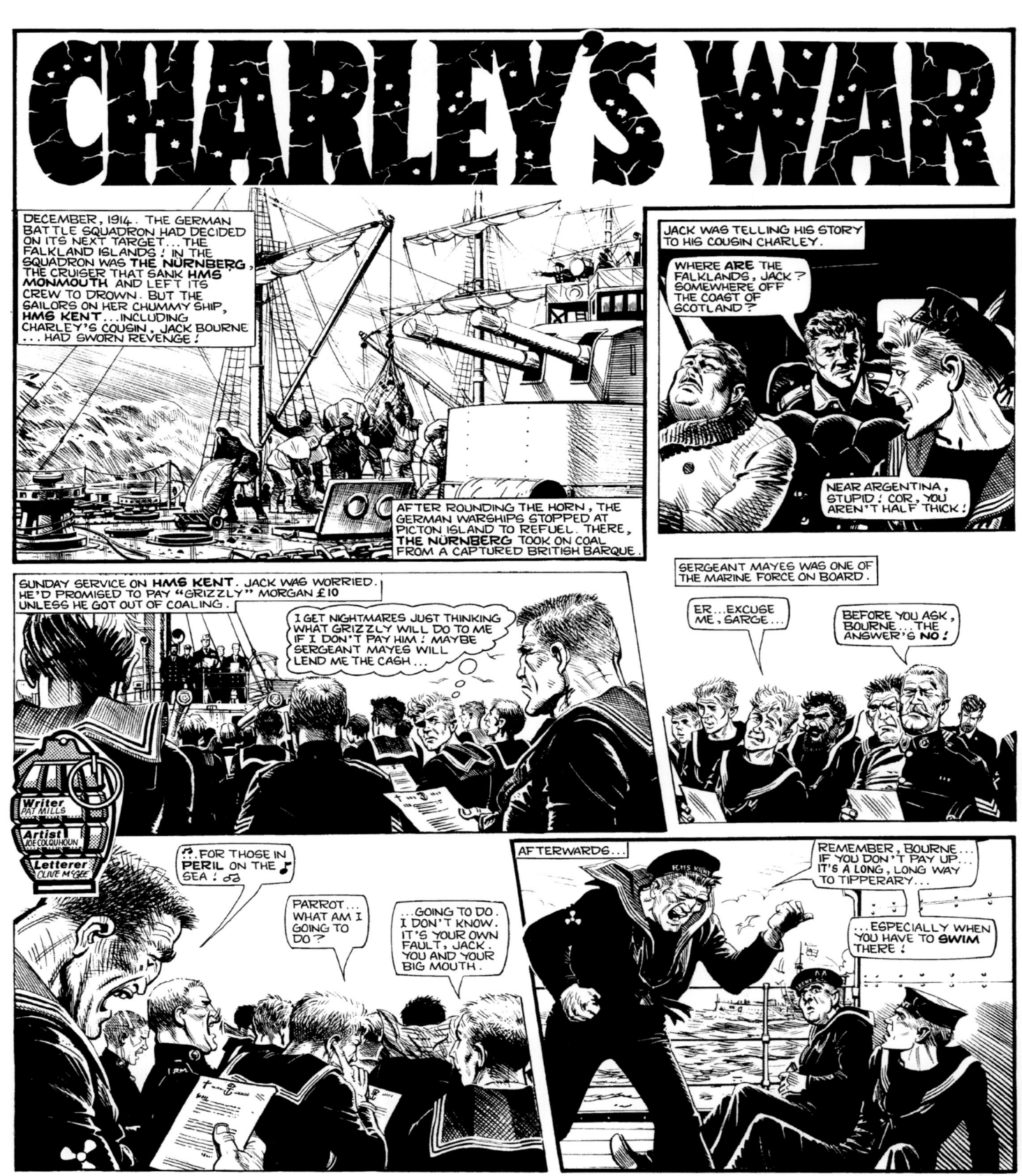

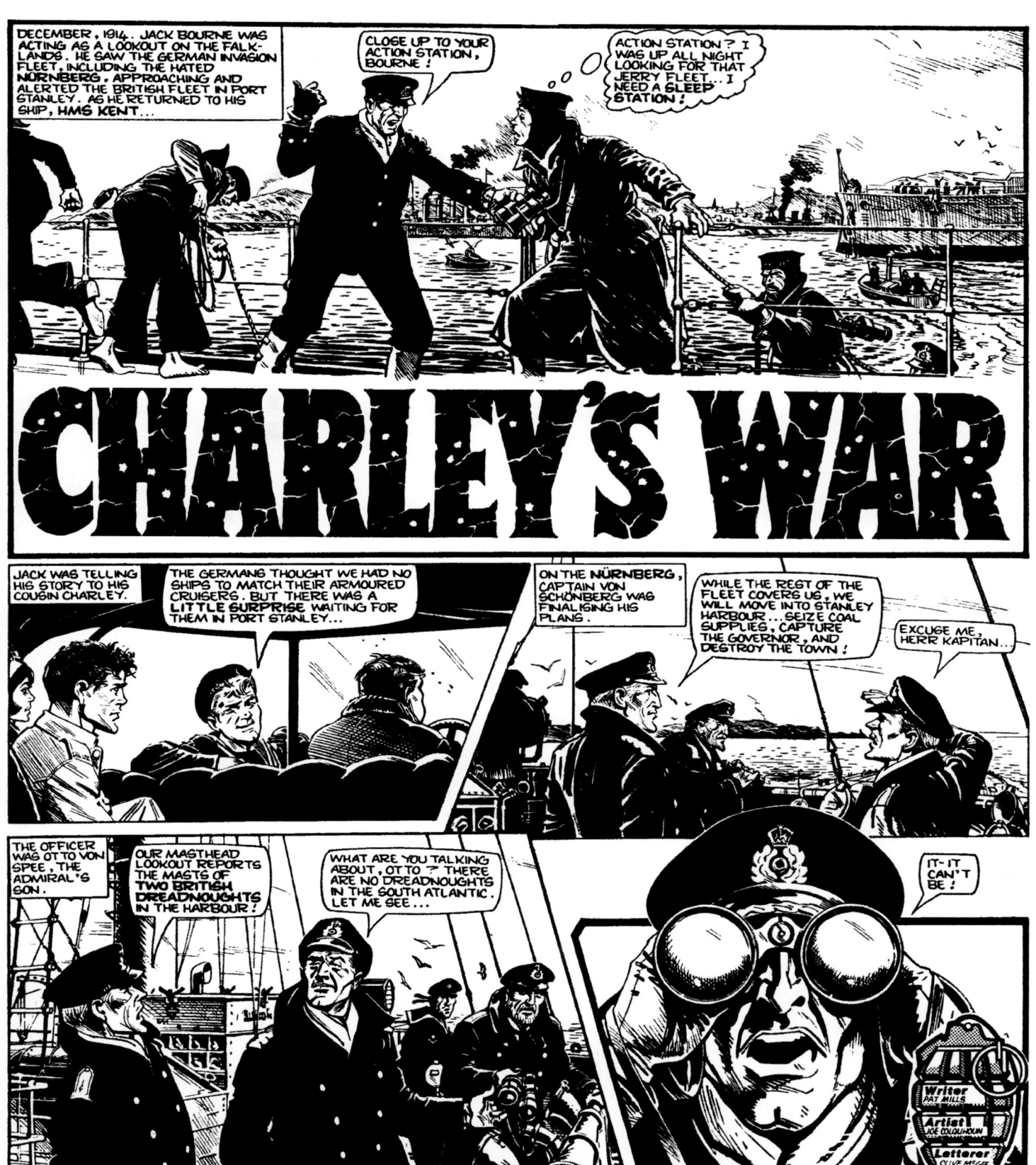

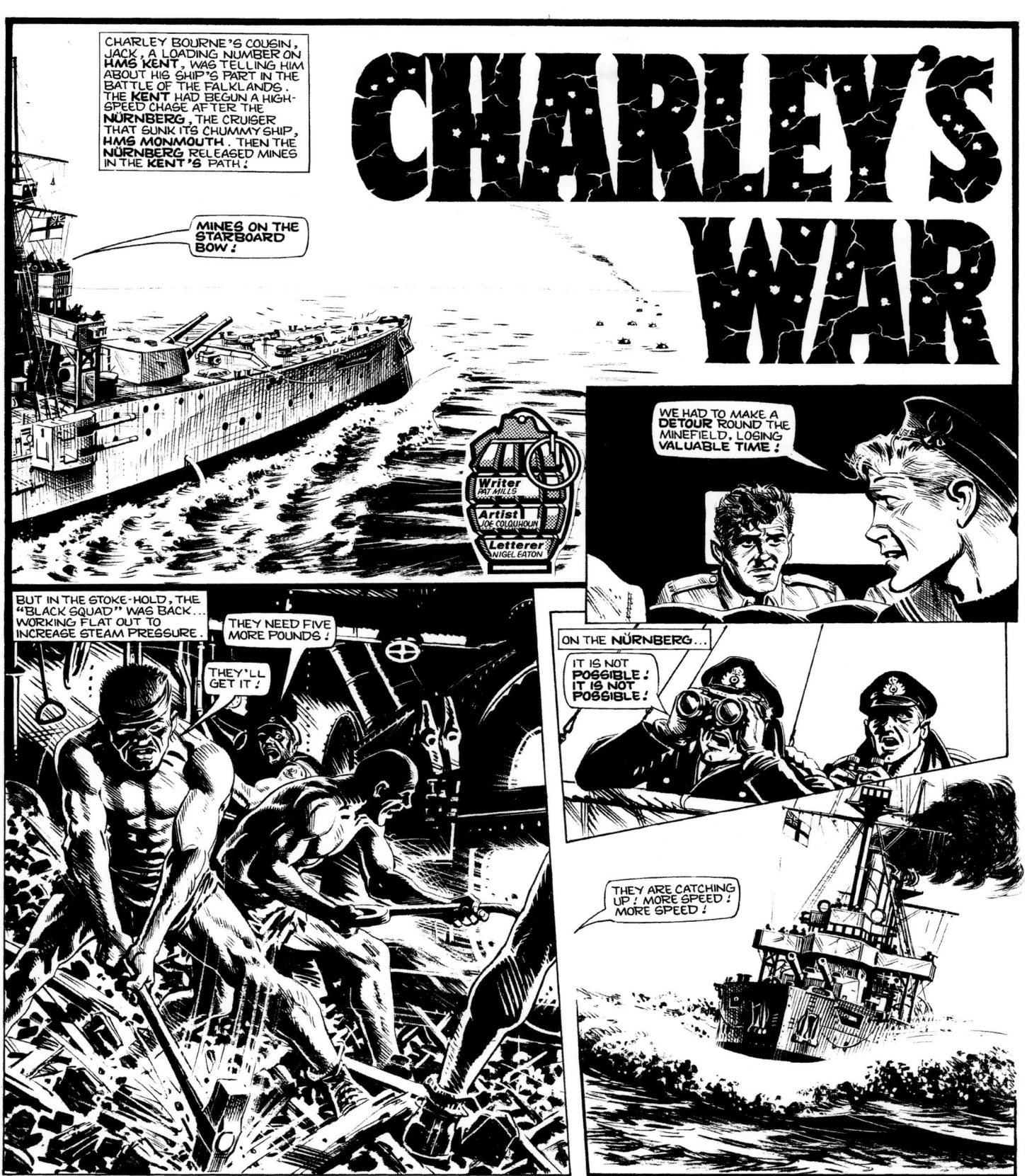

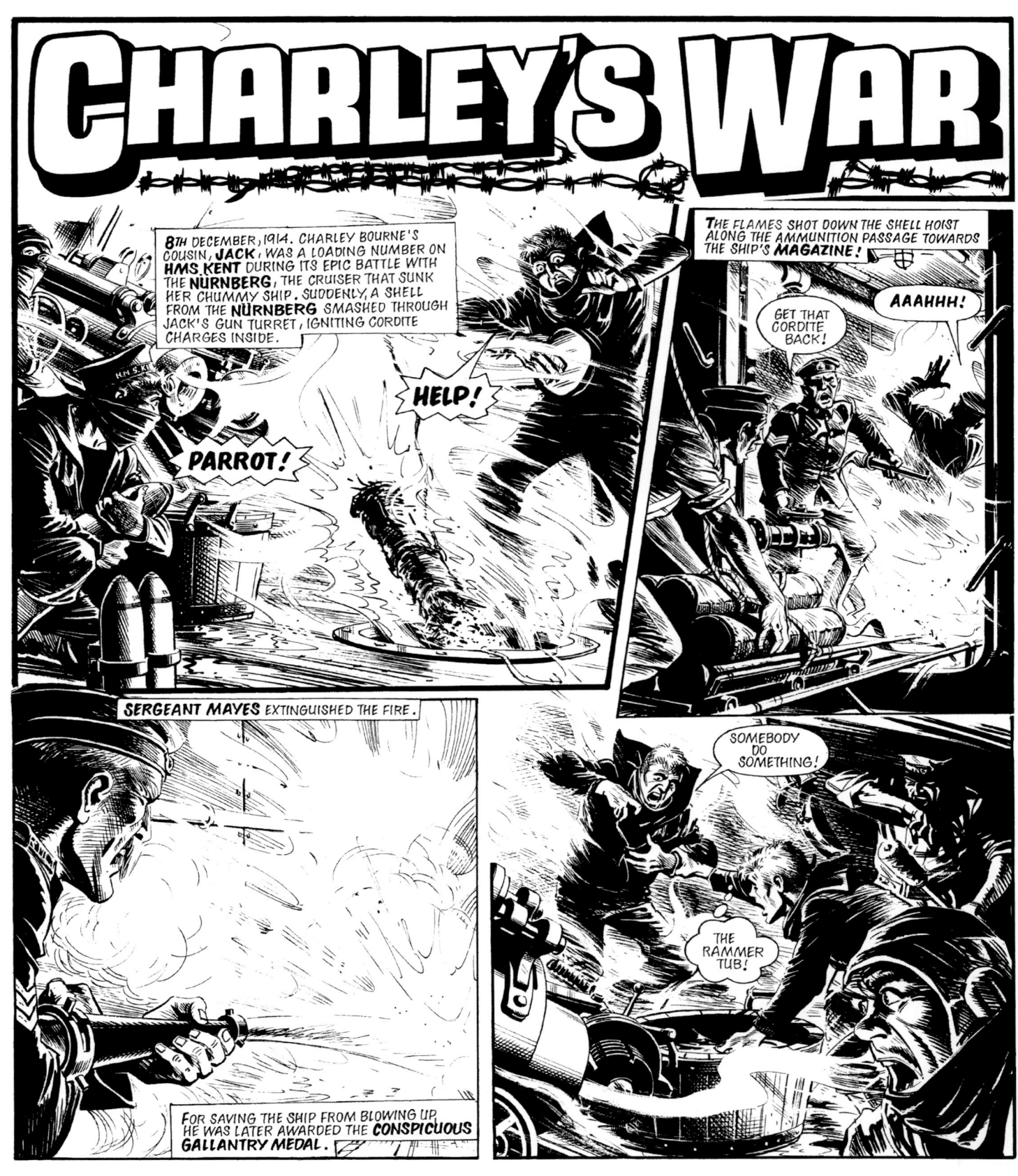

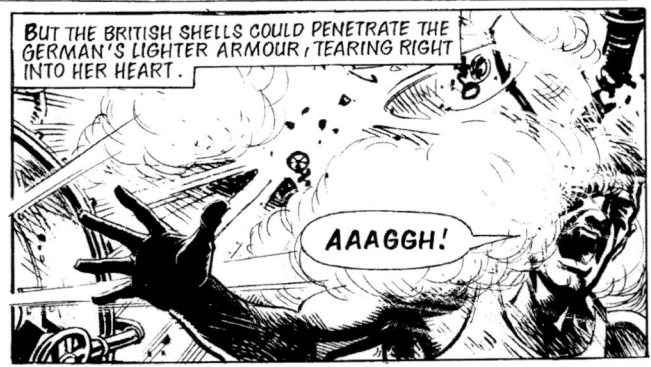

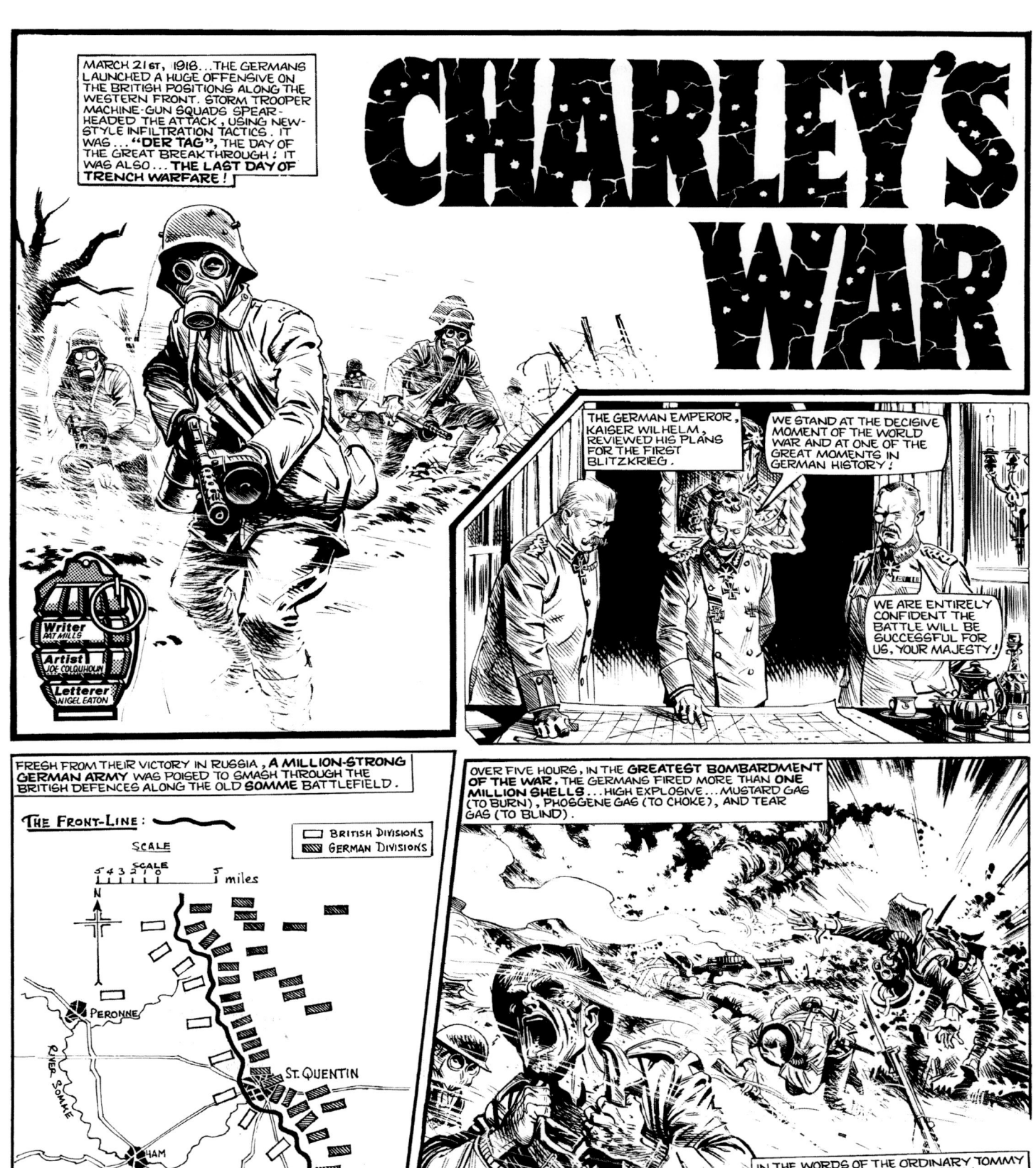

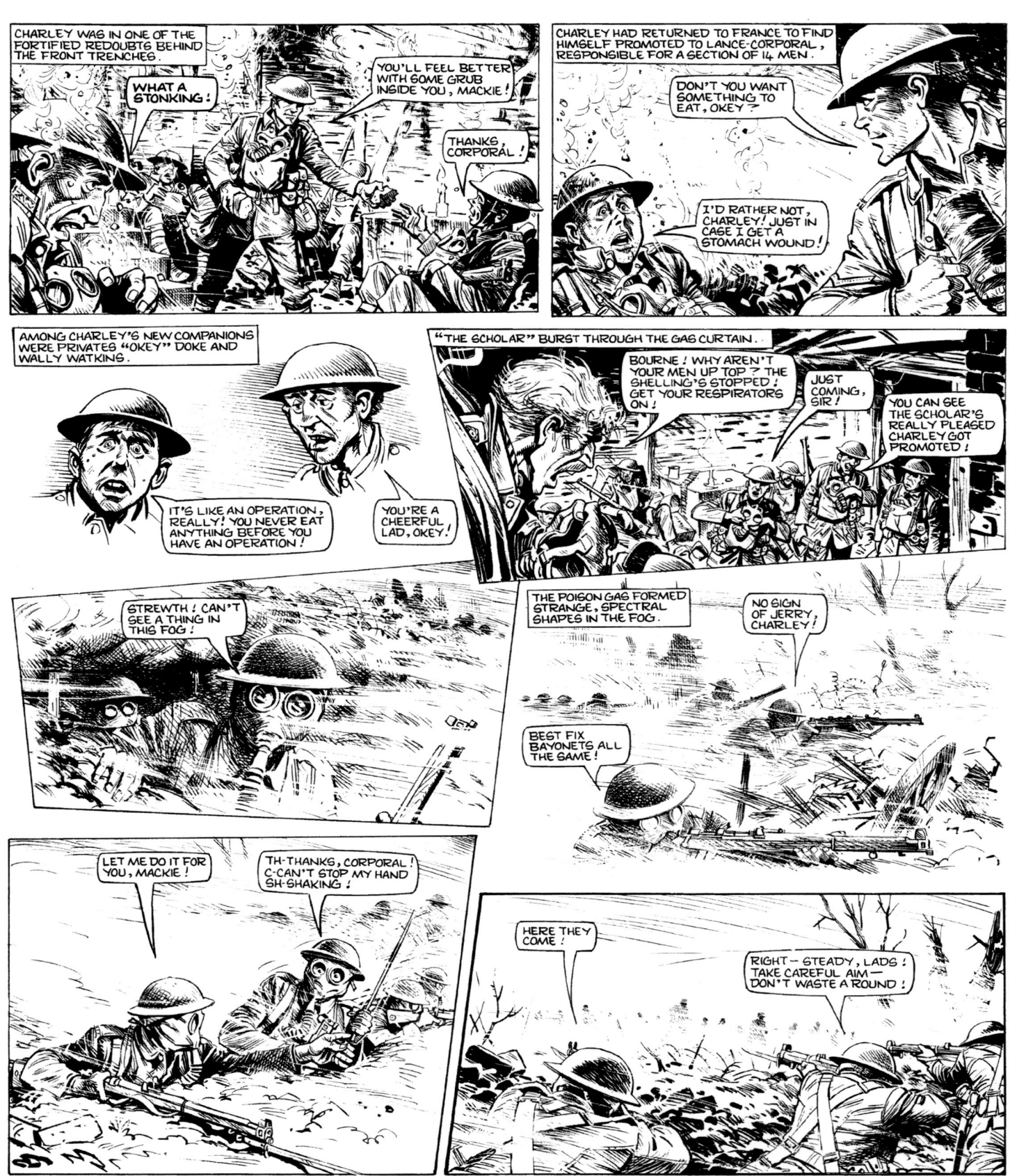

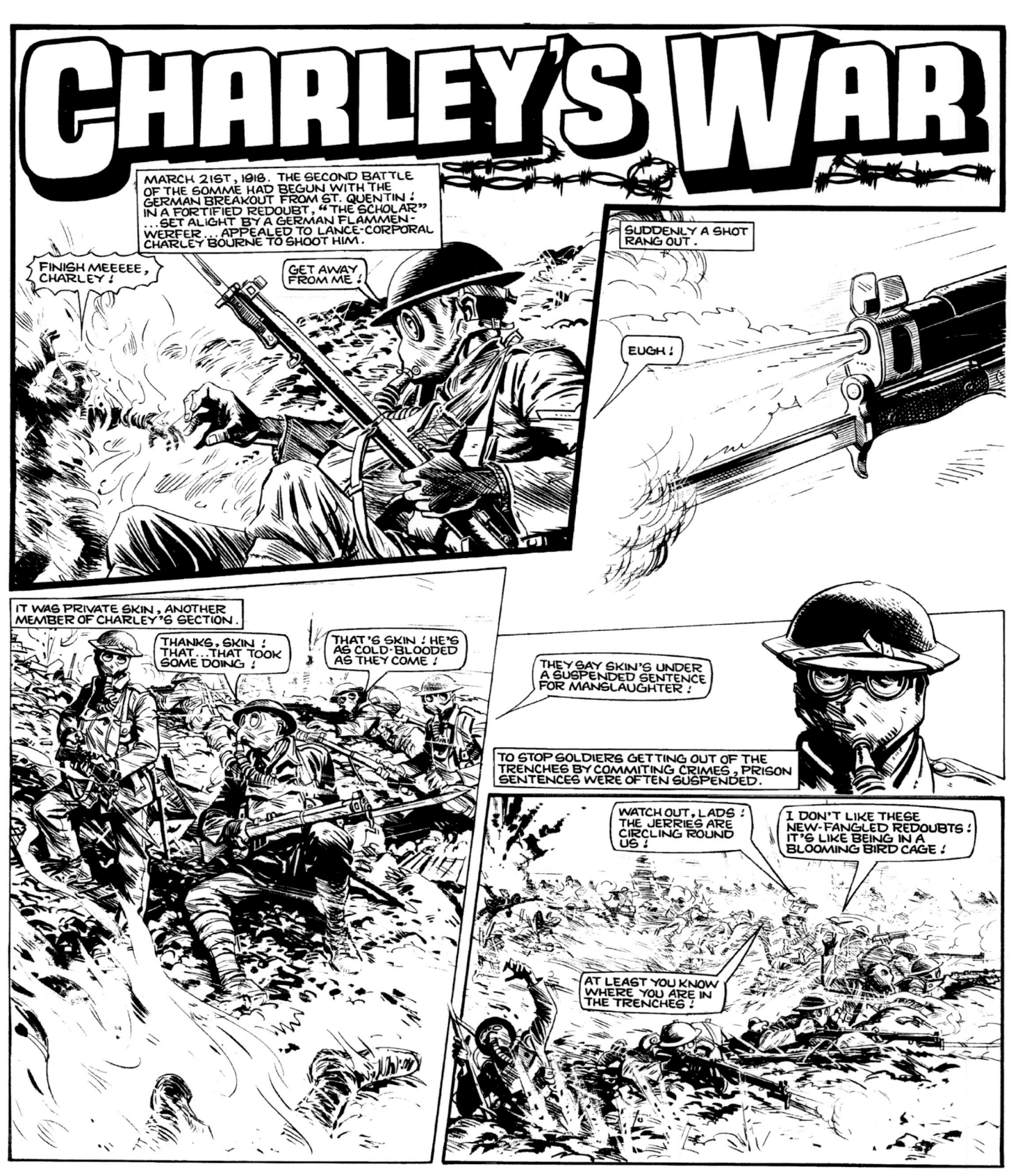

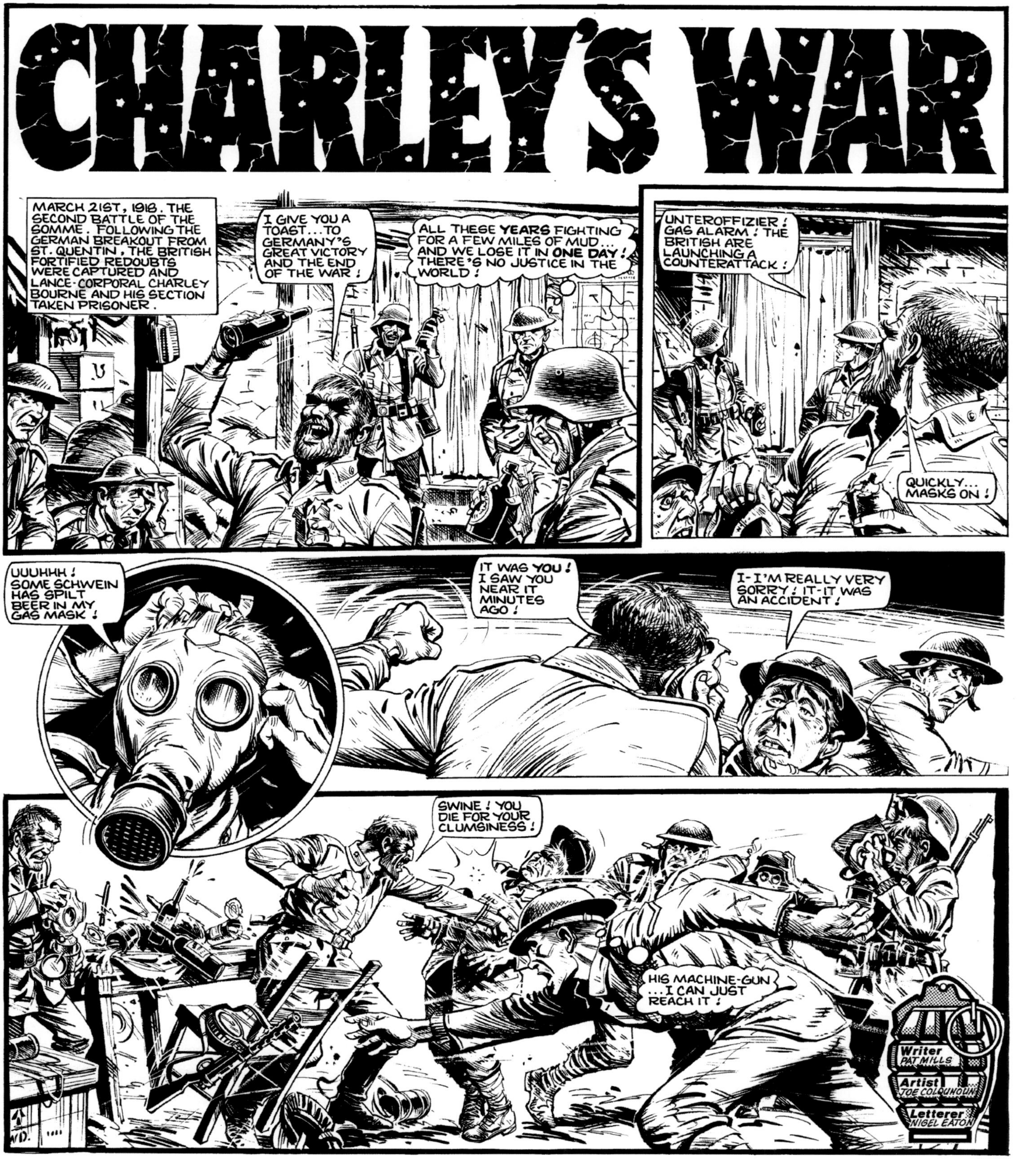

CHARLEY'S WAR

MARCH 21ST, 1918. THE SECOND BATTLE OF THE SOMME. FOLLOWING THE GERMAN BREAKOUT FROM ST. QUENTIN, THE BRITISH FORTIFIED REDOUBTS WERE CAPTURED AND LANCE-CORPORAL CHARLEY BOURNE AND HIS SECTION TAKEN PRISONER.

I GIVE YOU A TOAST... TO GERMANY'S GREAT VICTORY AND THE END OF THE WAR!

ALL THESE YEARS FIGHTING FOR A FEW MILES OF MUD... AND WE LOSE IT IN ONE DAY! THERE'S NO JUSTICE IN THE WORLD!

UNTEROFFIZIER! GAS ALARM! THE BRITISH ARE LAUNCHING A COUNTERATTACK!

QUICKLY... MASKS ON!

UUUHHH! SOME SCHWEIN HAS SPILT BEER IN MY GAS MASK!

IT WAS YOU! I SAW YOU NEAR IT MINUTES AGO!

I-I'M REALLY VERY SORRY! IT-IT WAS AN ACCIDENT!

SWINE! YOU DIE FOR YOUR CLUMSINESS!

HIS MACHINE-GUN ...I CAN JUST REACH IT!

Writer PAT MILLS
Artist JOE COLQUHOUN
Letterer NIGEL EATON

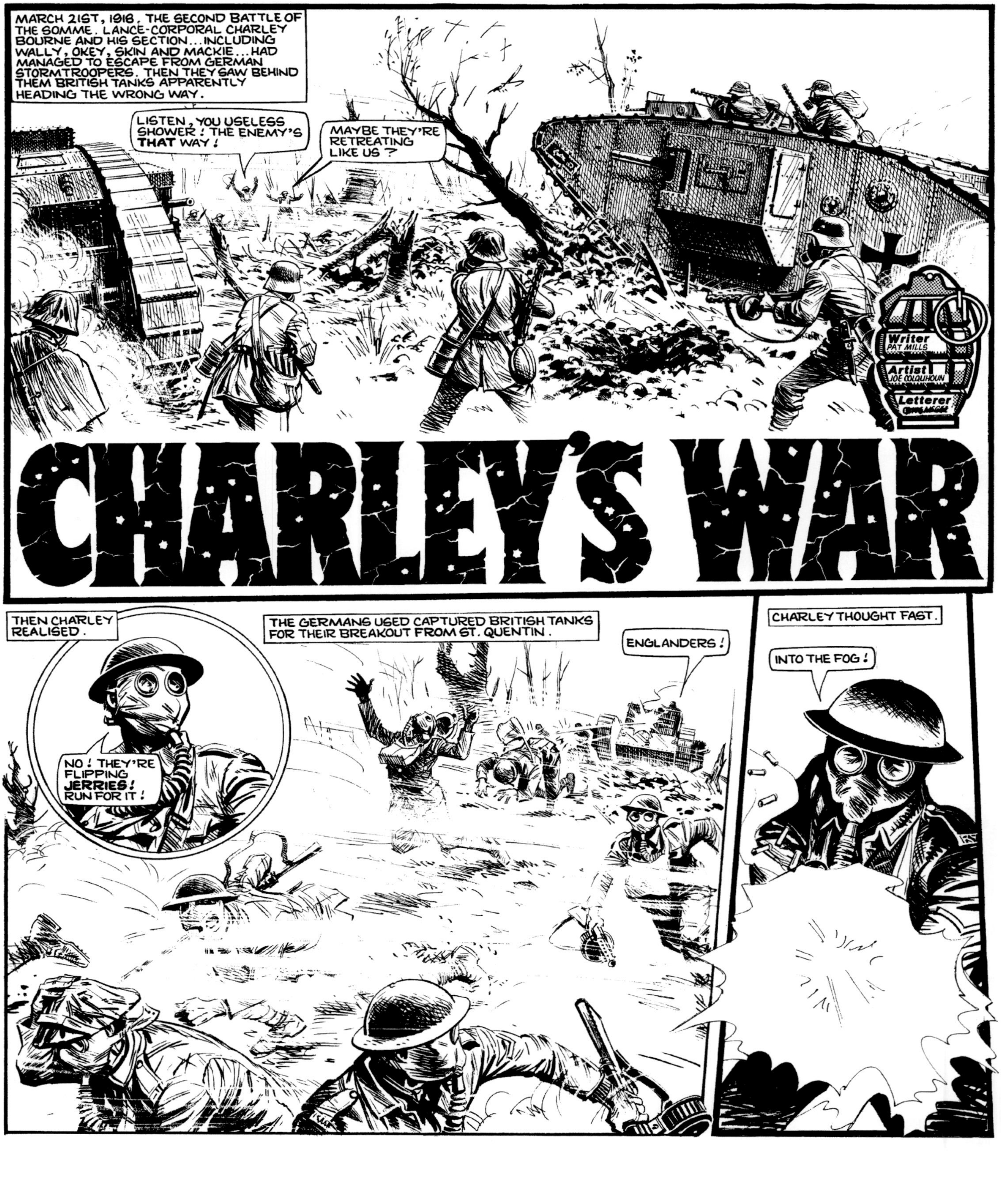

MARCH 21ST, 1918. THE SECOND BATTLE OF THE SOMME. LANCE-CORPORAL CHARLEY BOURNE AND HIS SECTION... INCLUDING WALLY, OKEY, SKIN AND MACKIE... HAD MANAGED TO ESCAPE FROM GERMAN STORMTROOPERS. THEN THEY SAW BEHIND THEM BRITISH TANKS APPARENTLY HEADING THE WRONG WAY.

"LISTEN, YOU USELESS SHOWER! THE ENEMY'S *THAT* WAY!"

"MAYBE THEY'RE RETREATING LIKE US?"

Writer PAT MILLS
Artist JOE COLQUHOUN
Letterer

CHARLEY'S WAR

THEN CHARLEY REALISED.

"NO! THEY'RE FLIPPING *JERRIES*! RUN FOR IT!"

THE GERMANS USED CAPTURED BRITISH TANKS FOR THEIR BREAKOUT FROM ST. QUENTIN.

"ENGLANDERS!"

CHARLEY THOUGHT FAST.

"INTO THE FOG!"

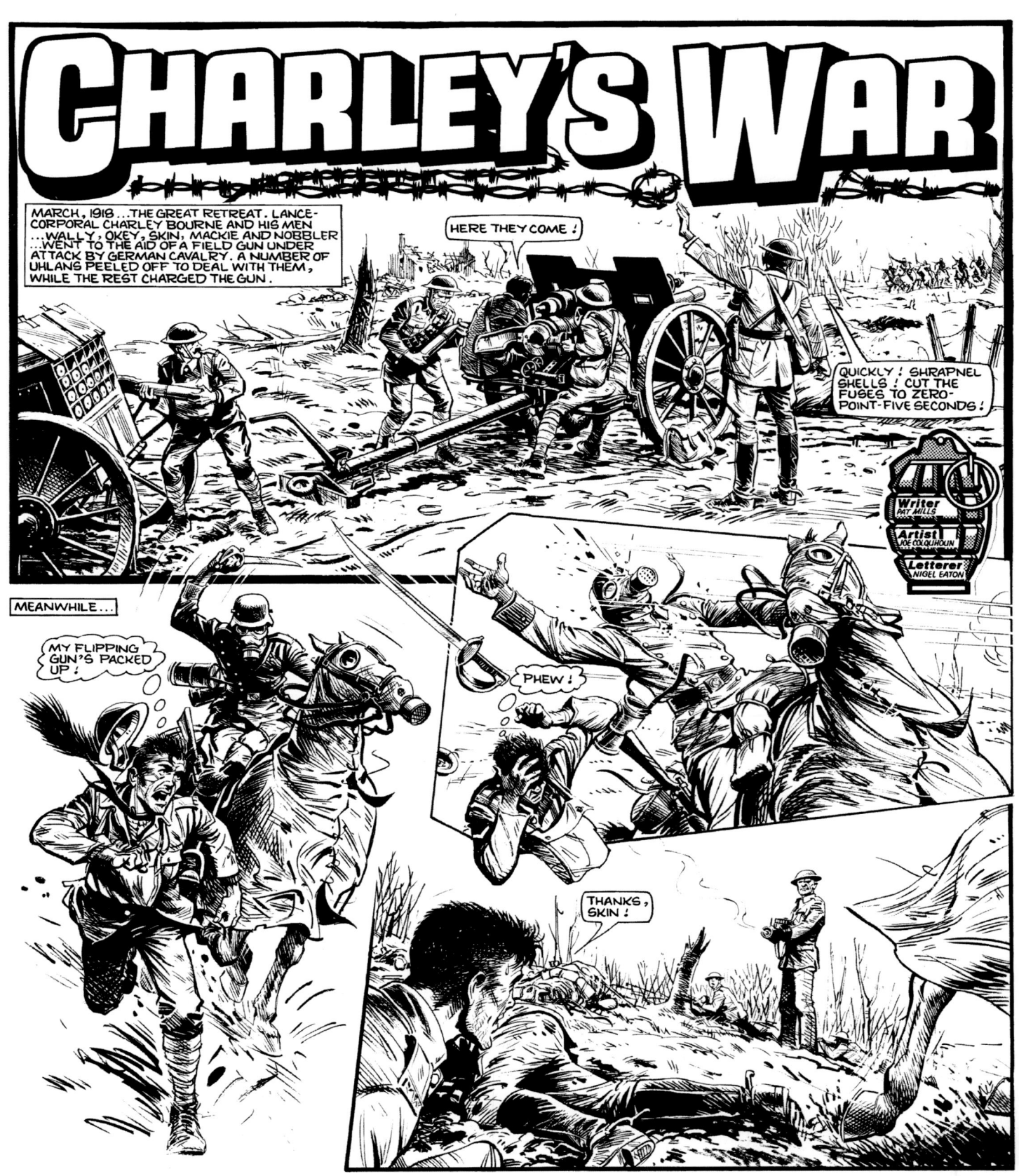

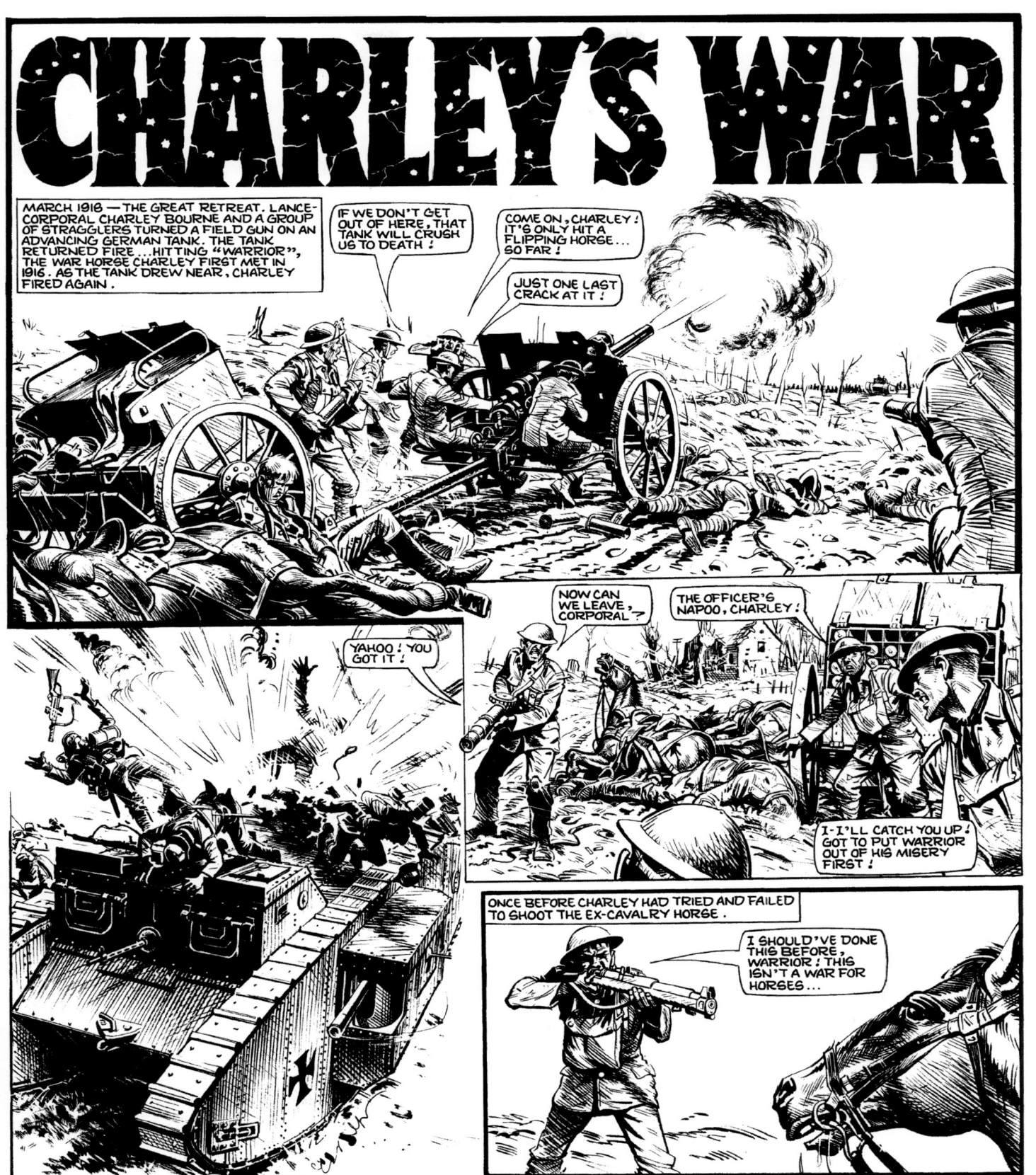

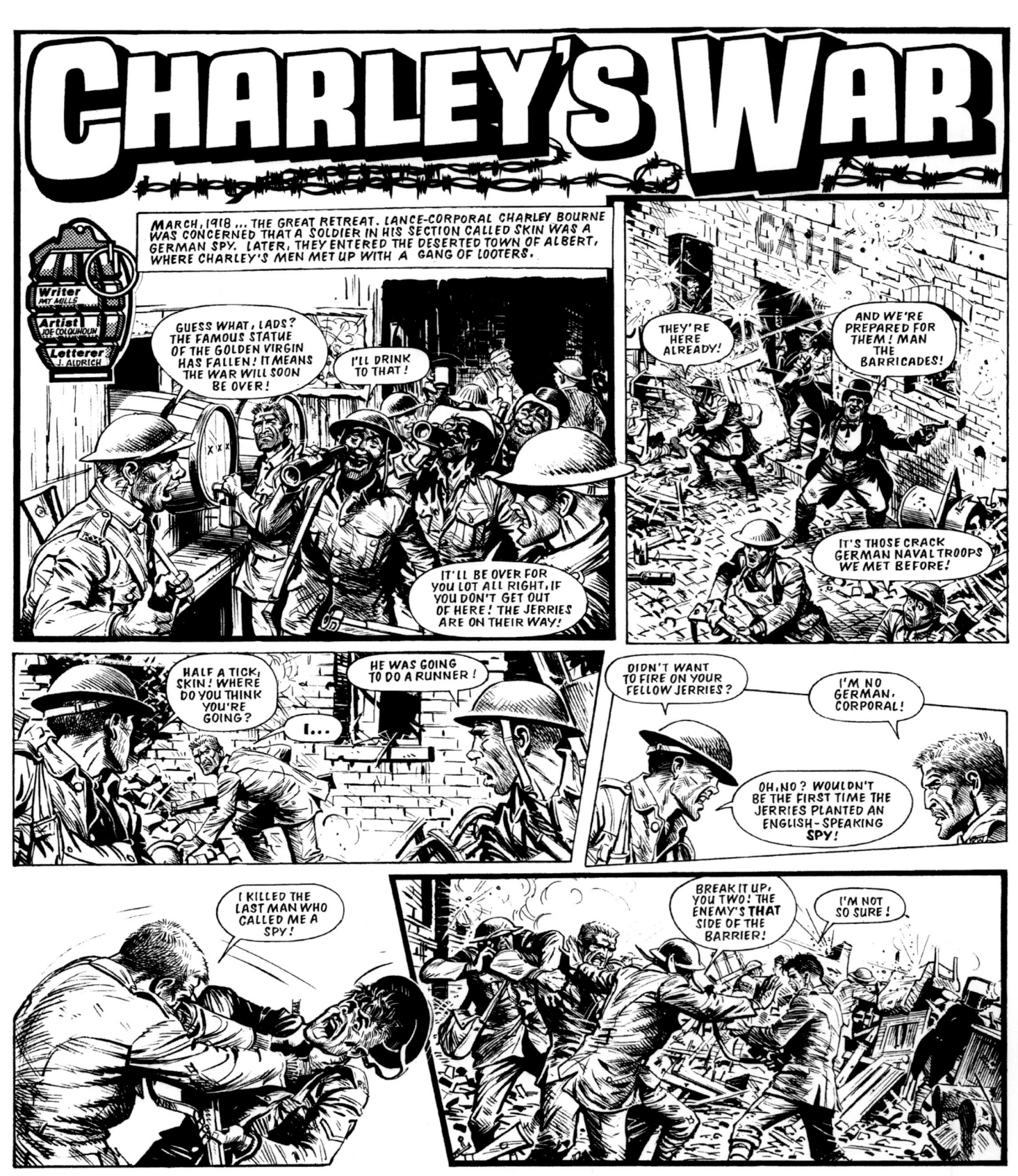

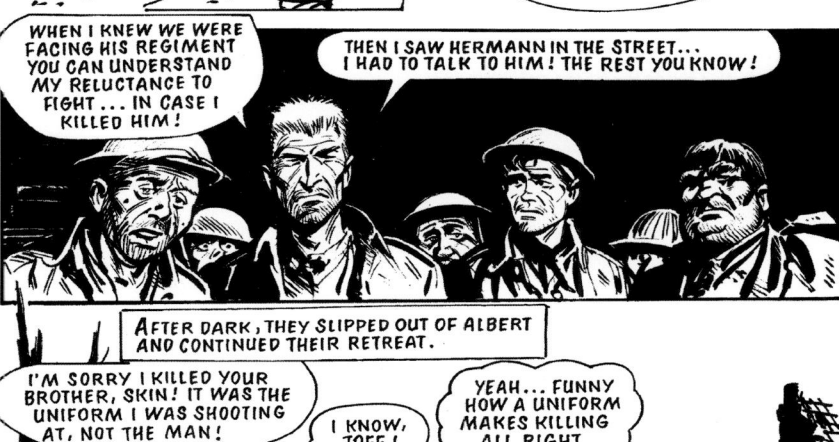

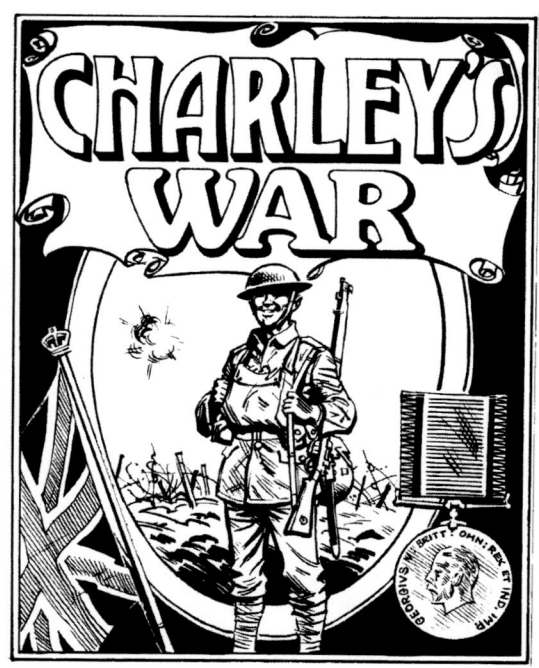

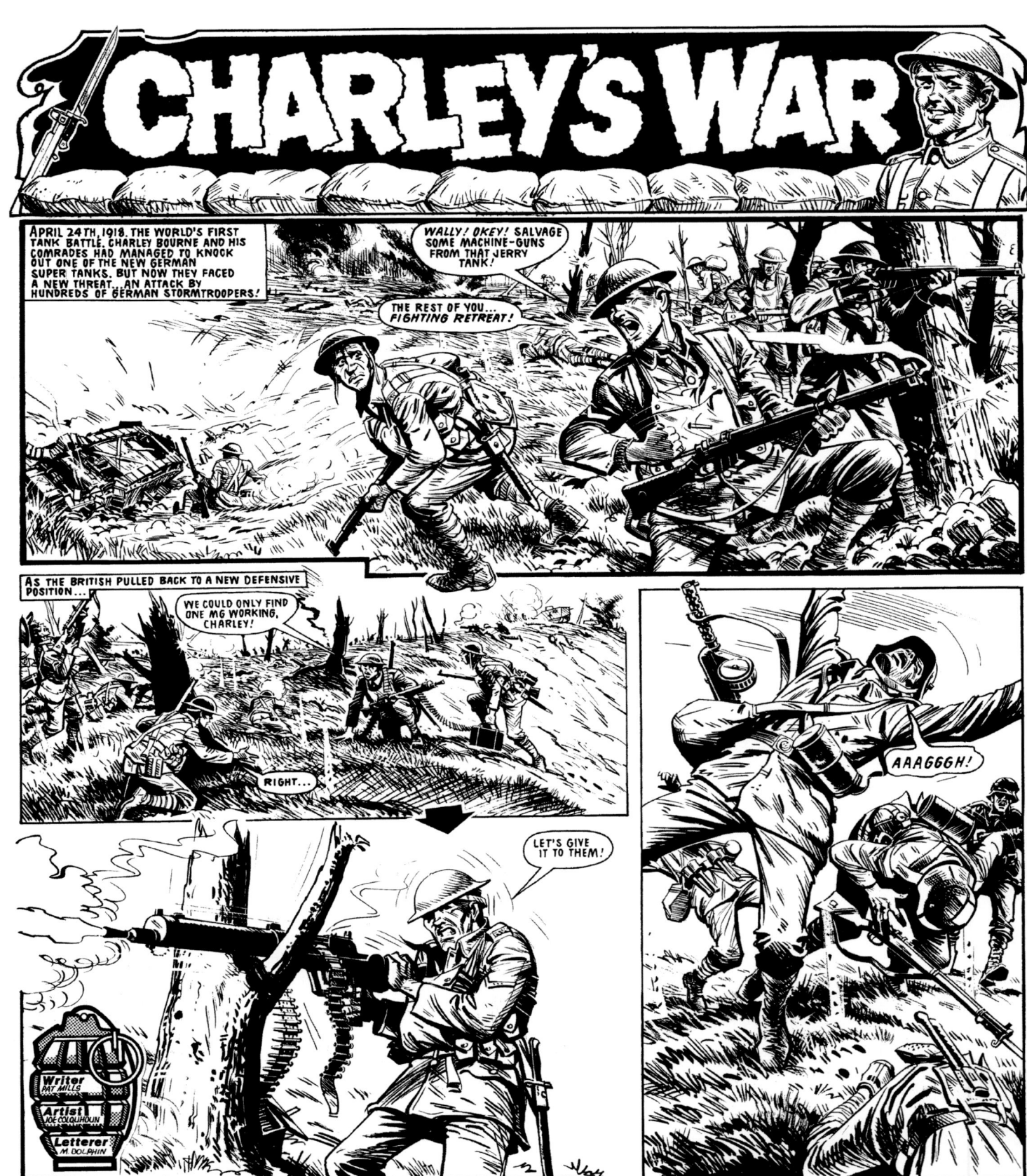

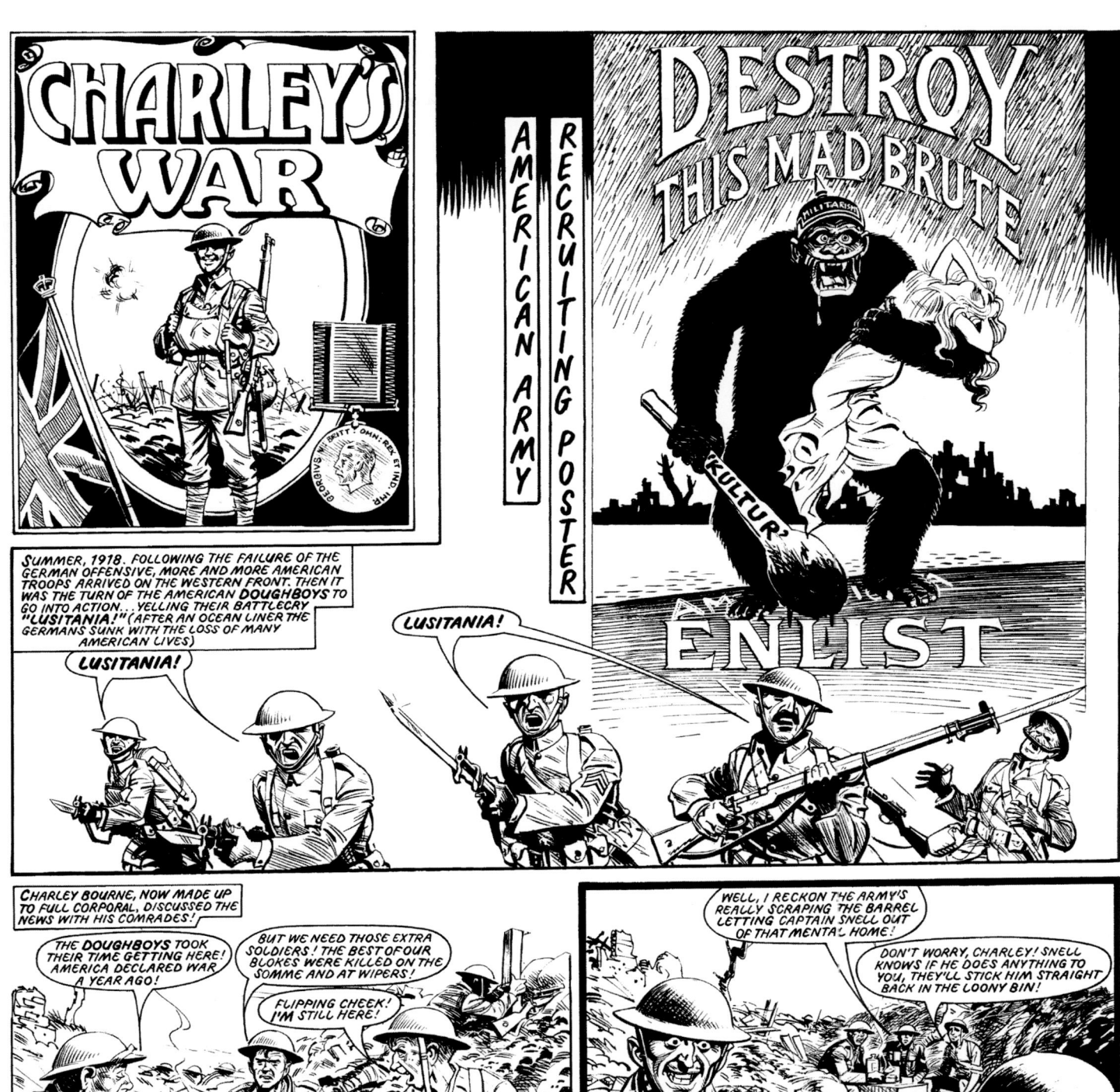

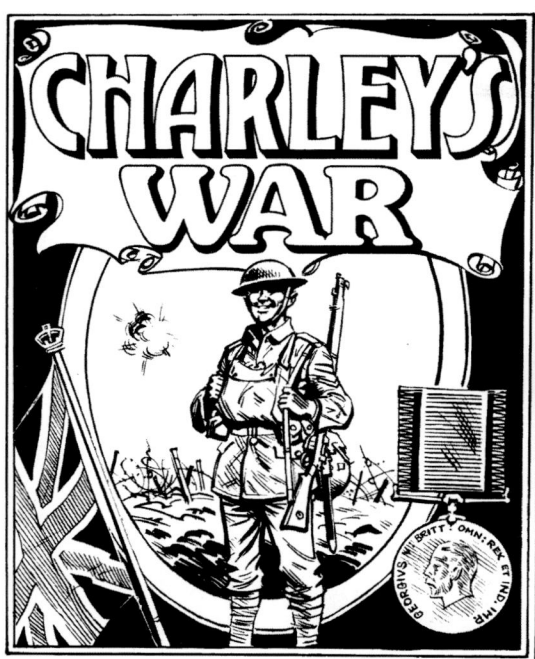

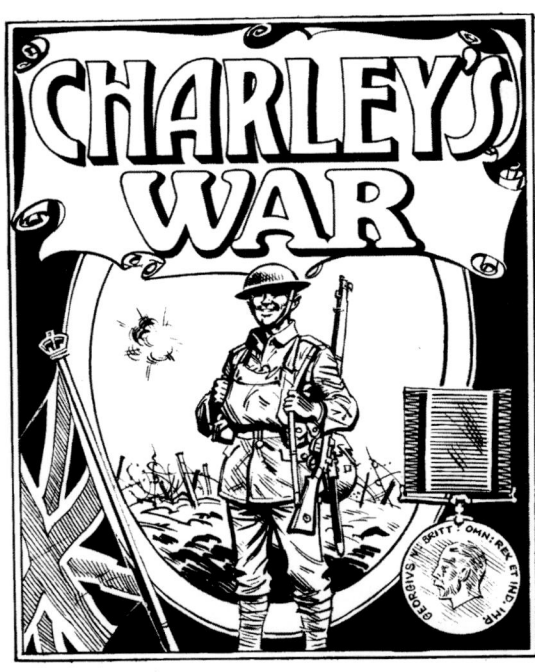

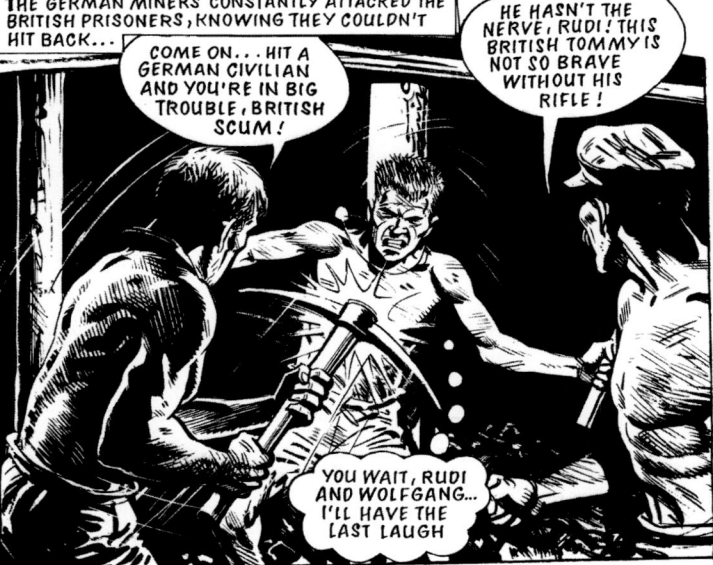

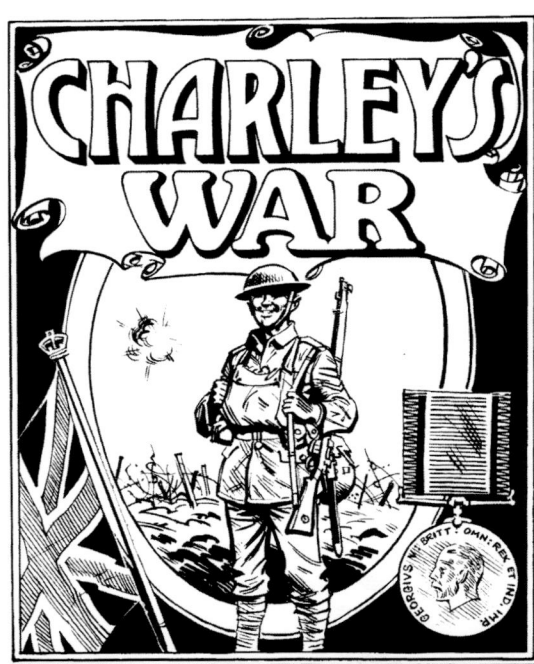

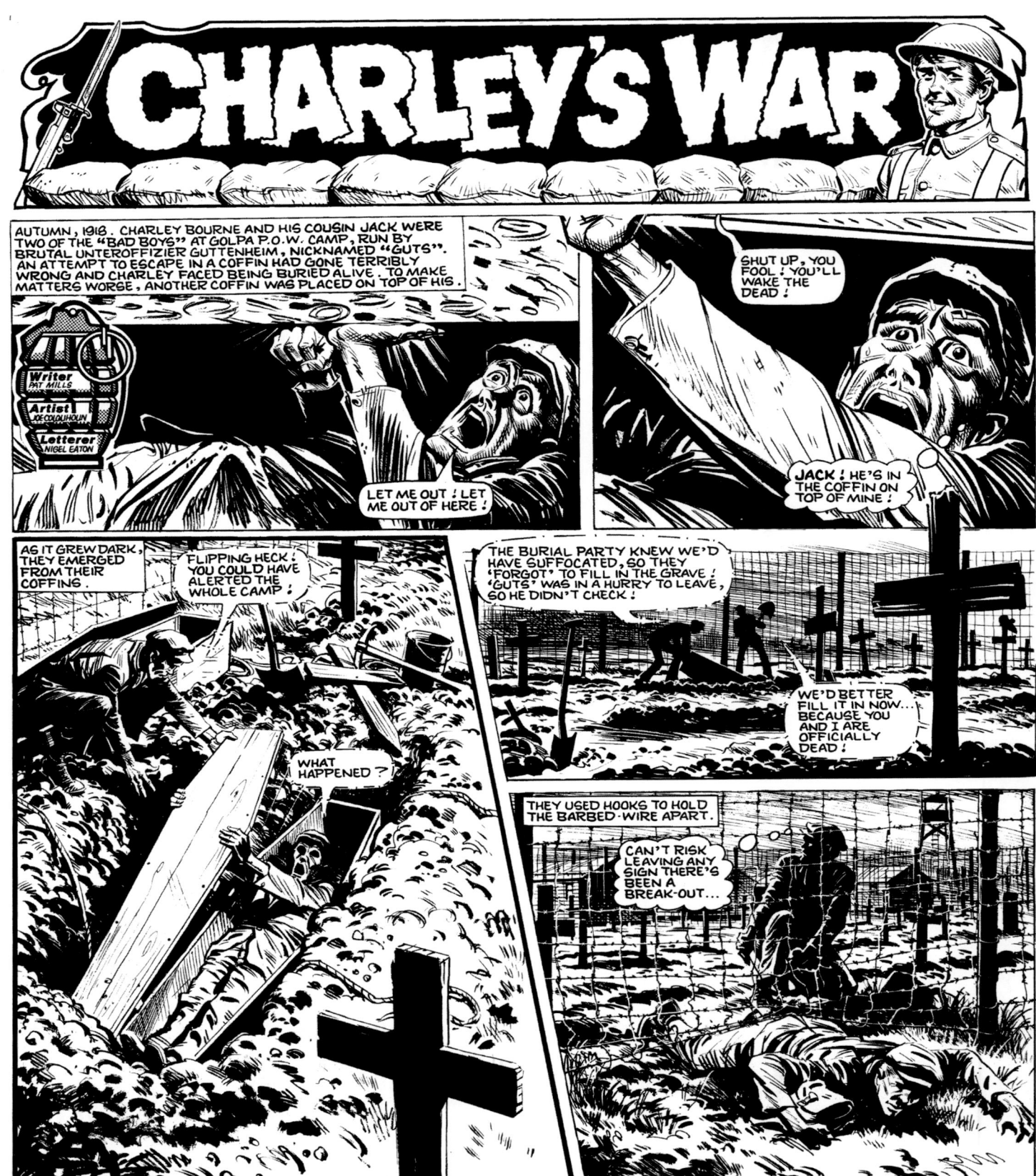

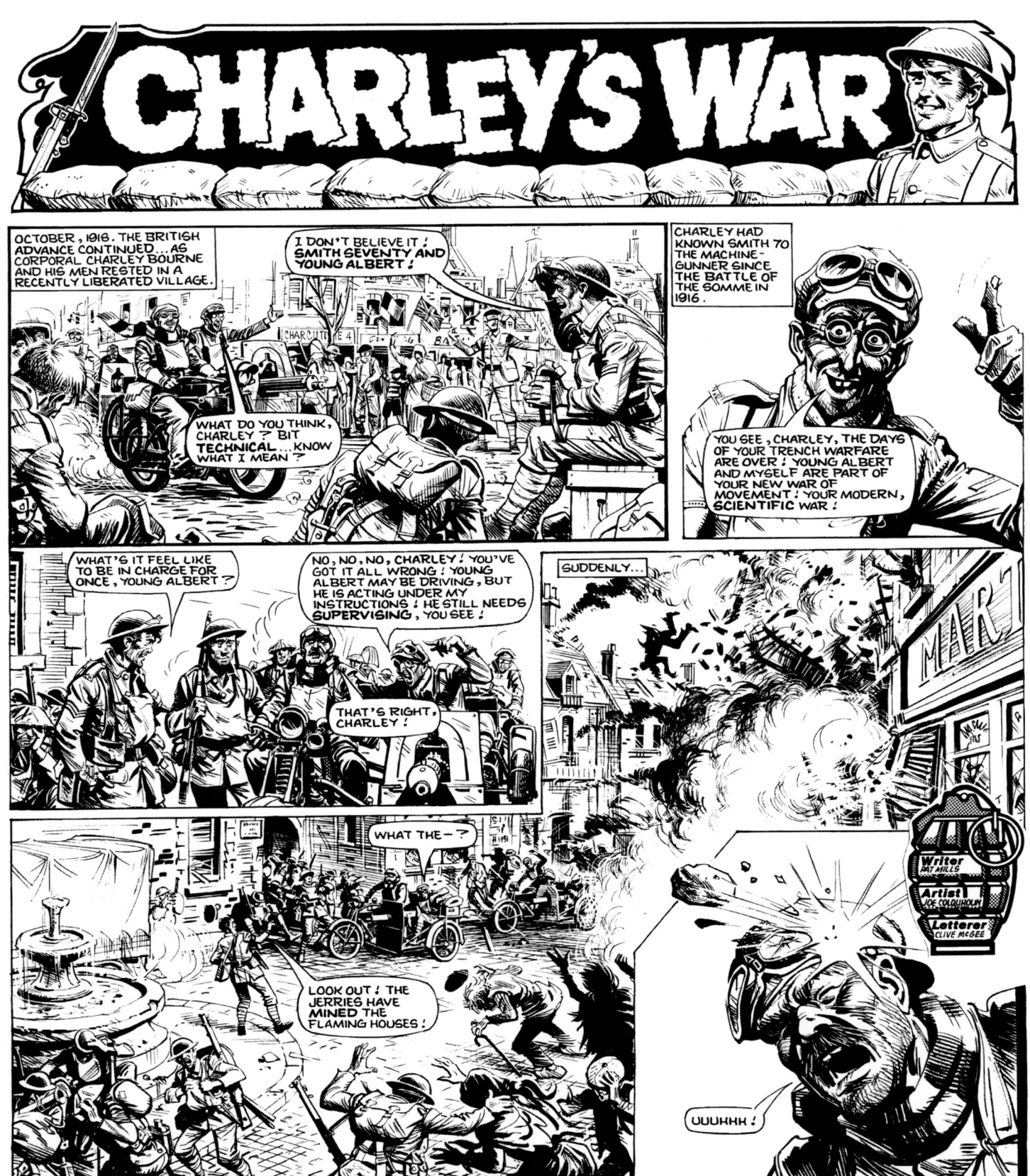

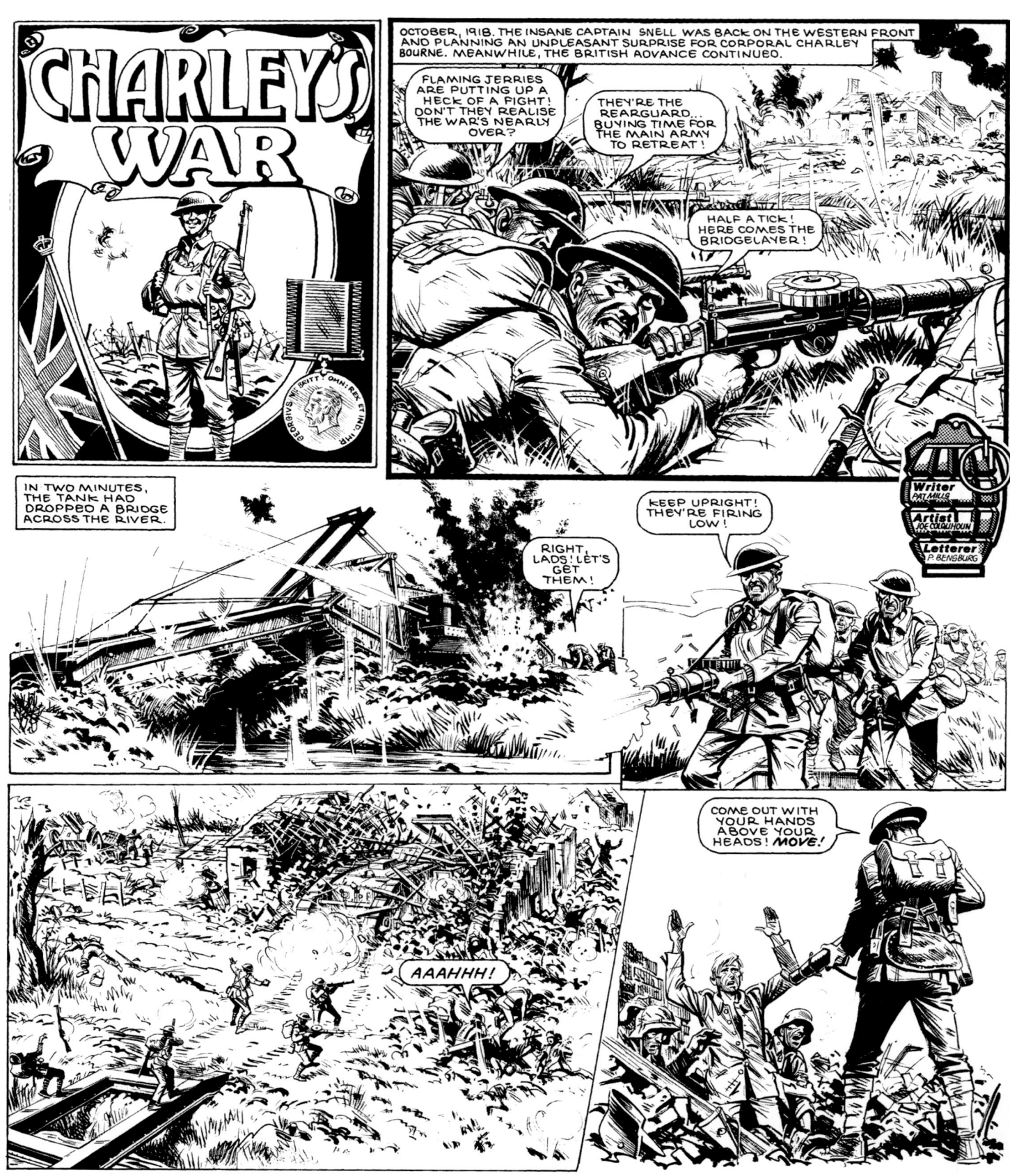

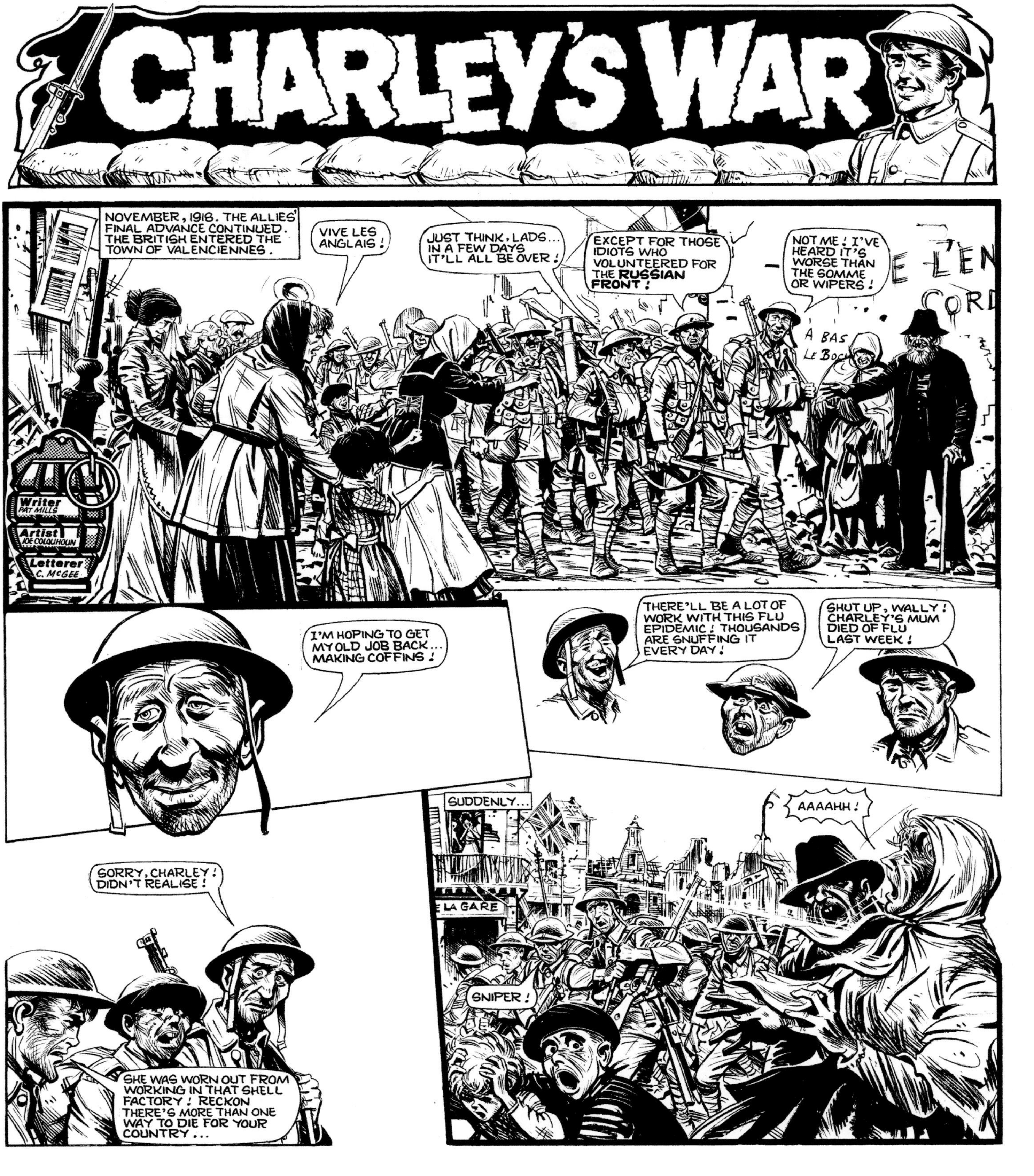

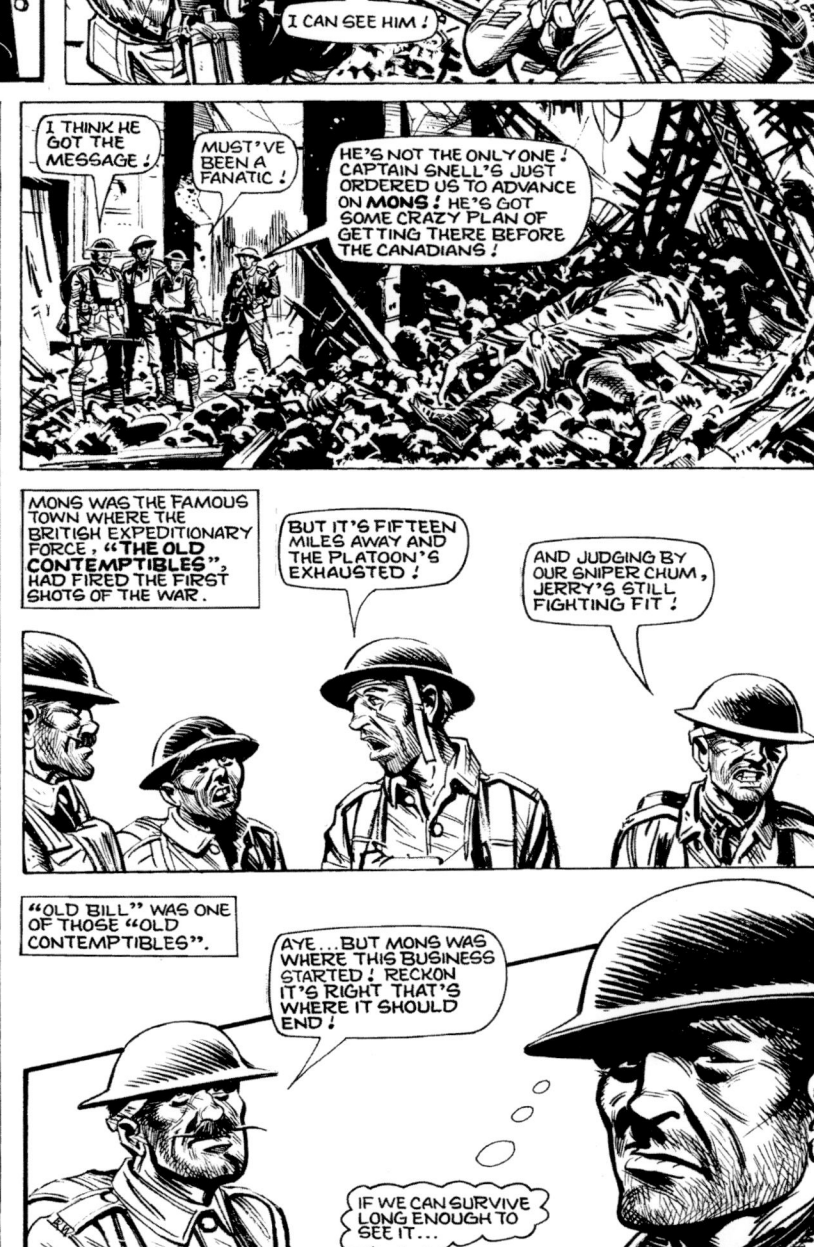

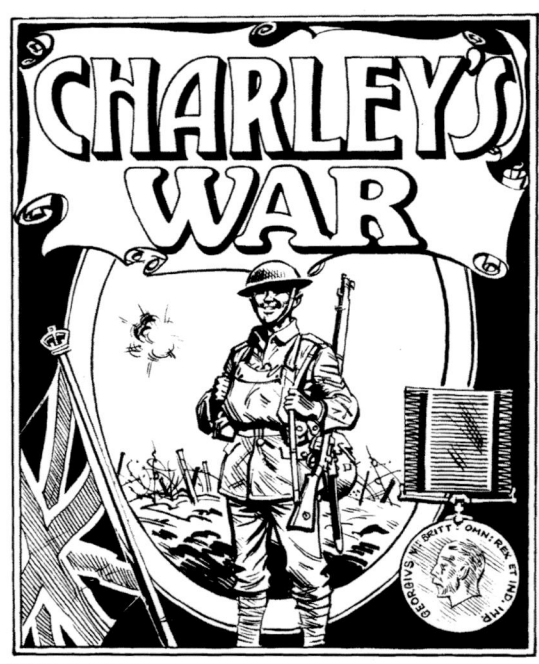

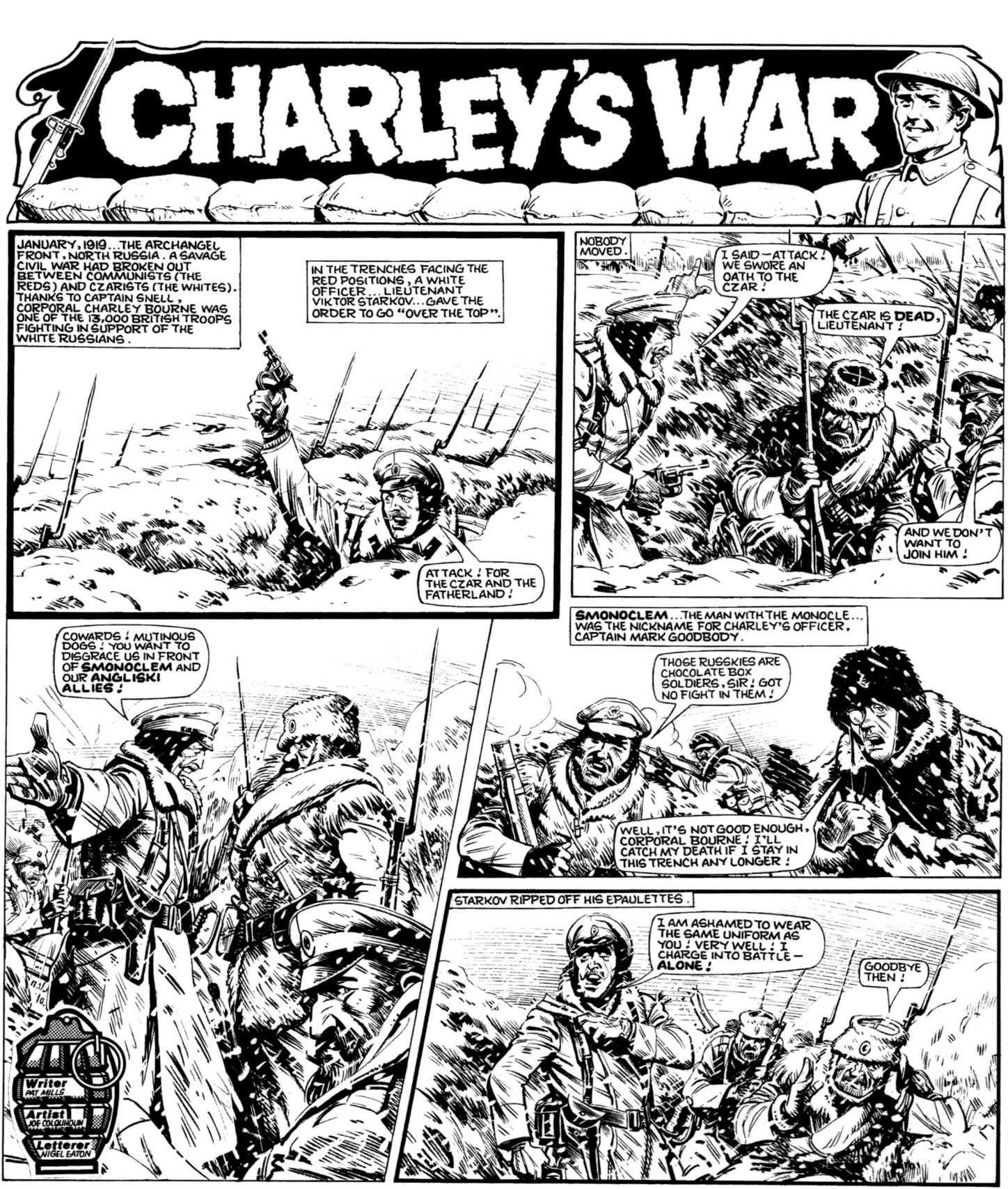

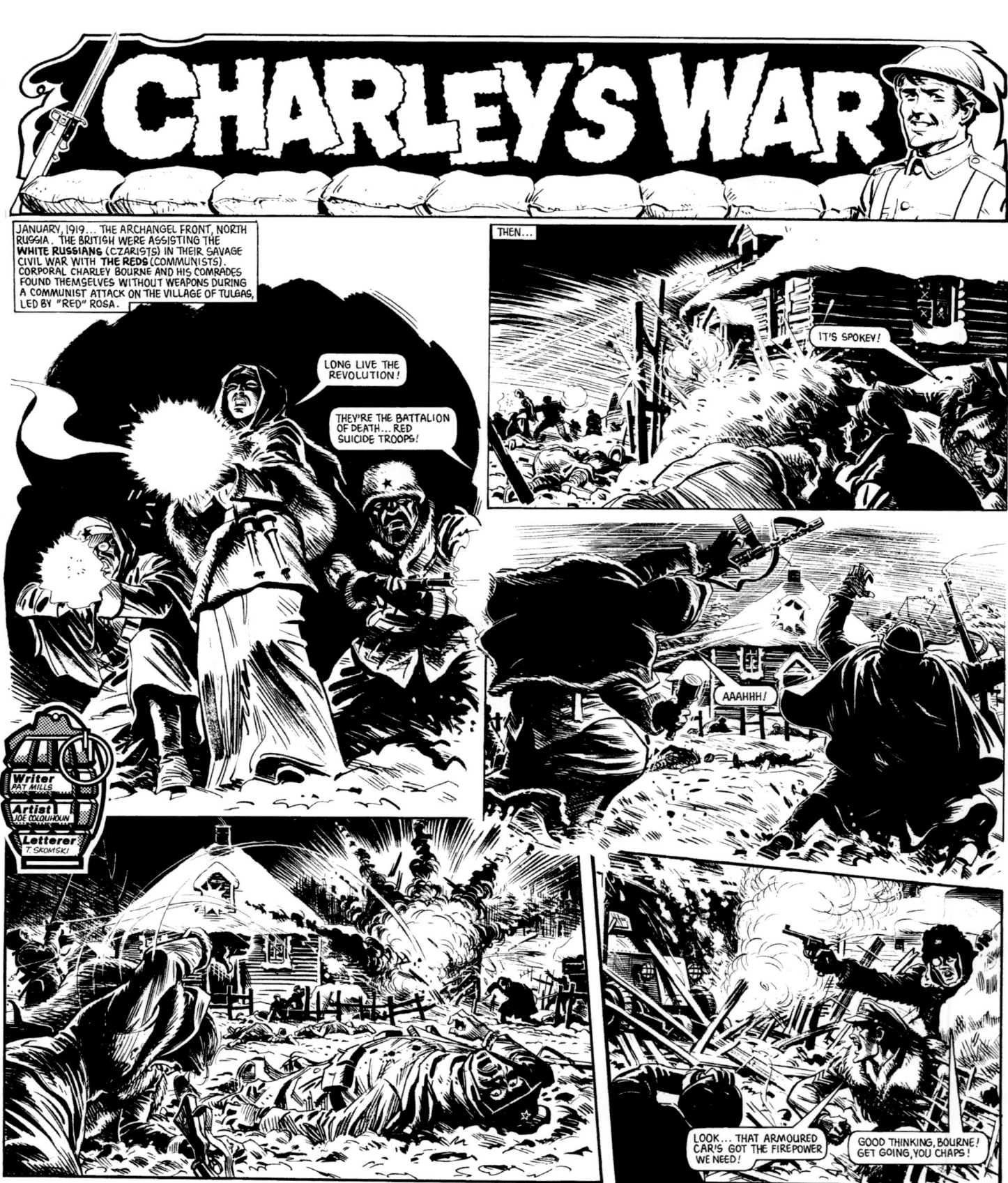

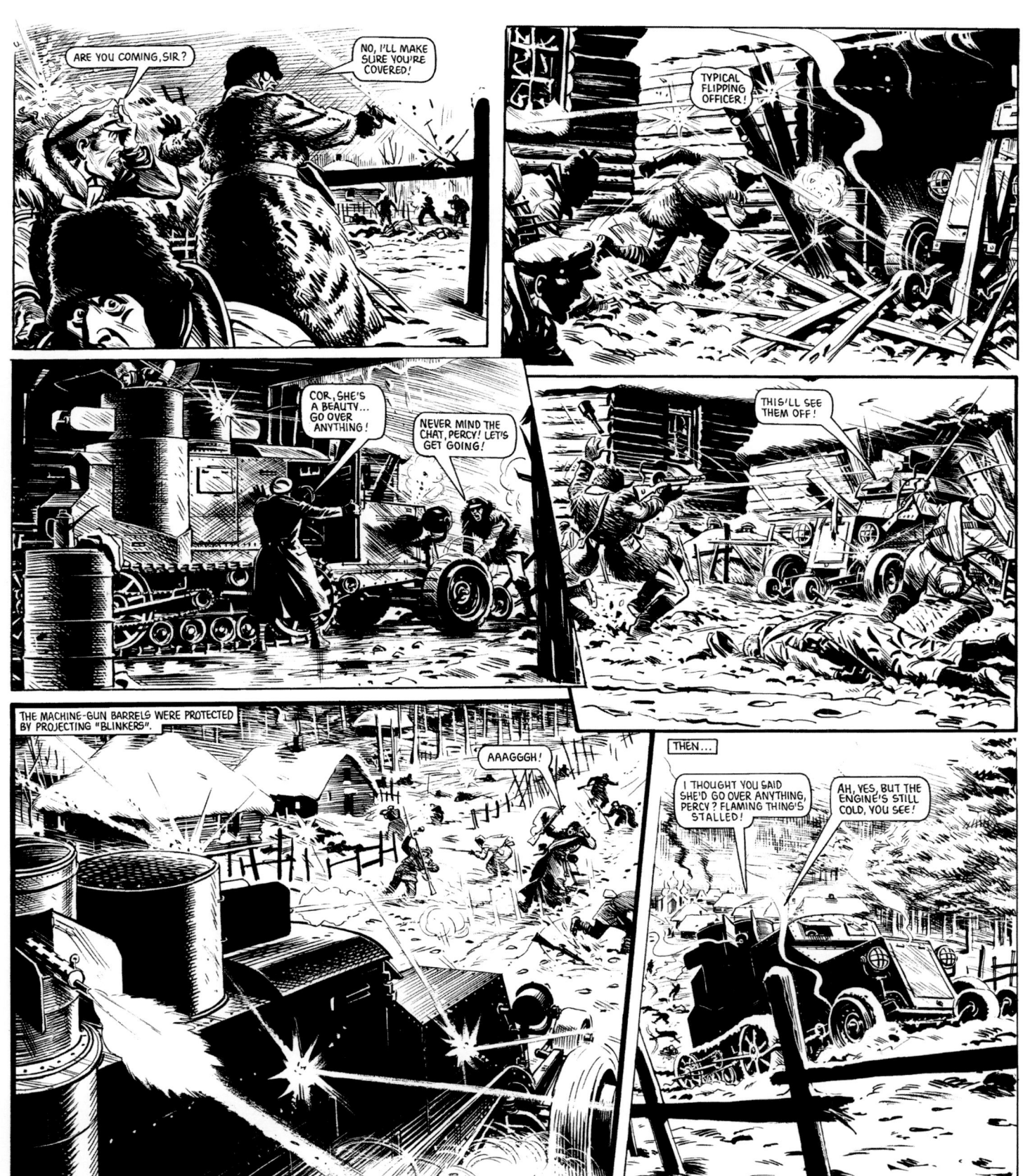

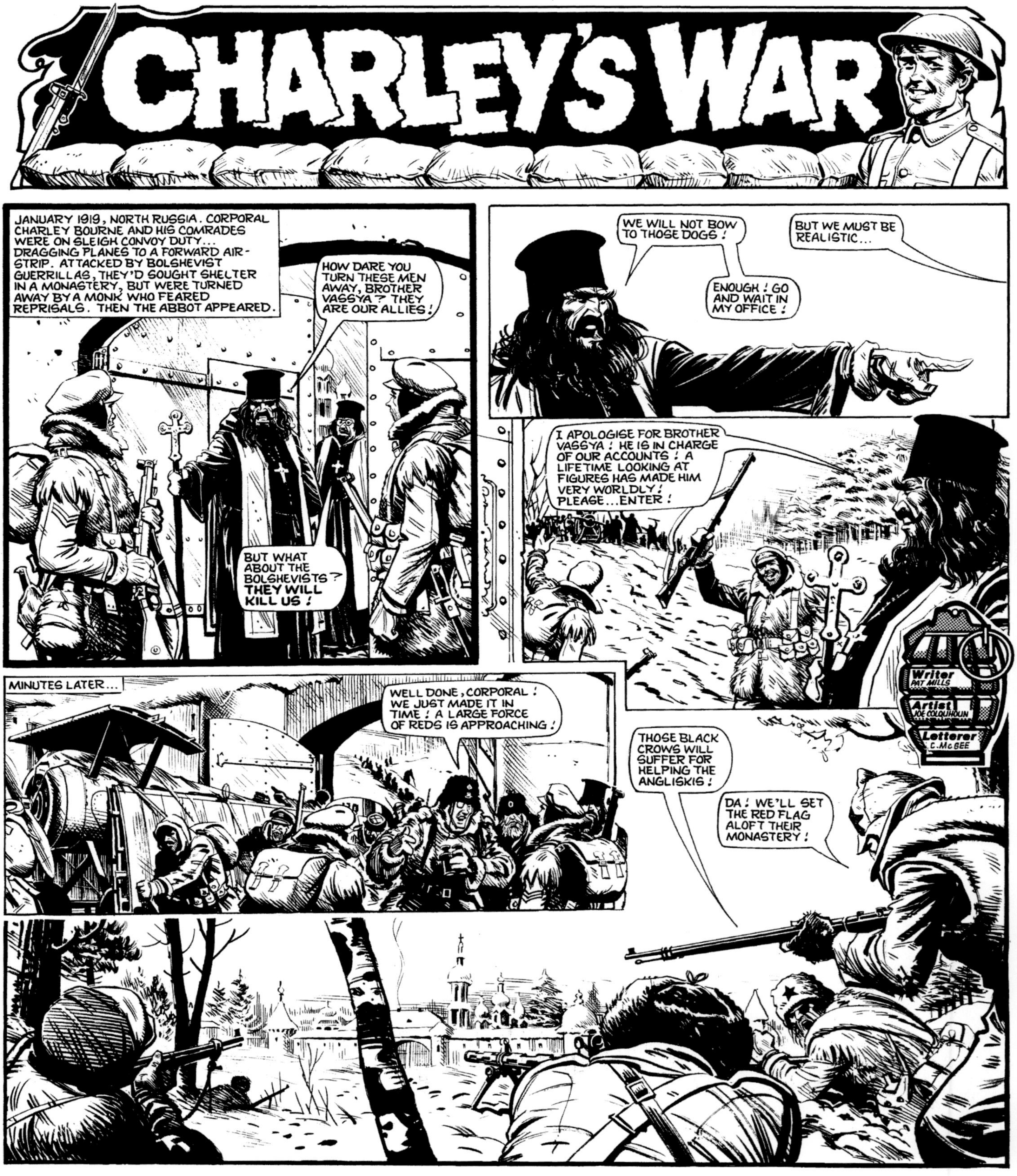

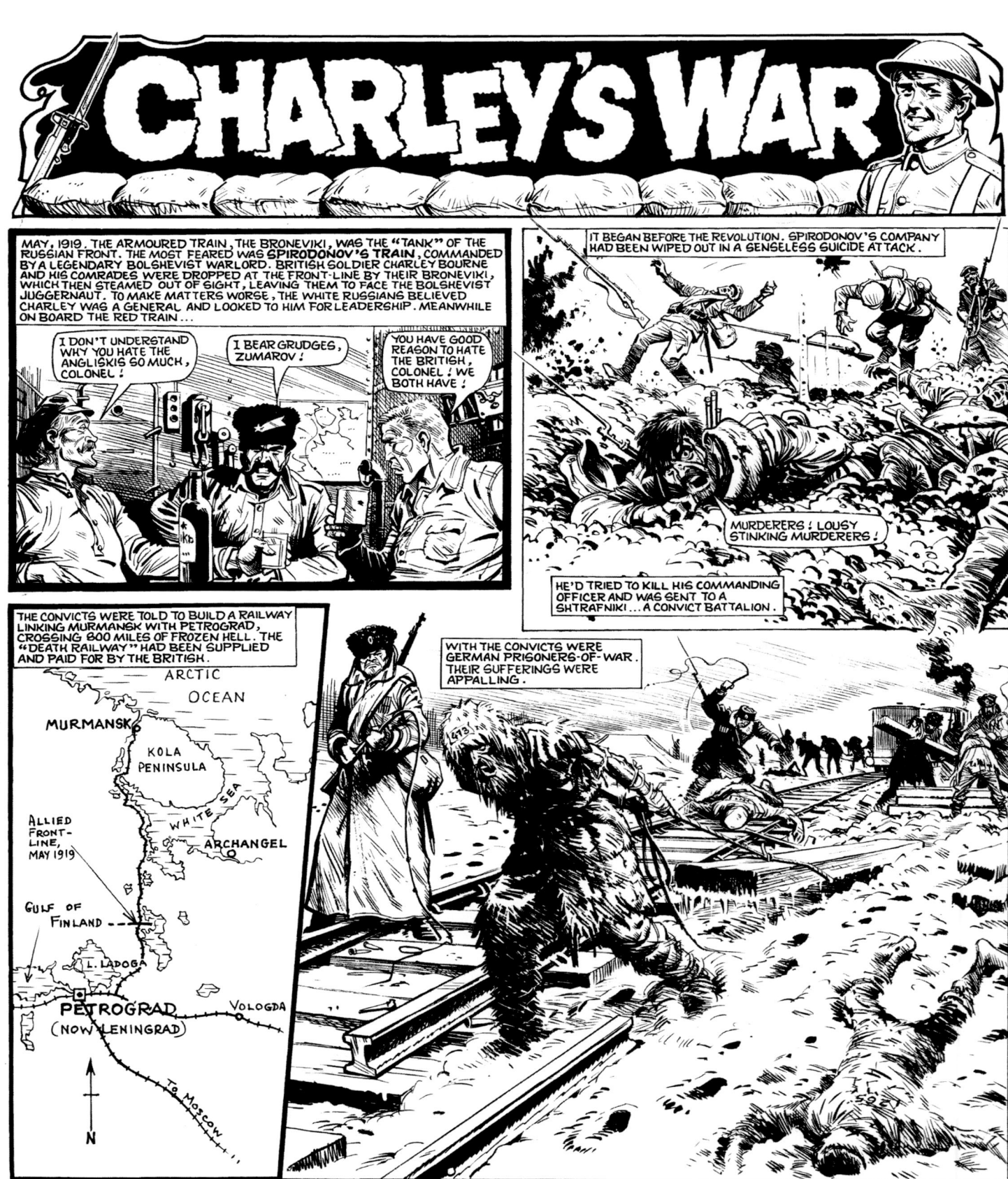

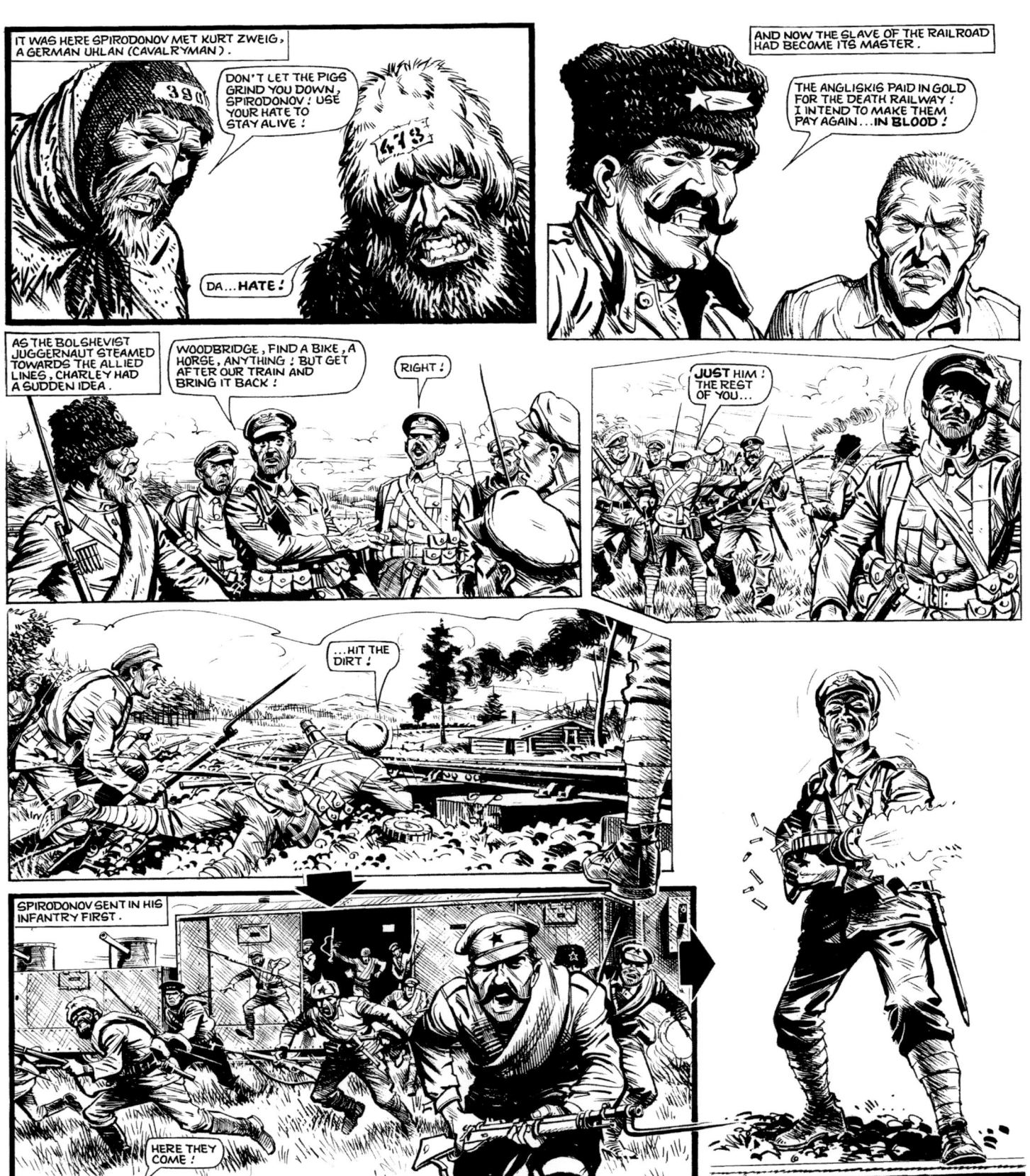

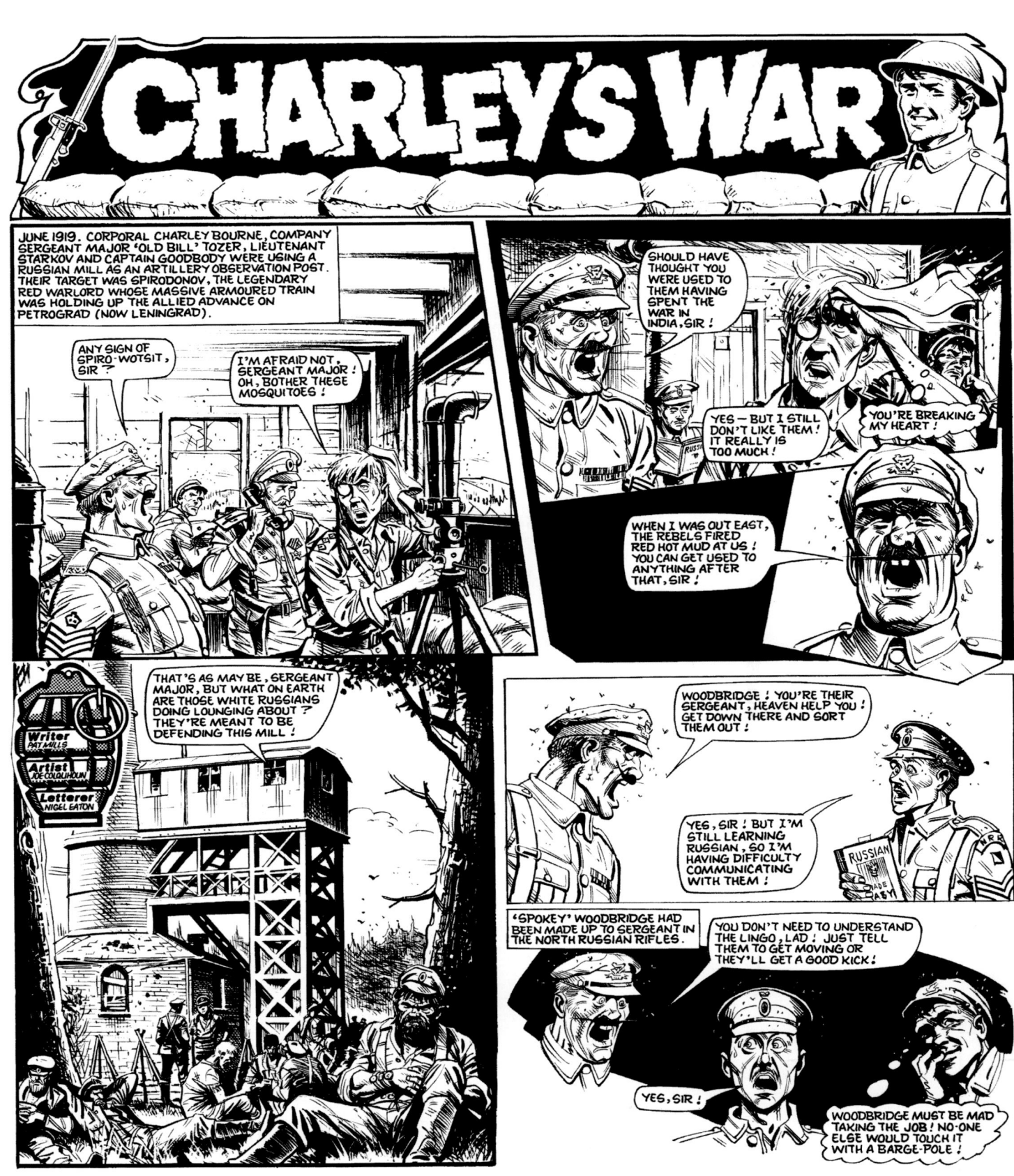

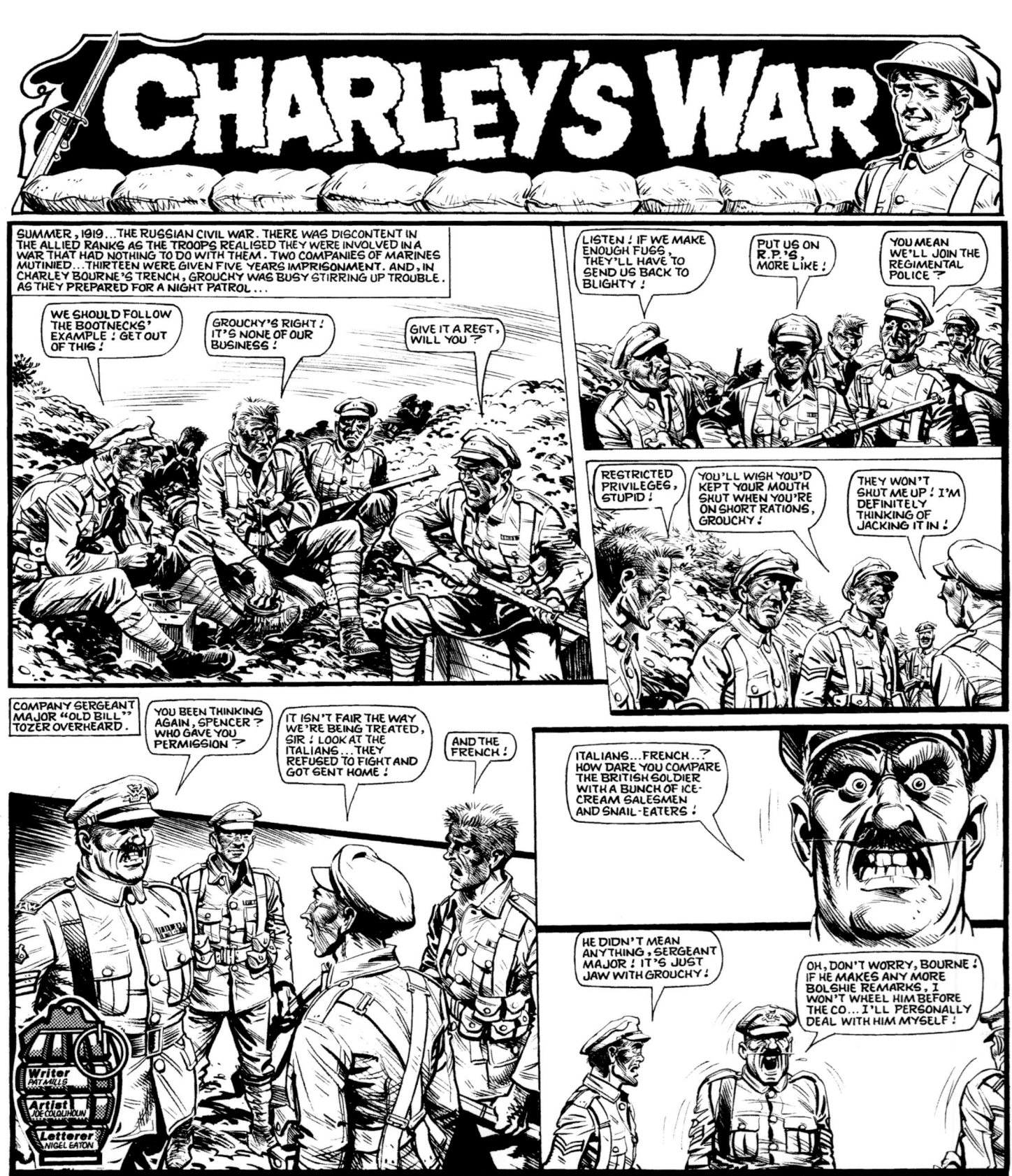

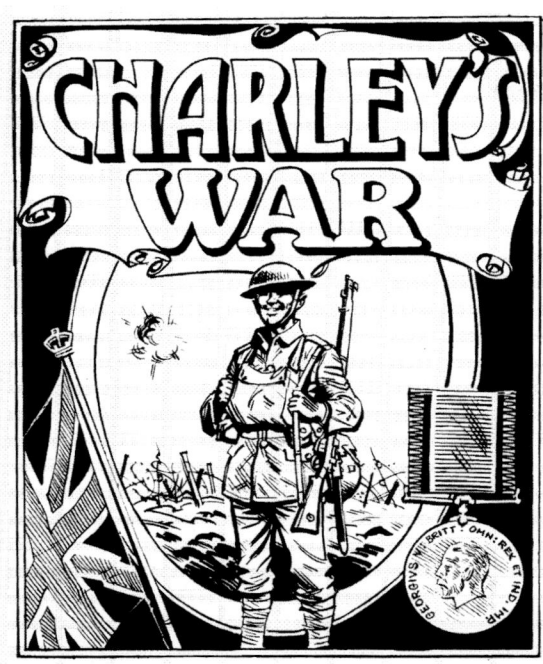

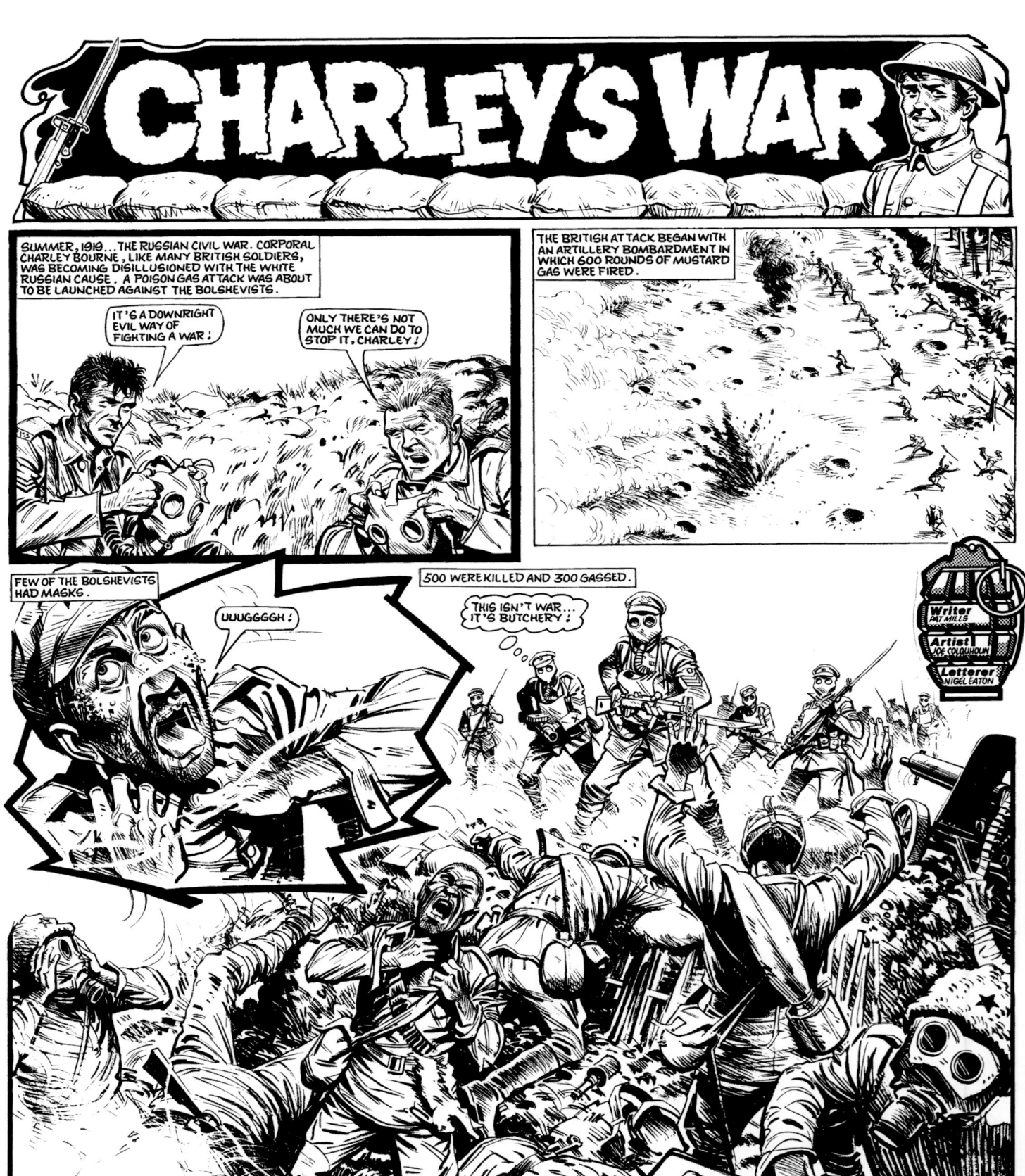

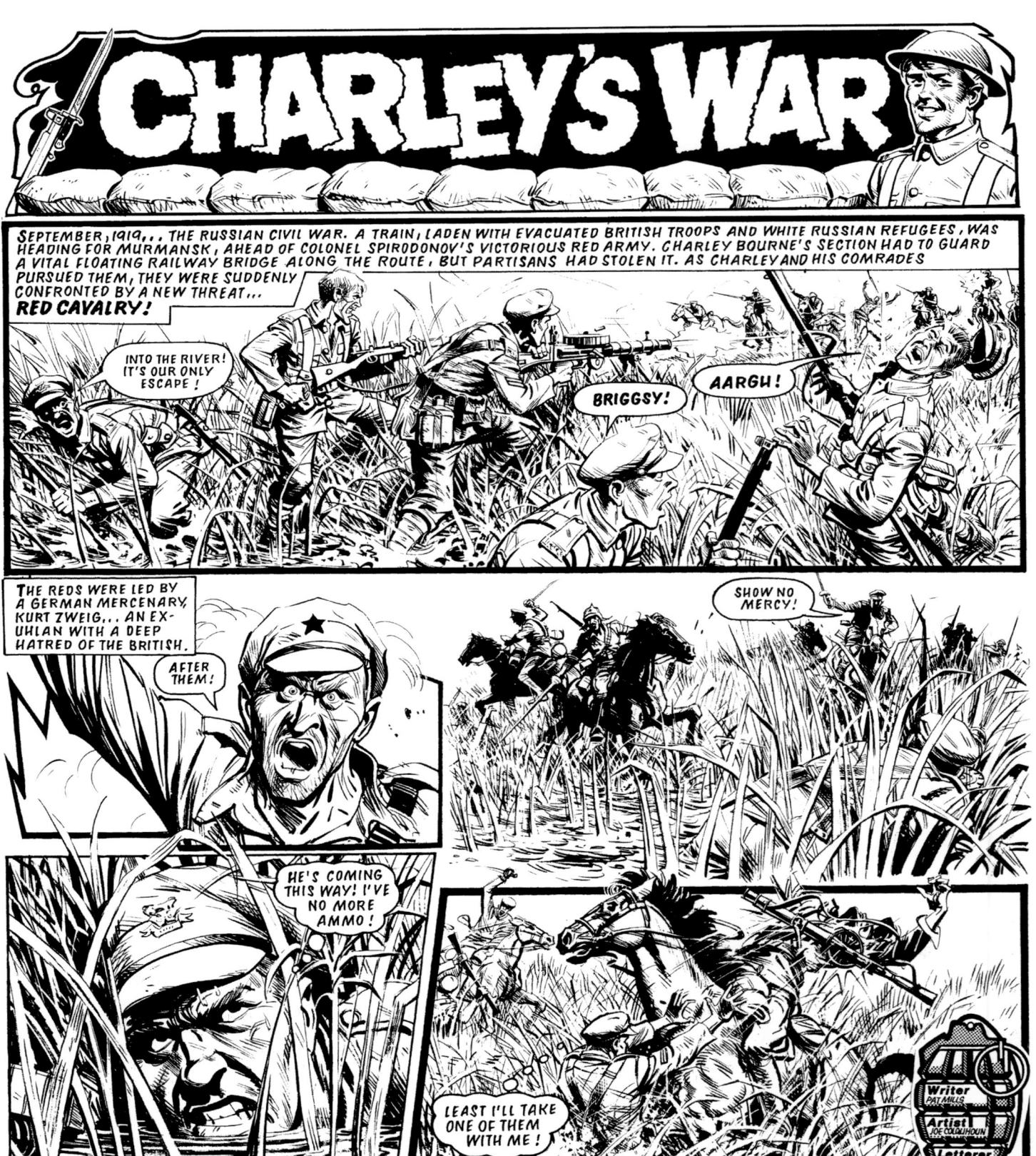

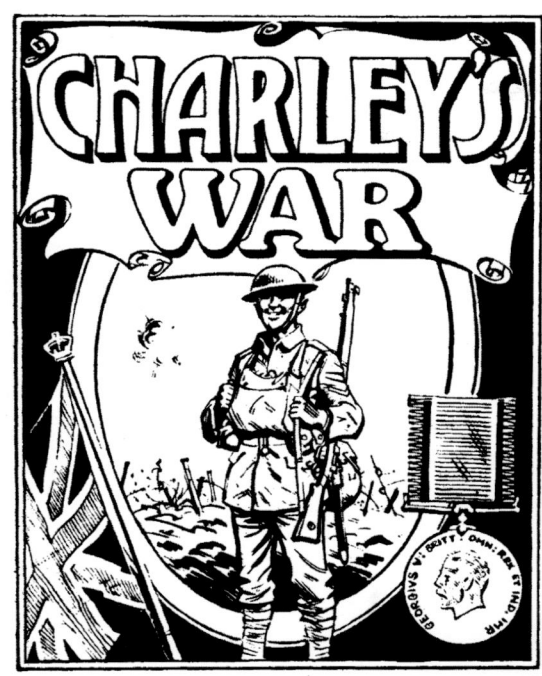

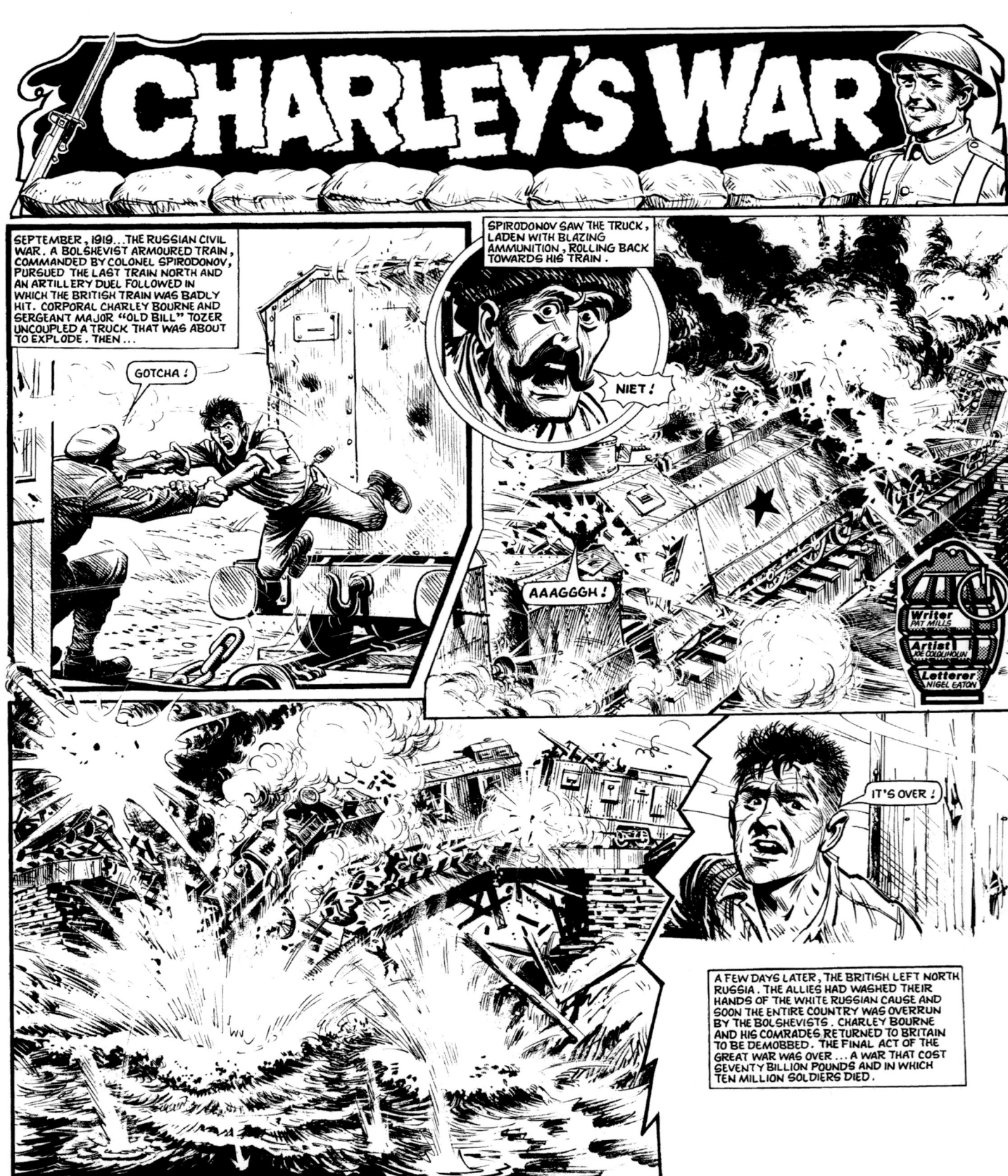

COMMENTARY

Volume 3

by **Pat Mills**

EPISODE 177 (Pages 4-6)
It was around this time that Joe was taken ill and there was a gap in the story. To fill it, by popular request, editorial reprinted the first three episodes of Charley. As Titan editor John Freeman told me, 'To the *Battle* editor's credit, virtually every other editorial during the gap refers to Joe either in hospital or getting better.' With this episode we are back on track.

EPISODE 178-180 (Pages 7-16)
The nightmare of Passchendaele continues. I was using original source material from books wherever possible, but I wish I'd been geared up to collect my own eye-witness accounts from veterans who were still alive at that time. This is an approach I prefer these days.

For instance, I recently wrote *The Ayatollah's Son* featuring the riots in Tehran. Published by Ctrl.Alt.Shift in their anthology *Unmasks Corruption* and superbly drawn by Lee O'Connor, it's the account of how a young man turns against his father, an Ayatollah, and becomes a revolutionary. His story was told to me by an Iranian journalist I met in Paris. If you come across it, you will recognize the modern day counterparts of Charley and his comrades and similar 'trench humour'. For example, an Iranian student is taken before an Inquisitor because he has been drinking – a crime punishable by thirty lashes He had the presence of mind to chew cigarettes first. The Inquisitor smelt his breath, 'Ugh! It doesn't smell of beer at all. It smells of shit!' and let him go. That's pure *Charley's War*! This actually happened to my Iranian contact when he was a student. The stories of such 'ordinary' heroes fascinate me. *Persepolis* has also proved that 'political' stories don't have to be boring and can be more entertaining than the meaningless adventures of men in tights.

I've put up *Ayatollah's Son* on a dedicated Facebook site. I hope to add to it with images from *Charley's War* and other political stories I've written. For example, the *Inspector Ryan* stories by myself and Alan Mitchell, drawn by the late John Hicklenton and my *You are Maggie Thatcher* book drawn by Hunt Emerson. I'm hoping it will create a possible forum for politically-orientated comic stories like *Charley's War*. It's under the heading PatMillsPoliticalComics. I welcome your feedback.

EPISODES 181-183 (Pages 17-25)
Difficult decisions for Charley and a drama involving poison gas. It's interesting to consider that in the year this story first appeared – 1982 – the Falklands War, the Russian invasion of Afghanistan and the Iran-Iraq war were raging. Poison gas was used extensively in this war against the Iranians and also the Kurds. The latter first had an experience of such a 'weapon of mass destruction' when it was dropped on them by the British in the 1920s, acting on Churchill's orders.

EPISODE 184 (Pages 26-28)
The blood transfusion episode. It seems unbelievable that blood should be pumped straight out of one soldier into another and yet it's all horribly true.

EPISODE 186 (Pages 32-34)
Fabulous artwork by Joe. The incident where General Haig only sees soldiers who have acceptable wounds is authentic. 'Nothing gruesome or upsetting. Like faces blown off…. He can't bear to look at the really horrible cases. They make him feel ill.' It's good that it's appearing at this time where there is an odious attempt by historians to rehabilitate Haig as some kind of misunderstood 'hero'. Although I doubt modern politicians visiting the war wounded from the Iraq and Afghanistan wars are any different to and only share 'photo opportunities' with soldiers who have 'suitable' wounds.

EPISODE 187 (Pages 35-37)
Joe's art continues to knock me out, particularly the last page and his view of the cattle trucks. I never thought any other artist would capture the combination of nightmare imbued with surreal comedy that is so often World War One. But recently I came across a book by artist Paul Slater: *Fried Eggs in Brine*. It is absolutely stunning. It contains surreal paintings with a very satirical view of British militarism. Do check it out.

EPISODES 188-189 (Pages 38-43)
The story of Charley's Last Carry. This adventure leads us up to the 'modern day' story of the tour of the war memorials. It reminded me of various attempts to have the Charley's War artwork exhibited in British war museums, including the Imperial War Museum, but so far without success. We have, however, been more fortunate in France and I'm told *Charley's War* was included in a French museum war exhibition.

France has always taken its comic books more seriously than Britain. I have fond memories of looking at a lush graphic novel, the 300-page *Le Cri du peuple*, set in 1871's Paris Commune by Tardi. This brilliant artist also produces superb stories on the French war in the trenches. I guess the Etaples Mutiny had much in common with the Commune; certainly red flags were carried by the mutineers. Then, and in the 1919 mutinies when British soldiers refused to invade Soviet Russia, there was serious talk of revolution.

It would impossible today to produce British equivalents in comic book form – e.g. The General Strike – for the Anglo-American comic market where fantasy rules. These days I have to sneak my interest in history and politics into my stories, but never too much in case a small but vocal section of my audience starts complaining once again that history and politics are 'not entertainment'. Sigh! Thus in *2000 AD's Defoe*, a science fantasy clockpunk adventure set in the 17th Century, Titus Defoe is the last Leveller and is guilt-ridden that he has sold

out to become the King's Zombie Hunter. This allowed me to explore the belief systems of the Levellers, the first socialists, and how they were betrayed by Cromwell. My critics haven't noticed. Don't tell them.

EPISODES 190-191 (Pages 44-49)

I think these two episodes of the veteran returning to Ypres in 1982 are probably the amongst the most powerful and emotional episodes of the entire *Charley's War* saga. Joe has surpassed himself with his characterisation and authentic detail.

EPISODES 192-193 (Pages 50-55)

The Battle of Cambrai. Charley doesn't feature in the action and I think this was deliberate – to show that major events do not always involve my central character, because that would be contrived and unrealistic. It was a reaction to traditional war hero stories – like Captain Hurricane – who featured in every major theatre in Europe and the Far East. At the same time, it was important to feature these momentous events, the courage of the Bantams and the criminal incompetence of the generals. Not to mention that ludicrous dummy tank which still makes me laugh. That said, I doubt I would write the story in this way today. I think I would have created a stronger sub-plot for Charley that made him more pro-active and engaged him in the central events in some other way. Perhaps with a stronger emphasis on the Home Front and how people really believed victory was in sight and the church bells rang in triumph.

News of events at the front was highly controlled and manipulated by the authorities and this continues into our own times. Excellent girls comic artist Charlotte Fawley told me how she used to draw images of battle for BBC2's *Newsnight* during the Falklands conflict and the first Gulf War. There was a ruling that photos could not be used but drawn images were acceptable. Sketched at *very* short notice, they are superb and have much in common with Joe's depictions of war.

EPISODE 195 (Pages 59-61)

This volume concludes with a sympathetic depiction of the Germans on their side of the trenches. With *Battle* and *Action* comics we went some way to showing Germans were heroes, too. I had pleaded with the IPC publisher to let me run a serial with a "good German" and he finally agreed. This became *Hellman of Hammer Force*, superbly written by Gerry Finley-Day and illustrated by Mike Dorey. However, information which shows the Germans in a positive light is still thin on the ground. For instance, I only recently discovered the story of the Edelweiss Pirates and the Roving Dudes – German teenagers who courageously fought back against the Nazis in the Second World War. These young heroes have never been recognized as a resistance movement, perhaps because they also fought against the British and Americans during the brutal first years of the Allied occupation of Germany (another largely untold story). They were regarded as 'a serious menace' by the Allies.

Although there will be many 'good Germans' in this next *Charley's War* story, the episode ends with one of my all time favorite cliff-hangers: the appearance of the young Adolf Hitler!

EPISODE 196-197 (Pages 62-67)

A film producer recently told me that what he particularly liked about Joe's art was the way the characters in *Charley's War* were portrayed in natural and unassuming poses. It's as if they are totally unaware they are being watched by us, the reader, or there is a "camera" (the artist) following them around, "filming" them. This is very much the case with the scenes with Hitler in the German dug-out.

This is the opposite of how heroes are portrayed in fantasy or sf comics. The more successful heroes are "self-conscious", invariably posing for the camera and striking iconic poses – whether it's super heroes running on one leg towards us, Slaine wielding an axe or Dredd leaping from his motorbike. This is what that audience looks for and is therefore valid in the world of fantasy; it's interesting that the reverse is highly regarded in the world of historical realism.

EPISODE 198 (Pages 68-70)

In John Toland's biography of Hitler he quotes an eerie poem written by the Fuhrer while he was in the trenches. It is reproduced in full below:

I often go on bitter nights
To Wotan's oak in the quiet glade
With dark powers to weave a union

*The runic letters the moon makes with its magic spell
And all who are full of impudence during the day
Are made small by the magic formula!
They draw shining steel—but instead of going into combat
They solidify into stalagmites.
So the false ones part from the real ones
I reach into a nest of words
And then give to the good and just
With my formula blessings and prosperity.*

Hitler's interest in the occult is well known and it would appear from this poem he was already trying to contact dark forces during World War One. I found this very chilling, especially when you consider his miraculous escapes from death in the trenches and later in World War Two.

EPISODES 199-201 (Pages 71-79)

I found myself sympathising with the Germans as they come under attack by the British snipers. Germans as positive figures in comics were relatively new when Charley's War was written. I had pioneered them in *Action* with *Hellmann of Hammer Force*, pleading with the publisher to let me include a German hero. At first he was reluctant, concerned that the British Legion might complain as well as the media who loathed comics, apart from the "educational" *Eagle*. But he eventually saw my point that this was the Seventies, and it was time we recognised the heroism of the enemy. I commissioned Gerry Finley-Day to write Hellmann and *Battle* ran *Fallmann, Fighter from the Skies*, about a German paratrooper – also written by Gerry, drawing on his parachute training in the TA.

Looking at Episode 200, I cringed at the text panel, "Powerful crossbows were used quite often by Germans." This was added by editorial and comes - once again - under the category of stating the bleeding obvious. But they are not entirely to blame; readers had previously cast doubt on the strange artefacts of World War One, such as dogs wearing gas masks. A reader cited them as an example of how stupid and unbelievable comics were. Even a soldier who served in North Africa in World War Two was sceptical that snipers wore medieval armour until I showed him the photo references. An example of World War One armour can be seen on page one of Episode 201.

EPISODES 202-203 (Pages 80-85)

The British join in the German "Hymn of Hate". A very British response, almost Pythonesque. You could never imagine any other nation doing it. I laughed out loud when I read this scene.

By World War Two, other songs had replaced the "Hymn of Hate" such as the German national anthem – "Deutschland Uber Alles". According to German reader, Josef Rother, this originated as a call for a united democratic Germany, rather than for Germany to conquer all. Arguably our "Rule Britannia" and the American "Twilight's Last Gleaming" are more jingoistic

EPISODE 204-206 (Pages 86-94)

I noticed there were several pictures with no dialogue and I'm pleased that they work well here. It's not always the case – sometimes words are needed to understand what's going on. Also to stop the page seeming empty. I'm not fond of comics, notably American super hero comics, where characters have long, unlikely, pseudo-witty conversations as they knock the stuffing out of each other. However, one artist colleague believes that words are needed with action sequences to slow the reader down, otherwise he will turn the page too quickly. I don't agree – if the pages are visually absorbing, the reader will take his time perusing them. Ideally, I'd like to see action scenes in comics written like film scenes with very little dialogue (e.g. the action scenes in *Kill Bill Volume 2*); but it doesn't always come off. With Joe, it works every time.

EPISODE 207 (Pages 95-97)

The Field Punishment Number One handed out to a soldier in this episode seems cruel, medieval and barbaric. But is the treatment handed out to an American soldier in 2011, Bradley Manning, for allegedly passing information to Wikileaks any less cruel, medieval and barbaric? The untried Manning is kept awake during the day, forbidden to exercise in his cell, and forced to present himself naked to his guards.

In this episode there is a reference to Hitler staying in Liverpool before the war. This fascinating possibility was explored by Beryl Bainbridge in her novel *Young Adolf*.

EPISODE 208-209 (Pages 98-103)

Episode 208 ends with a boxing match between a German and a Tommy and Charley's question "Wouldn't it be good if wars could be settled this way?" If that seems hopelessly naïve, it's worth noting America's most decorated soldier General Smedley Butler made equally "naïve" suggestions in his book *War is a Racket*. He proposed that only soldiers should have the right to vote on whether a nation goes to war and politicians and arms manufacturers should receive the same wages as soldiers as an acknowledgment of how the latter were risking their lives.

I wish I could have explored the sinister role of arms manufacturers further. The superb TV series, *Reilly Ace of Spies*, exposes the questionable activities of Vickers boss, Baron Zaharoff, one of the most infamous "Merchants of Death." He was notorious for selling to both sides in war. In Episode 209, Smith 70, the machine gunner, discovers his German opposite number has the same weapon. The Vickers machine gun. The profits made by "Merchants of Death" were astronomical. How apt therefore that in the background the Tommies sing, "Oh, it's the same the whole world over, it's the poor gets all the blame while the rich gets all the pleasure. Oh, isn't it a bleeding shame." The luxurious Christmas menu for the officers underlines the point.

By the way, my script originally had the authentic "ain't it a bleeding shame." Once again, a *Battle* sub-editor, obsessed with the Queen's English, has amended my dialogue.

The story of the anti-war General Butler is now the subject of a graphic novel *Devil Dog* by David Taylor and Spain Rodriguez, the celebrated underground artist.

The last page of the *Young Hitler* story feels rather condensed. I should have taken an extra page over it or perhaps even an episode. Probably the reason I didn't was because "slow" or "talking heads" episodes could get negative reactions from readers and editors were therefore wary of them.

EPISODE 210-212 (Pages 104-112)

Stunning aerial detail in *Wilf's War*. Joe benefited from having less pictures on a page in flying scenes and I think if we were doing this story today, I would be suggesting four pictures on a page or even double page spreads for "wide screen" drama to convey the complexities and the distances involved in aerial action.

Like *Blue's Story*, Charley doesn't feature in this adventure and once again the readers approved of the character "deviation" because it was in the same spirit as the trench war, showing the unsung working-class heroes of the RFC, rather than the high profile, middle and upper-class air aces.

EPISODE 213-215 (Pages 113-122)

I don't think there's any artist today who could draw something as visually demanding as the observer standing on the wing of a plane and directing the pilot. I'm sure the incident is authentic and the working-class subtext to the story stops it being a "ripping yarn".

EPISODE 216 (Pages 123-125)

The attitude expressed by the mechanic is an important one and relates to the theme of ambition that runs through *Wilf's War*. He says, "You shouldn't have tried to better yourself, Wilf. If you never try, you'll never fail. See what happens when you have ambition? Dreams? You end up as the smoke-bloke." I heard something similar from the editorial "old guard" when I was creating *Battle*, *Action* and *2000 AD*. They hated and feared change, wanting comics to remain the way they had been for decades. They told me nothing worked in comics anymore and it was best to just "coast" along, not taking any chances, until such time as they were all shut down and they would receive their redundancies. I'm sure that's what inspired me to include those lines.

Wilf ignores the attempts to drag him down into a morass of complacency and is constantly pro-active, even on the ground.

EPISODE 217-219 (Pages 126-134)

Wilf's pilot, Captain Morgan, is a fascinating character – he reminds me of the role played by George Peppard in *The Blue Max*, a German pilot obsessed

A FEW DAYS LATER, AFTER PHOTOGRAPHY LESSONS, WILF WAS SENT ON A RECONNAISSANCE MISSION, ESCORTED BY SINGLE-SEATER SCOUTS.

with aerial "kills" who will do anything to earn his "Pour le Merite", Germany's highest military honour.

I heard a rumour a year or so ago that Lord of the Rings film director Peter Jackson was interested in the British comic book serial Black Max. Then I discovered comic artist Chris Weston had also heard this rumour. To quote from his blog, "Black Max was a strip that originated in Thunder weekly comic way back in October 1970. Drawn by European supremo, Alfonso Font, it featured the villainous exploits of the German air ace Von Klorr, who used his flying skills and giant bats to fight the allies in WWI. After 22 issues, Thunder folded, but Black Max continued his adventures within the pages of Lion weekly."

The artwork on the Black Max was fantastic, in the same league as Joe's aerial art, although I don't recall being impressed by the stories. But it's a fun idea and, like Chris, I'd prefer giant bats to hobbits any day. I guess it's just a fanciful rumour, but if anyone knows more, do let us all know.

EPISODE 220-222 *(Pages 135-144)*

China's disfigured face, obscured by a mask, and the scene where a propeller cuts Jankers to pieces set me thinking once again about how much we should actually show in comics. I think we should go further – even for our original audience of boys aged 9 – 14, so they are aware of the true nature of war, rather than the Hollywood glamorization.

In General Butler's War is a Racket there are a grim series of photographs of the dead and wounded, including one where a soldier has lost half his face but is still alive. I truly believe if such photos were more widely shown it would make young men think twice before joining up. Of course it could never happen, because the media has a vested interest in concealing the real effects of "shock and awe", otherwise the recruiting offices would be out of business.

In fact, the media has always been hostile to war comics, believing that only Eagle and Look and Learn were "educational" and everything else was some kind of gratuitous penny dreadful that should be torn up or confiscated by school teachers.

When Battle first appeared, editor Dave Hunt was interviewed by John Craven for the BBC. Eagle-fan Craven asked Dave why a comic like Battle ran stories about the Second World War when the conflict had been over for thirty years? His concern was that children were being constantly exposed to the violence, hatred and trauma of yesteryear. Dave responded by pointing out that films about the Second World War were regularly shown on daytime BBC TV. Needless to say, his reply was cut from the transmitted interview.

For another graphic novel about the true reality of war, I'd recommend the recent Dougie's War by Rodge Glass and Dave Turbitt. Set in our times, it's about "one soldier's return from Afghanistan".

EPISODE 223 *(Pages 145-147)*

The death of Captain Morgan. I found this very powerful and exciting. But I wish I'd written it over two episodes to really give space to the key moments in this dramatic finale to Wilf's War.

Particularly because I think we're all interested in the primitive technology of the past. Here, Wilf uses an emergency stick to pilot the plane, as well as moving cables by hand! I wonder if there is a name for World War One and Two weird tech? For instance, 17 and 18th century weird tech is called "clock punk" (see my Defoe which features clockwork robots). 19th century weird tech is called "steam punk". Perhaps this is "propeller punk" or "prop punk"? Or is there another name already out there?

EPISODE 224-225 *(Pages 148-153)*

The detail on these two episodes is as mesmerizing as ever. The literal "tug of war" for a German body, for instance. But my favorite scene is on the last page of Episode 30, in the final bank of pictures. Old Bill quietly pockets the German marks that were on the corpse. The sly expression on his face is a joy to behold!

We also see Field Punishment Number One carried out under fire. Looking again at this outrageous brutality, I recalled the words of the Great War Prime Minister Lloyd George quoted in John Pilger's moving documentary The War You Don't See about the shameful and dishonest reporting of the Iraq War by the media.

Nothing has changed since December 1917. Back then, Lloyd George said to the editor of the Guardian, "If people really knew the truth, the war would be stopped tomorrow. But of course they don't know and can't know."

With Charley's War, I had an opportunity to show aspects of the war that are even to this day played down, avoided or not shown to a mass audience. An unimportant "kids comic" like Battle was largely ignored, so I could write what I liked. In the final two volumes, we will continue to show the result - "The Great War You Don't See."

Today, Charley is finally reaching a wider audience than ever. A French edition is now under way; it headlined an exhibition Comics and Conflicts at the Imperial War Museum in August 2011; and it is also used as a teaching aid in school. Jane Colquhoun, Joe's daughter, told us that a local school has been using it over ten years to support GCSE war poets study. Perhaps we are "educational", after all!

EPISODE 226 *(Pages 154-156)*

I recall reading how officers in the trenches sometimes had bells to ring for their servants, perpetuating the Upstairs and Downstairs class system. In this opening scene it's a gun, rather than a bell, and this seems the kind of ludicrous arrangement bored soldiers might well devise. I'd love to have seen it in Blackadder. "You fired, sir?" Smith 70 looks more like Baldrick every time he appears.

On the subject of Blackadder, I learnt recently that at Chalke Valley History Festival, eminent military authors gave a talk to rehabilitate the image of General Haig in "Lion Not Donkey: Haig & The Great War." They are doing this because, "Unquestionably, the legacy of the First World War has become distorted over the years. The poetry of men like Wilfred Owen and Siegfried Sassoon, films like Oh, What a Lovely War, and even Blackadder, have all helped create the myth that the vast deaths in the trenches of the Western Front were the result of military incompetence and that these lions were needlessly slaughtered because of the blunders by the antiquated donkeys who led them."

Myth…? I share the negative perspective of Haig best summed up by respected military historian Liddell Hart who was wounded during World War I: "He (Haig) was a man of supreme egoism and utter lack of scruple —who, to his overweening ambition, sacrificed hundreds of thousands of men. A man who betrayed even his most devoted assistants as well as the Government which he served. A man who gained his ends by trickery of a kind that was not merely immoral but criminal."

Blackadder puts it even better: "Haig is about to make yet another gargantuan effort to move his drinks cabinet six inches closer to Berlin."

It's disturbing that today's establishment historians – often with strong military connections – are so desperate to validate Haig and I wonder why. Thus there was the BBC's documentary in 2006, *The Somme – From Defeat to Victory*. The Somme *a victory*?! We live in Orwellian times.

EPISODE 227-228 (Pages 157-162)

Charley has what appears to be a self inflicted wound as he leaves the trenches for the last time. The war he will return to some months later will be a very different conflict. So this episode really is the end of an era. For other powerful visual images of the war in the trenches I recommend *Beyond the Wire* by Alys Jones published by Atlantic Press.

While he recovers, Charley is given a white feather by a nurse. She hates soldiers who incur self-inflicted wounds so they can get out of fighting. Good for them. To self-inflict a wound still takes a kind of courage and to be so desperate speaks volumes about the true state of the trench war. I'm reminded of the words of Albert Einstein, "The pioneers of a warless world are the youths who refuse military service'".

EPISODE 229 (Pages 163-165)

I found Charley's court martial riveting to read. In a modern comic, this story would have been told over six pages at least. It would allow more space for reactions, but I think it's still very effective in this condensed format.

EPISODE 230-231 (Pages 166-171)

The air war is drawn with astonishing accuracy and power by Joe. Today, we have been conditioned to the idea of civilians being a "legitimate" target or simply "collateral damage", but in 1918 the aerial bombing on non-combatants was rightly regarded as murder.

EPISODES 232-234 (Pages 172-180)

The drama of Captain Snell continues. I wonder what treatment they gave Snell to try and restore his sanity? Clearly it failed! It was too early for electric shock or insulin shock treatment which began in the 1930s. I suspect it was barbaric by today's standards. For instance, in Germany in the same period, Doctors wanted to check whether a patient was insane or faking his mental illness. Accordingly, they stuck pins under his nails, stabbed him in the back with a long needle and burned him with hot irons. When he didn't react they concluded he was mentally ill.

EPISODES 235-237 (Pages 181-189)

Romance and marriage for Charley. Comic heroes rarely seem to get married, even today, and I thought it was about time we entered the real world and had our characters behave like normal people. The middle-class family Charley has married into is beautifully rendered by Joe. In other less desperate times, they would certainly have been against the wedding to a working class lad, but by 1918 there was a shortage of young men and this would have serious implications after the war.

EPISODE 238 (Pages 190-192)

This episode makes clear there weren't sufficient air raid shelters for Londoners and parks and underground shelters were closed to them. Yet at this time Britain was the greatest and richest nation on Earth, but it could not provide such basic facilities for its loyal citizens.

The episode also features the famous and powerful poster, "Daddy, what did YOU do in the Great War?" It's still very effective. In a similar vein, the theatres ran recruiting plays such as *England Expects* exploiting young men's patriotism and suggesting that "the British Empire, as the chosen leaders of the world, shall travel along the road of destiny and progress, at the end of which we shall see the patient figure of the Prince of Peace." Many young men joined up in response to this call, firmly believing that God was on our side. Sound familiar?

EPISODE 239 (Pages 193-195)

The death of Wilf. I was very sad to see him go, but I needed to sustain the realism of the strip and the sense that death could be lurking round the corner for any of the regular characters.

EPISODE 240-241 (Pages 196-201)

The start of cousin Jack's naval adventures. Having successfully gone off on a rather risky tangent with Blue's story of the French at Verdun, and Wilf's story of war in the air, it seemed like a good idea to also feature the war at sea. I felt the lives of the ordinary seamen should be dramatized in the same way as the ordinary soldiers in the trenches. And, as this story originally appeared not long after the Battle of the Falklands, the naval Battle of the Falklands seemed like a good idea. I also knew that Joe had been in the navy in the Second World War and therefore would bring his first-hand knowledge to bear. Re-reading it for the first time since it appeared, I love his naval detail and I enjoyed both these episodes.

EPISODE 242-243 (Pages 202-207)

But no-one in comics had ever succeeded in making a ship story popular. Previously, John Wagner – the *Judge Dredd* writer-creator – had written *HMS Nightshade* and had conducted extensive research for it, including interviewing a naval veteran. Despite this, the readers hadn't voted for it in the voting charts that ruled writer and artists' lives. My naval story now also got the thumbs down from the readers and the editor told me not to pursue Jack's career any further. Re-reading these two episodes I can see why they didn't catch on. It's a complex scenario with many points of view and too many characters. It's easy to fall into such a trap with a naval story. If I was to write it today, I would drastically simplify the scenario and reduce the number of characters to make it dramatically effective.

EPISODE 244 (Pages 208-210)

I enjoyed this episode: a much simpler dramatic story of fuelling the boilers with the stokers as heroes. I also liked it because, all too often, it's the Captains who are shown as the main heroes in naval war movies. This diminishes the achievements of ordinary seamen and makes their efforts seem less important. There are so many middle and upper class heroes in fiction (Batman, Iron Man, Sherlock Holmes, James Bond etc) which gives the false illusion that somehow they are more interesting, more exciting, brighter, and funnier than ordinary people. We need more series like Sharpe, more working class heroes.

EPISODE 245 (Pages 211-213)

I had hoped – if this story had worked – to go on to feature Jack at the Battle of Jutland. This naval action, earlier in the war, featuring the nautical equivalents of Darth Vader's Death Star. It's a pity it never happened because this episode showed some of the potential; Joe's ships are powerful and exciting; imagine them at the Battle of Jutland! But for Jutland, I would have needed more pages, double page spreads to show the sheer size of the metal monsters, a stronger personal drama for Jack, a slower pace and some better writing techniques to really make it come alive. Tough to write and a hard sell to an editor!

EPISODE 246-247 (Pages 214-219)

Reading these episodes, it reminded me that last year the *Daily Mail* featured a newly-discovered German naval board game from 1916 which demonstrated how Germany was challenging Britain for control of the seas. In our own times, the board game *Diplomacy* – based on Europe in the Great War – also shows this superbly; we get a sense of the geographical problems both Britain and Germany faced and the strategies needed for victory. John Wagner and I were addicted to *Diplomacy*; so much so we even devised a Far East version for our own amusement.

EPISODE 248 (Pages 220-222)

The end of the naval battle. I was enthralled by this last episode, especially the albatrosses attacking the dying sailors. Jack then goes off on a secret mission. This would have been the Zeebrugge raid in April 1918. But unfortunately no more naval stories were permitted. Jack had been voted out by the readers.

A few years ago I related to an audience of *Charley's War* fans at the Cartoon Museum how ship stories had never worked in comics and the curator Anita O'Brien corrected me. She reminded me that there was one ship story that had been hugely popular : *Jonah* by Ken Reid!! Every week Jonah sunk a ship without fail! Maybe that's why it was so successful?! It's a brilliant series by a comic genius and deserves to be collected.

After Jack's departure, Oiley is called up again! Oiley reminds me of the loathsome Horatio Bottomley MP, editor of the patriotic *John Bull*, responsible for so many young men enlisting, but who never fought himself. "Would to God it were my privilege to shoulder a rifle and take my place beside the brave boys in the trenches. But you only have to look at me to see that I am suffering from two complaints. My medical man calls them anno domini and embonpoint. The first means I was born too soon and the second that my chest measurement has gone into the wrong place." Later, Bottomley was convicted of fraud and ended up in prison where Oiley also belongs.

EPISODE 249 (Pages 223-225)

The episode describes how, on March 21st 1918, the Germans launched the greatest bombardment of the war – more than one million shells fired at the Allied lines. Writers of war stories, myself included, tend to overlook the real villains here : the Merchants of Death, the companies who manufacture those million shells. Thus an American gunpowder manufacturer's profits were $6million dollars a year before 1914 and jumped to $58 million a year after 1914. Merchants of Death, then and now, need wars to boost profits. And if they're sociopaths, as apparently so many corporate bosses, generals, politicians and other leaders are, they're not going to care about the human cost.

EPISODE 250 (Pages 226-228)

There's an excellent dilemma for Charley here. Should he shoot the Scholar, an officer who has been set on fire and is desperate to die? His past stories with the Scholar makes it all the more powerful.

EPISODE 251-252 (Pages 229-234)

Incredible scenes of the German offensive conclude with a superb image of German cavalry looking like medieval knights. I've often wished we could have given Joe more space and time so all the pages could have been executed to this high standard. It would have resulted in *Charley's War* being an international success much sooner, I'm sure.

But as we approach the 100th year anniversary of the Great War there has been enquiries from several tv companies about producing a tv version of *Charley's War*. The French version is also proving very successful; it's attracted interest from museums in France and was on the official selection list for Angouleme 2012.

EPISODE 253-255 (Pages 235-243)

I haven't seen the play or film version of *War Horse*, but I really must, I'm told they're both excellent. The story of Warrior runs throughout *Charley's War* in a similar way. A sad, sad ending for Warrior even though it's deliberately and rightly underplayed, I feel, with no false sentimentality.

EPISODE 256-257 (Pages 244-249)

The war we're seeing now is very different to the trench war and closer to World War Two. The military campaigns of 1918 are often overshadowed by the earlier Battles of the Somme and Passchendaele, so it's fascinating to see the new dangers that Charley now has to face.

EPISODE 258 (Pages 250-252)

A poignant opening picture in sharp contrast to the new jingoistic logo with a smiling Charley that suddenly appears at the top of the page. It's old-fashioned and entirely inappropriate. Please ignore it!

In his speech to his troops, Haig, veteran of war in the Sudan, war in South Africa and Commander-in-Chief in India, talks of fighting "for the safety of our homes and the freedom of Mankind." I wonder if Mankind included black people? A British policeman described how they interrogated a Kenyan insurgent during the Mau Mau rebellion. "It got a little out of hand. By the time I cut his balls off he had no ears and his eyeball, the right one, I think, was hanging out of its socket. He died just before we got much out of him."

Or the Arabs in Palestine? Another British policeman relates how, "Most accidents out here are caused by police as running over an Arab is the same as a dog in England except we do not report it."

Just two of examples of the reality of our supposedly superior Empire bringing civilization to other peoples. One year after Haig's speech there was the Amritsar massacre in India where a thousand peaceful protestors, including women and children, were shot dead by British troops. No criminal action was taken against the officer responsible. "The freedom of Mankind" clearly didn't extend to Indians either. As Victorian writer Ernest Jones said about the British Empire, "On its colonies the sun never sets, but the blood never dries."

EPISODE 259 (Pages 253-255)

The German panzers lumber on. Recently I saw tanks up close at the Tank museum in Dorset where I was invited to give a talk on *Charley's War*. I found them really chilling. I also met Joe's widow and family at the museum and it was great to share memories of a man I regard as Britain's greatest adventure comic artist of the twentieth century.

EPISODE 260 (Pages 256-258)

Excellent cliff-hanger ending! Snell's back! However, I think that final text panel was added by editorial reminding us who Captain Snell was. By now Battle had a fixed readership and so it jars and seems quite unnecessary. I'm looking forward avidly to the last volume of the series and Charley's further battles with Snell.

Last volume? Yes, I'm afraid so. It will cover 1918 and the British invasion of Russia 1919 and will end my era on the story. Completists may wonder about *Charley's War*'s subsequent brief foray into World War Two with another writer and a very different tone, but long-term fans I consulted agreed with me that this series should end in 1933 with my final episode. That said, Joe continued to do a great job, so there's a case for the best pages from the abortive sequel being collected, perhaps in an *Art of Joe Colquhoun* book.

EPISODE 261 (Pages 259-261)

I obtained the gorilla poster from the Imperial War Museum. Its hate-filled message seems ludicrous now, but I'm sure it was effective at the time. I've often wondered if it was the inspiration for the film *King Kong*. Pity about the lettering "American Army Recruiting Poster" – so strange and awkward looking!

There are conspiracy theories about the sinking of the *Lusitania*. It's now confirmed it was carrying arms for the Allies – a dive team estimate four million rounds of ammunition – and there's the possibility the British knew there was a German submarine in the area but failed to alert the ship. Winston Churchill wrote shortly before the sinking, "It is most important to attract neutral shipping to our shores, in the hope especially of embroiling the US with Germany." The sinking brought the isolationist United States into the war. Given how often the technique of appearing to be the innocent, injured party has worked successfully for Britain and America, from Pearl Harbour to the present day, it seems not unlikely. Americans were told, falsely, that German children were given a day off school to celebrate the sinking. The emotional myth – "Remember the *Lusitania*" – becomes more important than the reality. The scientist Carl Sagan summed it up well, "One of the saddest lessons of history is this: If we've been bamboozled long enough, we tend to reject any evidence of the bamboozle. We're no longer interested in finding out the truth. The bamboozle has captured us. It's simply too painful to acknowledge, even to ourselves, that we've been taken."

EPISODE 262-263 (Pages 262-267)

There's no racism in this story which, of course, there would have been. It was all censored by the *Battle* editor, Terry Magee. So he cut out my references to white American soldiers being members of the Klu Klux Klan because he told me in a phone conversation, "We don't want to offend anyone". Offend who? The Klu Klux Klan?! FFS! So we're not meant to tell kids about racism. It would have been most unlike me to have presented the characters in this bland and typically crap comic-book way. The dialogue is most unconvincing. I recall the way I wrote the Harlem Hellfighters was rather different. But anything "offensive" has been removed.

I put up with it because I wanted to slip the forthcoming Russian serial through – where I write about Britain's truly shameful invasion of Russia which, potentially, could offend a lot of people. So I figured it wouldn't be wise to get on the wrong side of Terry. We all used such techniques to get through the censors. Thus Kevin O'Neill's – later art editor on 2000 AD – favorite technique was to feature something obvious for them to censor, so they wouldn't notice something far "worse" he wanted to get away with. I'm delighted to say it worked pretty well!

EPISODE 264 (Pages 268-270)

There's a reference to the famous Zeebrugge raid here which I had originally intended to dramatise, featuring Charley's cousin Jack, but readers weren't keen on ship stories – so I left it at a single image recording Jack's supposed death.

EPISODE 265-270 (Pages 271-288)

I love this whole adventure where Charley becomes a prisoner of war and meets up with his cousin Jack. It gives us a fascinating insight into conditions in Germany. I like Mad Bob and his pet brick. I suspect he was based on some authentic character I discovered. The German gaoler Guts is brilliantly depicted by Joe. He reminds me of some Weimar republic character from Erich Kastner's children's book *Emil and the Detectives*. Or *The Good Soldier Svejk* by Jaroslav Hasek. The plot moves at a break-neck speed – too fast for my taste today – but it did ensure there were no quiet or slow episodes. There's a great emotional dilemma for Charley – should he stay and face a firing squad or escape and betray his fellow prisoners? Then a hair-raising scenario where Charley is buried alive and compares himself to Count Dracula. Bram Stoker's novel was published in 1897, so it's plausible he would have heard of it, even though the film had not been made yet. Finally, there's the comedy of Jack claiming Charley is a halfwit. Thanks to Joe, a laugh out loud moment.

EPISODE 271 (Pages 289-292)

Should you feel Captain Snell's cruelty is untypical of officers, consider what a Lt Colonel S C Marriott wrote:

"The last time we went down for a rest I had as many as 31 men tied to the wheel (the crucifixion punishment) at the same time...Even Eckes, my second in command, had his faithful servant strung up for forgetting to put his anti-gas helmet over his shoulder one day..."

A contemporary account describes how this crucifixion was meted out to half-a-dozen Liverpool 'Pals', who had lost their gas helmets in a marsh. "They were tied by the neck, waist, hands and feet to wheels for one hour". One of them died.

But the Tommies were starting to fight back against their oppressors. Grievance committees were formed and their demands included, "The stopping of exploitation by officers who required the men to do private jobs for them, to be treated as men, not as children by the officers."

EPISODE 272 (Pages 293-295)

Smith 70 makes a welcome reappearance. He was based on my art editor Doug Church – who designed 2000 AD and is responsible for its early iconic imagery, and the idea of Judge Dredd's Mega-City One. I'm delighted to say Doug is still around and as exuberant as ever, a real character, and recently gave an interview to online fan magazine Hibernia.

EPISODE 273 (Pages 296-298)

There are now references to how bad things will be in Germany and Britain after the war. There was a revolution imminent in Germany but Britain was also close to revolution, although this is played down by establishment historians. Certainly in 1919 soldiers were mutinying: fifty army mutinies in two weeks involving tens of thousands of troops. Soldiers' unions were formed. Soldiers' delegations marched on Whitehall and demanded to see the Prime Minister. The Chief of the Imperial General Staff said, "The soldiers' delegations bore a dangerous resemblance to a *Soviet*. If such a practice were to spread, the consequences would be disastrous." General Haig wanted to shoot the leaders of a mutiny in Calais after officers were thrown out of a camp. He warned, "The state of the army is deplorable. It is rapidly disappearing." General Wilson agreed. "We dare not give an unpopular order to the troops and discipline is a thing of the past."

There were massive workers strikes. The police also went on strike. Churchill, predictably, wanted to smash the workers. But Lloyd George made some concessions, including pay increases, fast demobilization and reducing the number of troops sent to the Russian Front, to take the steam out of the situation. Another way he achieved this was by removing in June 1919 the restrictions on the notoriously poor quantity and quality of beer, so the working man could just get pissed again and forget his troubles. The Russian communists did the opposite: destroying vodka stocks after October 1917 so the workers were sober enough to continue the revolution and bring their rulers to account.

EPISODE 274 (Pages 299-301)

November 1918 and just a few days until the end of the war. "Except for those idiots who volunteered for the Russian front." The Tommies had no desire to fight their fellow workers in Russia and there were "Hands off Russia" demonstrations and mutinies, so effective that the numbers sent to the Russian front were dramatically reduced. Lenin wrote at the time, "Attempts to conquer Russia, which require a long-term occupation army of a million men, are the most certain road to the most rapid extension of proletarian revolution."

But there was another war also looming – the Irish War of Independence which Churchill and Lloyd George tried to brutally suppress with the infamous Black and Tans – unemployed veterans from the trenches; and the Auxiliaries, a paramilitary police force made up of British officers. My neighbor's grandfather enlisted in 1918 at age fourteen, eager to fight for his country. When the army discovered his age, they didn't discharge him: instead they sent him to Ireland as part of the Army of Occupation.

EPISODE 275 (Pages 302-304)

November 11, 1918. The last day of the war. Snell wants to make history with a final glorious charge. Sadly, once again, this is no comicbook caricature but is how a certain breed of officer thinks. Thus there's a legendary British officer who died in a hail of bullets seeking glory in the Falklands War. What is not so well known is that if the Argentinians hadn't killed him, there were some of his own men who vowed to do so. Because he wanted to die, "using the bodies of his men to cover himself in glory". What's also not so well known is the Falklands War was the last close contact war where soldiers would remember forever the bodies of young Argentinian conscripts dying on the ends of their bayonets, and many would be driven insane by the memory. Today, war is more remote and there's a new generation of British officers like Prince Harry, who compares his missions killing Afghan insurgents with playing a computer game. The spirit of Captain Snell lives on.

Finally the guns stop at the eleventh hour. Today, we are deliberately and offensively encouraged to remember it as primarily a noble "sacrifice". Sacrifice for *what*? To protect the interests and profits of the ruling classes. Harry Patch, the last survivor of the Western Front, saw it differently. He died in 2009, aged 111. "At the end, the peace was settled round a table, so why the hell couldn't they do that at the start without losing millions of men?" he said. "War is organised murder, and nothing else." Alan Bennett makes a related point in *The History Boys* when his history teacher admits that Britain was "partly responsible" for the war and the loss of millions of lives. And he suggests the true purpose of the war memorials and the two minute silence: "It's not lest we forget, it's lest we *remember*."

EPISODE 276 (Pages 305-307)

Charley pursues Snell, intent on "Judgement at Mons".

It's a tragedy that the war criminals on the British side – the politicians, the generals and the arms manufacturers – never faced the "Judgement at Nuremburg" they imposed on the Nazis in 1945. Amongst *their* war crimes were the executions of 306 British soldiers shot "for cowardice or desertion", in reality usually post-traumatic stress disorder. Soldiers such as 25 year old Private Farr, whose auditory nerves were affected by the guns so he couldn't stop shaking. After several months of fighting, he requested to see a medical orderly but was refused. In Farr's court martial papers, the Sergeant Major is quoted as saying "If you don't go up to the f*****g front, I'm going to f*****g blow your brains out" to which Farr replied "I just can't go on." The court martial was over in **20 minutes**. Farr had to defend himself. General Haig signed his death warrant and he was shot at dawn.

I see Snell as the representative of all those who should have faced a war crimes tribunal in 1919 and been punished for the "organized murder" of a generation.

EPISODE 277 *(Pages 308-310)*

Snell has "volunteered" Charley to fight in Russia! I wish I'd written an interlude story with Charley back in Blighty between November 1918 and January 1919. But there was little information available at the time and much of the unrest in Britain came later in 1919. In any event, the chances are Charley would have been shipped straight off to the Russian front from France.

My wife, Lisa, who loves modern history, had no idea the British invaded Russia – and on three fronts. I doubt it was ever on the national curriculum. So she asked her friends on Facebook if any of them knew. Here are a few of their amusing replies:

Dave of the Dead: Nope. Is it cos we didn't win?

Liam Child: I knew! 15 countries invaded Soviet territory in support of the Russian "White Armies". They bumped into the Anarchist Black Army in Ukraine and got battered (as did the Red Army). History was simpler when armies were colour coded.

Michael Bostock: The Red Army used captured English tanks to invade Georgia in 1921.

Robert Staveley: ... It was in support of Georgie (the King) cuz of the Tsar. Since he had finished kicking the shit out of the Hohenzollern and Hapsburg cuzzins, he decided to help out. After all, you can't have bleeding commoners kicking the shit out of Royals, only other Royals can do that!

The full extent of British interference in the affairs of Russia will probably always be concealed. But it included the Lockhart plot: an attempt by a British secret agent – Sidney Reilly – to assassinate Lenin and overthrow the Bolsheviks.

EPISODE 278 *(Pages 311-313)*

The Russian story sometimes makes for uncomfortable reading because our hero – Charley – is clearly on the wrong side. It's one reason why I had considered subsequently featuring Charley in the British occupation of Iraq in the 1920s but decided against it. It was a war where weapons of mass destruction – poison gas – were dropped on the civilian population of Iraq on the orders of Churchill and "Bomber" Harris.

But this episode also made me laugh as I got into Joe's beautifully designed characters. The comedy and the drama reminded me of *Auf Wierdersehen Pet* in Cuba – where none of the lads have a clue what's going on. There is something very funny about the British abroad!

EPISODE 279-281 *(Pages 314-322)*

The Orthodox monks are great characters, especially "Rasputin". Joe seems to have a special affinity for drawing all things Russian as we know from his superb *Johnny Red*.

EPISODE 282 *(Pages 323-325)*

The highpoint of the Russian saga has to be the armoured train war, which seems like something out of steampunk science fiction. Only Joe could have drawn Spirodonov's train with such awesome and menacing detail. The episode where "General" Charley is left in charge of the White Russians as Spirodonov's juggernaut approaches is one of the best cliff-hangers of all time. It demonstrates the power of the weekly comic. If I was a kid, I'd be at the newsagents the next Saturday desperate to find out what happens next. But with graphic novels, all we have to do is turn the page! And Spirodonov – based on a real life armoured train commander – is an excellent villain.

EPISODE 283-290 *(Pages 326-349)*

The British really don't come out of this story well. There's the use of British officers and NCO's in White Russian units and as "military advisers", much as they are used today. Thus Britain can officially deny it is interfering in the internal affairs of other countries. There's the British first use of poison gas in Russia. And a German mercenary's bitter comment, "In the Fatherland our children are starving because the British won't allow food in!" There were similar deliberate moves by the Allies to starve the Germans *after* World War Two was over. Millions died: a crime that amounted to genocide. (See *Crimes and Mercies* by James Bacque.)

There's a welcome lighter note when Charley and Co. guard a bridge which then gets nicked by the enemy and floats away before their eyes. I thought this was hilarious. A real movie moment, beautifully drawn by Joe, with great drama that follows.

EPISODE 291 *(Pages 350-352)*

I wish I had used double page spreads to really bring out the scale of the Red cavalry charge and the massive armoured trains. My lack of vision – I should have changed the whole scale of my storytelling to convey the "widescreen" nature of the war. A touch of *Doctor Zhivago* and David Lean was needed! Although it's worth noting there were comic critics back then who thought the more pictures on the page, the better value for money. Today, I'd have written it with perhaps four pictures on a spread and four pictures on a vertical page. Imagine what Joe would have done with that kind of space! But we still get the detail and the power as he works within the cramped confines of a traditional comic strip. That's how brilliant and conscientious he was. I swept much of that thinking away with *2000 AD*, but sometimes I think I didn't go far enough.

EPISODE 292 *(Pages 353-355)*

Charley would have said "'alf a mo'" – it was meant to be his authentic Cockney catchphrase – but editorial, with their usual lack of understanding, have changed it to "Half a tick". The drama builds to an exciting finale with the revelation that the train is laden with gold. And an excellent last cliff hanger for our hero.

EPISODE 293 *(Pages 356-358)*

I really should have lingered longer on the end of Spirodonov and showed Charley's return to Blighty, but I was too conditioned by the weekly format and the necessity for action in every episode. Stories that didn't have action, no matter how well established they were, usually received significantly less votes in the weekly vote chart and this would lead to a story being swiftly axed or a storyline changed. So comic scriptwriters tended to avoid non-action sequences, although we all cursed the tyranny of the vote charts that dictated our storytelling. Consequently, I only had two non-action pages left to complete the saga. A great pity. I originally intended Charley to also meet Smith 70 and Young Albert again, but there just wasn't the space.

So those two pages, then and now, are very significant. Firstly, I'm saying goodbye to old friends I've enjoyed spending time with again over these last ten years and ten volumes. The fact they're fictional doesn't make them any less real. Fortunately, it's not the last I will see of them, because there are plans for a deluxe version of *Charley's War* in 2014 and there are also the French editions. Secondly, because they are a damning indictment of the politicians who promised "A Land Fit For Heroes" but betrayed our servicemen.

It's a painful parting, and hard to look at these last two beautifully drawn pages knowing they're finally ending this astonishing saga. The image of King Kong is particularly poignant, as we began this last volume with the same gorilla, symbolizing militarism. Of all my stories, I always say *Charley's War* is my favorite – because I know it made a difference. But it also showed another road comics could have taken but, sadly, never did.

A Working Class Hero

Afterword

by **Pat Mills**

I had intended *Charley's War* to continue into World War Two. After all, my hero was 39 years old in 1939 and he also had a son who would join up. But I was determined that it should sustain the anti-war flavour of the Great War. I knew it was possible. My uncle – a World War Two soldier – once told me that the conflict was nothing like the popular image we are all familiar with, but promptly went quiet and changed the subject when he saw my interest. It will probably take another generation or two to reveal the truth, so we can look back on Churchill the way many Slavs now look back on their great war hero Marshal Tito. In a Sarajevo cinema in 2000, I watched a hilarious movie *Marshal Tito's Spirit*, which savagely criticized their savior to the considerable amusement of the audience. Could you imagine such a film criticizing *our* savior Churchill? Instead we have the "feel good", safe and sentimental *The Gathering Storm*. The establishment just has too much invested in the myths of World War Two.

The words of President Kennedy are relevant here: "The great enemy of the truth is very often not the lie – deliberate, contrived and dishonest – but the myth – persistent, persuasive and unrealistic."

But there is a truth that needs to be told that I wanted to tell in *Charley's War*.

Recently, a reader "Aptaz" wrote on my blog: "My grandfather was a Major at Dunkirk and when he and his men arrived at the beaches they were refused entry onto evacuation boats because he wasn't a Colonel or above in rank. Leaving his men by the boats he wandered off down the beach until he found the body of a Colonel and casually swopped jackets with him. Returning to the boats, the same officer who had refused him minutes before let him and his men on the boats based only on the number of pips now showing on his epaulettes." Somewhat different to the classic myth of Dunkirk, this was the kind of incident I was looking for.

But at the time books like *Unpatriotic History of the Second World War* by James Heartfield or Clive Ponting's *1940: Myth and Reality* were yet to appear. So I didn't know that the British government had secretly funded and was thus responsible for the rise of fascism and Mussolini. That officers had pushed in front of their men to escape at Dunkirk. Or about Churchill's bombing of Berlin *first* so the Nazis would retaliate with the Blitz. How the King and Queen and Churchill were booed in Charley's East End. How Churchill ignored the famine in India. That British and American troops were ordered to take no Japanese prisoners and this was the real reason so few surrendered. And during the time the East End was battered in the Blitz and its people camped in the London Underground, which Churchill had tried to prevent them entering, the upper classes, particularly members of the government, lived a life of luxury in hotels like the Dorchester. "Half London seemed to be there… Our bill must have been immense for we had four magnums of champagne. London lives well. I've never seen more lavishness, more money spent, or more food consumed than tonight and the dance floor was packed."

No different to the Great War, is it? A friend in publishing had already told me that the kind of World War Two stories I was looking for were unpublished memoirs stored in the vaults of the Imperial War Museum. So the only way I could continue *Charley* would be if I interviewed British Legion veterans and found out their truth. Despite the story's huge popularity, the managing editor refused to give me a small research budget. So with great reluctance I decided to end *Charley's War*. Joe asked if I'd mind him carrying on with another writer as he was close to retirement. Of course I agreed. But the story was a flop because it wasn't anti-war, and came to a premature end. That is why original *Battle* readers I consulted, Titan Books and I, all agreed the series should conclude with Charley on the dole in 1933. At some point there should be a chance to see Joe's excellent artwork on the World War Two version in a collection of his art or in a *Battle* anthology, but it's

not *Charley's War*. Currently, in collaboration with Repeat Offenders Ltd., I'm finally developing the natural sequel to *Charley's War*. Entitled *Rebels*, it dramatizes the lives of British, French and German teenagers on their respective home fronts.

In 2014, the 100th anniversary of the Great War will be remembered. The indications are that it will be more cleverly disguised jingoism. The same tired old apologies for empire that I was taught as a kid will be trotted out yet again, possibly given a new lick of paint for the 21st century: Britain going to the aid of plucky little Belgium (responsible for the murder of 10 million Congolese). The supposed "impossibility" of stepping back from the brink; the notion that war was sadly "inevitable". Even though it was perfectly possible to step back from the brink in the Cold War, notably during the Cuban Missile Crisis. Britain's brutal and greedy enslavement of its colonies, its determination to crush its unpleasant, upstart rival in the slavery business, will be carefully avoided, along with Germany's peace proposals and their rejection as early as December 1916. And above all – the secret role of oil, brilliantly and amusingly revealed in Robert Newman's *A History of Oil*.

Words like "sacrifice" will be used in preference to "murder" which was Harry Patch – the last Tommy's – word for it. Because then the Great War can be used to justify the murder of more young squaddies who have been given a twisted version of why they were fighting in Iraq, Afghanistan, Libya, and perhaps soon in Syria and Iran. It's still the *Imperial* War Museum and *Great* War is still the term used. Not – as one *Guardian* reader suggested – "Shit War". (16th October 2012)

Our Prime Minister tells us he wants to remember those who "gave their lives for our freedom". Seumus Milne's excellent rebuttal in the same issue of *The Guardian* was: "Those who died didn't give their lives 'for freedom'; they were the victims of an empire that was a stain on humanity, the cynicism of politicians and the despicable folly of the generals."

A stain on humanity indeed. Britain was – and remains – a Dark Empire. It just has better spin doctors than Darth Vader. But occasionally the mask slips. As it did recently when the head of the British Legion, Lieutenant General Sir John Kiszely, was forced to resign. "In a sting operation in which reporters posed as representatives of a South Korean arms company, Kiszely said his role at the legion gave him access to important figures in defence, and described the annual remembrance events as a "tremendous networking opportunity." (*Guardian* 15th October 2012)

All the spin in the world, the acknowledgement of his "exaggerated and foolish claims" can't repair the damage. This is who *they* really are, this is how *they* think, and this is the ongoing danger *their* arms deals represent to young men and women who will die in future disguised imperial wars and their "sacrifice" remembered on Remembrance Sunday by the successors of Sir John. "Sacrificed" so *they* can grow richer.

The need for working class heroes like Charley is more important than ever. Because the majority of popular culture heroes reinforce *their* perspective and are often written by its leading members. (From Fleming, Wheatley, Buchan and Conan Doyle onwards). The most popular story ever in *Battle* comic, *Charley* demonstrates that it is possible to write an exciting, anti-war, anti-establishment serial about a not very bright kid from the back streets every bit as enthralling as stories about his "betters". It also reveals that readers would *prefer* an anti-war story over powerful rival pro-war stories in a war comic. That has profound implications and is an uncomfortable nettle no one, even today, will grasp. All the years I wrote the serial, I was aware of the impact it was having on the minds of 150,000-plus young readers – many of whom might be termed "working class" – and it was a surprise to me and others that no-one pulled the plug on it. It simply slipped under the wire. Doubtless no-one thought a seditious three page story in a cheap bog-paper comic was worth worrying about. But when the truth is suppressed in government-controlled and manipulated media, it's all there is. Thus we're unlikely to see the superb *Monocled Mutineer* ever again on prime time TV because of protests from Tory MPs. It might give today's squaddies ideas. But if you want to know the truth about the day our forefathers heroically rose up against their "betters", you can still find it in *Charley's War*.

I hope the series will inspire someone to write its equivalent today. It's long overdue in a now largely safe, escapist, and middle class comic industry that focuses on graphic novels for adults and rarely caters for or is interested in the original popular culture market of kids aged 9–14 from which it grew. And that's a pity because as John Lennon said, "A working class hero is something to be."

Pat Mills
March 2013